In memory of Mary McIntosh

Bestselling authors of *The Sugar Girls*

Duncan Barrett & Nuala Calvi

GI Brides

The wartime girls who
crossed the Atlantic
for love

HARPER

HARPER

An imprint of HarperCollins*Publishers*
77–85 Fulham Palace Road
Hammersmith, London W6 8JB

www.harpercollins.co.uk

First published by HarperCollins*Publishers* 2013

1 3 5 7 9 10 8 6 4 2

A catalogue record for this book is
available from the British Library

ISBN 978-0-00-750144-1

Printed and bound in Great Britain by
Clays Ltd, St Ives plc

1

Sylvia

As the 8.10 to Charing Cross pulled out of Woolwich, Sylvia Bradley could barely contain her excitement. At fifteen and a half, she had only just left school, and was thrilled to be joining the crowds of glamorous women who took the train 'Up West' every morning to work in the capital's grand hotels and shops. Her blonde hair had been perfectly curled for the occasion, and her brand-new lipstick applied.

If Sylvia's mother had got her way, she wouldn't have been there at all. A talented seamstress, Mrs Bradley had been a furrier before the war, working from home sewing the false eyes and noses on fox furs for a West End shop. Applying the wartime philosophy of make-do-and-mend, these days she prided herself on keeping her family well turned out, despite clothes rationing, by finding old garments in second-hand shops and working miracles on them so that they looked brand new. She had easily found her eldest daughter a position with a local tailor in East London, sewing trouser hems.

But Sylvia, who had grown up surrounded by the fox furs that her mother took in and hearing about the fashionable shops where they were sold, dreamed of one day working in the West End. She couldn't help admiring Dolly Stickens, who lived on the next road over, and who her mother sometimes did sewing work for. Dolly worked in the Piccadilly Hotel, and every day she set off for town looking incredibly smart, her face well made-up.

'Look at her, at her age, wearing all that make-up!' Sylvia's mother tutted. Mrs Bradley would never have rouged her face, let alone dyed her hair a shocking red like Dolly's.

But to Sylvia, the other woman looked like a movie star.

Dolly's job was selling theatre tickets from a little kiosk at the Piccadilly, and one day she heard that the hotel was looking for a couple of young women for the billing office. 'Perhaps your Sylvie might be interested,' she said.

'Oh, no, she wouldn't want to work so far away,' Mrs Bradley said dismissively.

Sylvia saw her chance drifting away and quickly piped up. 'I wouldn't mind. I think I'd like it.'

'Well, I'll put in a word for you then,' said Dolly with a smile. 'Ta-ra!' She was gone before Mrs Bradley had a chance to protest.

Sylvia was ecstatic when, a few days later, Dolly gave her the news that she was to be given a trial period as a comptometer operator. She had no idea what that meant, but she didn't care. All she knew was that she would be joining the stylish women who headed into town every morning.

When she arrived at Charing Cross, Sylvia was almost knocked over in the fray as everyone bustled off the train and hurried to the exit. She had only been into central London once before, when she was a child and her father had taken her to Madame Tussauds. Although she was older now, she was still struck by how big everything was, and how busy it felt compared to Woolwich.

Dolly had given Sylvia written instructions for getting the bus up to Piccadilly, which she followed carefully, finally alighting outside the hotel's grand Palladian façade. The billing office was up a little spiral staircase at the side, and when she arrived a rather intimidating manageress called Miss Frank showed her how to clock in with a card. Then she sat Sylvia down in the office and explained how to use the comptometer – which turned out to be an adding machine for processing the hotel's bills.

Sylvia did her best to listen, but her attention was caught by a large half-moon window that overlooked the street. Below, Mayfair thronged with exotic-looking men, from Free French and Polish soldiers to various foreign dignitaries.

'Here comes our maharaja!' one girl shouted, and all the others ran to the window, as a handsome Sikh in a bright-blue turban walked past.

'Comes past the same time every day,' said a girl called Peggy, who sat at the desk next to Sylvia's. 'I reckon he's got a princess hidden away in one of the hotels who he goes to visit secretly.'

'Back to work, girls,' Miss Frank said, and they all returned to their machines.

Over the course of the day, Sylvia learned that the people-watching was considered the best part of the job at the Piccadilly, and took up much of the girls' time. And increasingly, it was Americans who were the main players in the movie unfolding outside their window, as the whole area was taken over by the soldiers of the 'friendly invasion'.

The first GIs had come to the British Isles in January 1942, less than two months after the bombing of Pearl Harbor, and by the summer there were tens of thousands of them arriving every month. Mayfair had become known as 'Little America', since the US Embassy and US Army headquarters were on Grosvenor Square, and its grand Georgian houses had been turned into accommodation and offices for US admin staff. An Englishman on the streets of Mayfair now looked like the odd one out.

Directly opposite the Piccadilly Hotel was the USO Club, and Sylvia and her colleagues could see the GIs swaggering in and out in their smart uniforms. They were quite unlike the Tommies of the British Army in their heavy serge – the better cut and higher-quality material of the Yanks' outfits made it hard to tell an officer from a private. The stripes on their sleeves, which were upside down from the British perspective, only confused matters further. Then there was the way they moved – often seen slouching with their hands in their pockets, or leaning against a wall chewing gum, they lacked the straight-backed gait of British military discipline. Their relaxed marching style, carried out in rubber-soled boots, had even earned the nickname 'the soft-shoe shuffle'.

Their approach to women also seemed confident and direct by local standards. From her window at the hotel, Sylvia watched countless young American servicemen chatting up attractive young women in the street, sometimes employing the 'reverse handkerchief trick' where they dropped a coin in the woman's path so that she would pick it up and begin a conversation.

Despite the apparent confidence of the GIs she watched, however, Sylvia couldn't help feeling sorry for them. 'I reckon they must be lonely,' she told Peggy. 'They're so far away from home.'

'Not lonely for long, I'll bet,' her colleague laughed, gesturing towards a GI who had just hooked a young English girl onto his arm.

Sylvia gravitated towards Peggy, thanks to her cheeky sense of humour, and much of the rest of their day was spent in fits of giggles, which they tried to suppress whenever Miss Frank was within earshot. By clocking-out time, Sylvia left the Piccadilly Hotel happy that she had made a new friend, and looking forward to her next day working 'Up West'.

A few days later, Peggy came into the billing office buzzing with excitement. 'Guess what, Sylvia?' she said. 'The American Red Cross are looking for girls to volunteer at their clubs. We could go and sign up after work.'

The Red Cross had set up numerous clubs in central London to cater for the GIs based there, as well as the thousands who would pour in from all over the country when their two days a month's leave came up. On Piccadilly Circus was the famous Rainbow Corner club, open twenty-four hours a day, where the GIs could shoot pool, play pinball, eat hamburgers and waffles, and generally get a taste of 'home'.

'I will if you will,' Sylvia replied enthusiastically. She was delighted at the thought of doing something to help the Americans, and Peggy seemed quite keen on the idea too, if the grin on her face was anything to go by.

After work that day, the two girls took themselves to the US Embassy for an interview. A Red Cross lady in a military-style blue uniform took down their names and addresses, and asked what their parents did for a living. *I hope they don't only want posh girls,* Sylvia thought to herself, as she explained that her dad worked at Greenwich Gas Works and her mum made shell casings at Woolwich Arsenal.

But the American woman didn't seem to be put off by anything that Sylvia said. 'The most important thing is being warm and friendly,' she told her. 'Whatever problems you have in your own life, you check them at the door. Our boys deserve a good welcome the moment they step inside a Red Cross club.'

She explained that Sylvia and Peggy would be sent to the Washington Club on nearby Curzon Street, and would be expected to work there two nights per week. Sylvia's first three-hour shift would be the following Tuesday, while Peggy would start later in the week.

When she arrived on Curzon Street after work on Tuesday, Sylvia found the club easily. It was housed in the Washington Hotel, which had suffered bomb damage during the Blitz but had recently reopened, and as she passed under a big blue awning and through the revolving front door, she felt a thrill of excitement go through her.

Inside, she was met by a young woman in Red Cross uniform. 'You must be the new volunteer,' she said. 'Follow me.'

Sylvia was aware of music playing in the distance, as the young woman led her down a corridor leading further into the hotel. On either side of them were racks of American newspapers and magazines from various states, with pride of place given to the *Stars and Stripes*, the servicemen's newspaper, written by American journalists in London and distributed by the *News of the World*. As they passed into a large room at the end of the corridor, the music got louder, and Sylvia could make out the final bars of 'I'll Be Seeing You' giving way to the lively beat of Glen Miller's 'In the Mood'.

The room was filled with GIs – some playing pool, some jostling for control of the jukebox, and others taking dough-nuts from a silver machine in the corner – while half a dozen young women rushed around serving them. A smell of apple pie suffused the air, and Sylvia could hear snatches of conversa-tion in a variety of distinctive American accents, from the rapid, nasal speech of New York to the lazy drawl of Alabama. It really did feel like being in another country, she thought.

The kitchen was a small affair at the back of the room, and inside Sylvia could see volunteers peeling potatoes and wash-ing dishes. 'So, what can I do?' she asked, keen to get stuck in.

'You can start by clearing the plates off the tables,' the other girl told her.

Sylvia didn't need asking twice. She put away her coat and bag and got to work straight away.

Clearing the GI's tables, Sylvia found she learned a lot about American eating habits. For a start there were the strange combinations of sweet and savoury items on a single plate, such as bacon and eggs topped with strawberry jam. Then there were the soft drinks that went along with them. Many of the GIs were sipping a dark substance that looked like some kind of fizzy vinegar, and Sylvia learned it was called Coca-Cola.

But the most striking thing about the GIs' meals was the sheer size of them – a single plateful might constitute half a week's rations in England, and they often left much of their food uneaten. Sylvia felt guilty as she threw away plates full of perfectly good food, aware of how much her mum struggled at home to feed the family.

The GIs were keen to chat to her as she worked. 'Hey, beautiful, don't forget my plate!' one called out. 'Aw, honey, why don't you come sit down with me?' shouted another.

At first Sylvia blushed shyly at their remarks, but after a while she got used to laughing them off like the other girls did. She remembered what she had been told about giving the men a warm welcome, and when they wanted to talk to her about their homeland she was a willing listener. One young man told her about living in North Dakota, where it snowed for six months of the year. Another described growing up in sophisticated San Francisco, while a third, from Arizona, told her all about life on the border with Mexico.

Sylvia loved to hear their tales of America, and she could see it helped them too. Beneath the bravado and charm, they were lonely young men in a strange country, far from their families and facing an uncertain future. They knew they hadn't been sent to England just to have a good time – one way or another they were preparing for an invasion of the Continent, which they described rather poetically as 'the far shore'. Sylvia knew there would be dark days ahead for many of the men in the room, but in the meantime, the least she could do was keep their spirits up.

As she worked, she began humming along to the music issuing from the jukebox. Her dad had always described American music as 'twaddle' when it came on the wireless, but Sylvia loved the swing sound of Glenn Miller and his 'Chattanooga Choo Choo', and soon she was singing her heart out.

With Sylvia volunteering at the Washington Club, her mother became worried that she would be pursued by GIs. Like many parents, she was distrustful of the Americans, who had quickly gained a reputation for being 'overpaid, oversexed and over here'. She knew her petite blonde daughter, with her big blue eyes and hourglass figure, would be sure to attract their attention.

Mrs Bradley was extremely protective of Sylvia, and had already had to fend off the advances of several local boys. When she was fourteen, a boy Sylvia had known since childhood had suddenly come to see her in a new light. Arthur was eighteen and already a pathfinder in the RAF, and his parents were friends of the Bradleys. When both families were in The Castle pub one night, he asked if he could walk Sylvia home. 'All right, but you better behave yourself,' her mother replied.

When they reached the doorstep, however, Sylvia's beau went in for more than a peck on the cheek. They were necking away, when she suddenly felt Arthur's hand wandering over her breast and pulled away in shock.

'You might be a pathfinder in the Air Force, but you ain't making no paths over me!' she said, rushing into the house and slamming the door.

Mr and Mrs Bradley returned from the pub a few minutes later. 'Mum, that Arthur just tried to touch me on the chest,' Sylvia said.

'Oh, he did, did he?' Mrs Bradley replied, her eyes flashing. She took an umbrella and went straight out onto the street. Arthur was still walking up the road, and she ran after him.

'Oi!' she shouted. 'You keep your hands off my Sylvie!'

Arthur didn't have a chance to turn around before the first blow of the umbrella landed on the back of his head. He put his hands up to shield himself as a second, third and fourth blow followed, and began running away as fast as he could, never to darken the Bradleys' door again.

When Sylvia started at the American Red Cross club, her mother insisted on sending her into town armed with a cigarette and a box of matches with which to defend herself from unwanted attention. 'If one of them Yanks tries it on, just light the ciggie and stub it out on his hand!' she instructed her.

Since Sylvia didn't have occasion to use the cigarette, after a while it fell to pieces in her handbag, and when her mother discovered this she came up with a new plan. 'Here's the pepper pot,' she said. 'If a bloke starts getting funny, throw some in his face.'

'Yes, Mum,' said Sylvia, hoping she would never have to resort to a pepper attack.

Despite Mrs Bradley's efforts, Sylvia was soon dating GIs. The first one to take her out was a shy, lanky young man with blond hair called Melvin Anderson – 'Andy' – who hailed from Eureka, California. She spotted him gazing adoringly at her from his table as she was singing along to the jukebox, and when she came over to collect his glass, he told her admiringly, 'You're so full of life!'

'Um, thank you,' Sylvia said, laughing at the strange compliment. He was softly spoken and a little reserved – nothing like most of the Americans who came into the club. She didn't have the heart to turn him down, so she agreed to accompany him to the movies the following night.

He turned up to meet her outside the Piccadilly Hotel clutching an enormous bunch of flowers and a box of chocolates. Sylvia had never been given presents by a man before. I'm living the high life now! she thought, as she breathed in the sweet smell of the flowers. The GIs were rich by English standards, since even the privates earned almost five times the salary of their British counterparts, and they could afford to flash the cash on dates. Like most Americans, Andy also made an impression with his impeccable manners and gentlemanly behaviour, which compared to her experiences with English boys made her feel like a queen.

But however courteous Andy was, Sylvia knew her mum wasn't going to be happy at the idea of her dating a Yank. 'I want you to bring him home so me and your dad can meet him,' Mrs Bradley demanded. 'A mother's got a right to know what sort of fella her daughter's associating with.'

'Yes, Mum,' Sylvia replied, dreading what her mum would make of poor Andy.

As she opened the door to the young GI, Mrs Bradley eyed him suspiciously.

'Evening, ma'am,' Andy said, taking off his hat. 'Thank you for welcoming me to your home.'

Sylvia could see her mother was disarmed by his politeness, and tickled by his use of the word ma'am.

'Good to meet you, sir,' he added, shaking Mr Bradley's hand.

Sylvia's younger sisters, Audrey and Enid, sniggered at Andy's funny accent. 'Don't you be rude to our guest,' Mrs Bradley chastised them. 'Andy, why don't you come and sit down?'

She led him into the kitchen, where she was laying out the dinner.

They sat down to eat and Andy complimented Mrs Bradley on the food, while she started asking him all about his experience of being in England with the US Army. Sylvia was surprised to see that, in the presence of the handsome young man in uniform, Mrs Bradley became increasingly girlish and giggly, fluttering her eyelashes like a woman twenty years younger.

The longer they chatted, the more her mother seemed to be enjoying herself, and Sylvia found she was barely getting a word in edgeways. 'Oh, this takes me back, Andy,' Mrs Bradley told the embarrassed young man. 'Do you know, I went out with a couple of Australian soldiers in the last war. One of them took me to a dance at the barracks and I was wearing my long knickers – which I made myself, you know – and we were dancing the Gay Gordons when the string on my knickers broke! Here I am, hopping around, and my bloomin' knickers fall down! I just stepped out of them, rolled them up, stuck them under my arm and carried on!'

Andy's tears of laughter only encouraged Mrs Bradley, who spent most of the rest of the evening regaling him with tales of her youth.

'You have a real sharp mom,' he told Sylvia approvingly, when he finally left for the night.

'Thanks,' she replied, wondering how it was that her mother seemed to have enjoyed the date more than she had.

'You go out with as many Americans as you like,' her mum told her afterwards. 'Just make sure you bring them all home, won't you!'

Against all expectations, the GIs had won over yet another Englishwoman.

2

Rae

Rae Brewer got out of the Underground at Acton, West London, and found her way to the address she had noted down from the newspaper. She had chosen a day when she knew her mother and stepfather were out at a wedding and wouldn't notice her absence. No one else knew it yet, but Rae was about to join up.

She was only seventeen, but for some time she had been itching to follow her older brothers, Vic and Bill, into the Army. Despite having cascading brown locks and a striking kind of beauty, Rae had always been a tomboy, dressing herself in her brothers' trousers, rather than the skirts her mother wanted her to wear. Her real name was Rosetta Mae, but from childhood she had gone by her less girlish nickname. She had been pleased to get a job as a drilling operator after school, but after a while she began to long to do something that would make a real difference in the war.

She had good reason to want to fight the Germans. During the Blitz, her family had been bombed out twice in Holloway, North London – both times on the same road. Her real father had been gassed by the Germans early in the First World War and spent most of the conflict in a prison camp, returning so emaciated that he had to wear a sign around his neck with his name on it so his wife could recognise him. During the first few years of Rae's life he was bedridden and continually fighting tuberculosis, which he had picked up in the camp. By the time she was four, he had died.

At the recruiting office of the Auxiliary Territorial Service, physical exams were being held for the potential recruits. The girls were sent two to a cubicle to undress, and then were given the standard medical examinations. Rae felt confident that she would pass – she had always been a sporty girl, and had been an avid swimmer, before the local pool had been turned into a morgue for Blitz victims.

Then the girls were sent to the eye doctor to check their sight. Rae's heart sank. She had never had good vision in her left eye, and though she had learned to cope with it, she knew it would let her down.

The doctor saw her distress. 'How badly do you want to get in?' he asked quietly.

'Pretty badly,' Rae whispered.

The doctor raised her to an A3, and she was in. Rae was ecstatic.

When she got home, her parents were still out, but her elder sister Mary was there. 'Mary, I just went down to Acton and joined the ATS!' she told her nervously. 'I don't know how I'm going to tell Mum.'

Before she had a chance to answer, the door burst open and in walked Mr and Mrs Burton, slightly tipsy. As soon as she saw the look on her daughter's face, Rae's mother knew something was wrong.

'What's happened?' she asked.

'I joined the Army, Mum,' Rae replied.

Her mother was quiet for a moment. 'You know I could stop you,' she said. 'You're still only seventeen.'

'Yes,' said Rae, 'but they'll get me anyway in the end.'

'All right then,' her mother sighed. She knew there was no point in arguing with Rae once her heart was set on something.

On the long train journey to Glencorse Barracks, a few miles south of Edinburgh, Rae's enthusiasm and excitement only grew with every mile. Her contingent of raw recruits arrived at 11 p.m. and was met by a brusque Scottish sergeant with flaming red hair, who led them on a march to the camp. This was no mean feat, given that many of the women were wearing heels, and they couldn't help laughing at themselves as they clip-clopped along while she barked 'Left! Right! Left! Right!'

The recruits made slow progress, but finally arrived at the barracks and marched into a parade ground. They were led inside a large building and told to line up with their hands on their hips, while a doctor went down the line giving each of them an injection in both arms. Next, they were taken for a hair inspection, to ensure they were free of head lice and that their hair was the regulation two inches off the collar.

Rae hadn't been bothered by the injections, but she was bothered now. Even when rolled up, there was no way her hair was going to be two inches above her collar.

'You'll need to have that chopped off first thing in the morning,' the sergeant told her.

'You're not cutting my hair!' she retorted. She viewed her long, dark locks as a source of pride.

'Aye, we are,' the woman replied. 'Report back here at 6 a.m.'

Before Rae had a chance to reply, the women were marched to the mess for dinner. Having lived on meagre rations, she was looking forward to a good feed, but even so she couldn't help finding the fatty mutton that was served up almost inedible. The recruits were expected to eat every last morsel, however, and a scary-looking woman stood on guard duty by the bin, just in case any of them thought of discreetly disposing of it.

Next they were led to the corrugated-iron Nissen huts where they were to sleep, eleven to a hut. Each girl had a little wooden bed frame on which there were three individual squares of mattress, one next to the other. The girls soon found that these thin squares had an annoying tendency to move if they turned over in the night, throwing out the arrangement and giving them sore hips. Even more troubling was the cold – it was February, and in Scotland that meant sub-zero temperatures in the metal hut.

The next morning, the girls were woken at 5 a.m. as the sergeant flung open the door, letting in the bracing Scottish air, and told them to be ready in ten minutes to be issued with their uniforms. Rae remembered she was expected to report for her haircut, and felt as angry as she had the night before. However much she wanted to fight the Germans, she wasn't going to put up with this. She opened her suitcase and began to pack.

When the other girls were gone, the sergeant came looking for her. 'What do you think you're doing?' she demanded.

'I'm leaving.'

'I've got news for you, lassie,' her superior replied. 'You've accepted the King's shilling, so you're not going anywhere.'

Rae realised there was nothing she could do. Gritting her teeth, she put the suitcase away and followed the sergeant into one of the brick huts. There, she sat in angry silence as her hair was lopped off and fell to the floor.

Next, the recruits were given their uniforms: a tunic jacket, two skirts, three shirts and a tie, along with a pair of clumpy lace-up shoes and several enormous pairs of bloomers, which were known unofficially as 'passion killers'.

Once the girls were kitted out, they were led into the parade ground for their first drill practice. This time, no giggling or stumbling about was tolerated, as they circuited the ground over and over again, bellowed at by the sergeant, until their feet fell in perfect rhythm.

After a good half-hour, the girls felt ready for a break, but instead they had to set off into the Scottish countryside to wear in their new shoes with a five-mile march. Rae could feel blisters forming, but there was no let-up as the sergeant shouted, 'Left! Right! Left! Right!'

By the time they returned to the barracks, the young women were exhausted and miserable, and many of them were close to tears. They now greeted the sight of the spartan Nissen huts with relief, and once inside, gingerly peeled the socks off their blistered feet to bathe them. But before long, they could hear the sergeant's shrill voice again. 'Everybody out!' she shouted. 'Report to parade ground for drill practice!'

It was a routine that grew crushingly familiar as the days and weeks at the barracks wore on, and Rae, like her fellow recruits, learned that her life was no longer her own, but the Army's. They were told when to march, when to salute, when to eat and sleep and shower. They were forced to run through the Scottish hills in the driving rain, to negotiate a punishing and muddy assault course, to iron their shirts and polish their buttons.

Rae grew more interested, however, once their combat training began. The girls mastered the basics of unarmed combat, learning how to break a hold and throw an enemy onto the floor. They learned how to shoot a rifle, and how to thrust and lunge at the enemy with a bayonet. They practised getting wounded comrades onto stretchers, and mastered first aid. These unladylike tasks prompted much giggling from some of the girls, but Rae was pleased that she was finally learning to become a fighter. 'Good, Brewer,' the sergeant shouted, seeing her enthusiastic attempts to spear an imaginary German.

After a few weeks of training, Rae realised she was beginning to enjoy herself, despite the rigorous discipline. The fresh air and physical exertion suited her, and she had even come to take pride in making her uniform look perfect for the daily inspection, keeping her shirts and tunic pressed by laying them under her mattress every night, and polishing her buttons and shoes until they gleamed.

One day, on the assault course, she was racing as fast as she could when she came up to a rope hung over a ditch. Without slowing down to judge the distance she leaped for it and missed, falling onto the ground below. Her whole weight came down on her left ankle, and she cried out in pain as she felt the joint twist.

Rae was helped to the barracks nurse, who iced the ankle and wrapped it in a tight bandage. 'Keep it elevated,' the woman told her. 'You'll have to rest up for a couple of weeks.'

While some might have been glad of the rest, Rae was frustrated at not being able to join the others. Once her injury was healed, however, there was even worse news.

'You'll have to join the next intake,' her sergeant told her. 'You can resume your training – from the beginning.'

Rae watched helplessly as the rest of the girls left Glencorse Barracks without her. She joined the new group of fresh-faced recruits and started the endless process of drill practice all over again.

After completing their training in Scotland, the girls were posted around the country. Rae was sent to Derby to the Royal Army Ordnance Corps, who were responsible for the supply and maintenance of vehicles and weapons. She couldn't believe it – after all those weeks of army training, she was confined to a clerical role, processing orders.

In Derby, the ATS girls were billeted in a Victorian orphanage, and it was still as grotty and depressing as it had been when its previous inhabitants were there. The work was dull, involving hour upon hour spent memorising the code numbers that corresponded to every piece of equipment and every part from nuts and bolts upwards. The tedious rote-learning was unbearable for Rae, who desperately wanted to be doing something. Many of the other girls felt the same, and they all tried to put in for transfers.

Luckily, after three weeks, Rae got a call to say she was being sent to Chelmsford, Essex, as part of a bold new experiment: training women in the manly art of welding. Just twelve ATS girls had been chosen from across the whole country, and Rae was among their number thanks to her experience working as a drilling operator back in London. Finally, she would be doing something practical for the war effort.

The girls were sent to technical college to learn their new craft. The teacher had never taught women before and it was clear he wasn't quite sure what to make of the new group of students. He greeted them awkwardly, but was soon demonstrating how to weld two sheets of aluminium together, holding the flame to a welding rod until it melted into the joint between them, sparks flying off in all directions. Rae was transfixed. This was worlds away from the boring codes she had been learning, and she couldn't wait to get her hands on one of the torches.

Soon he showed each girl to a bench, on which sat a pair of plates to be welded, along with a welding rod. He distributed gloves and safety goggles and showed them how to hook up their torches to the cylinders that stood on little trolleys behind them. 'All right, you can light your torches now,' he told them.

Rae was thrilled when the torch came alive in her hand and she felt the powerful heat of the blue flame. She took her rod and gently touched the flame to it, watching it sizzle and spark and the molten metal drip gently onto the plate below. It was extremely satisfying to see the metal transform under her influence.

At the end of the eight-week training period all but two of the candidates passed, including Rae, who had proved an excellent welder even with her bad eye. Now came their real test: being sent off to depots around the country to ply their new trade among their male counterparts.

Rae was sent to a workshop in Mansfield, a town about fifteen miles north of Nottingham, where she was the only female welder. She couldn't wait to put her training to use, and before long she found her skills were in demand all over the workshop.

Her first task was to help a corporal with re-bending some springs for a car. Rae warmed the metal with her torch and he teased them back into tightly sprung coils. Next, she was sent to the tin-bashers, who were working on damaged fenders. Again, Rae heated the metal, which was then coaxed into shape much more easily. Then, she was sent to the blacksmith to heat up the metal he was pounding with his hammer. She was soon a popular presence throughout the workshop, and to say thank you, the blacksmith toasted a piece of bread for her on his fire.

Although she was the only female welder, Rae was not the only woman at the workshop, and she was billeted in a house full of other ATS girls. The house was run by a Scottish sergeant by the name of Helen, and sharing a room with Rae were Irene, a motorcycle despatch rider from Birmingham, and Eileen, a Liverpudlian who worked as the colonel's chauffeur. Rae flourished in the company of both girls, glad that she was no longer the only tomboy.

In the ATS, Rae was entitled to a week's leave every three months, and she generally visited her family in London. On one such trip, she and her sister Mary decided to go out in the West End, but Rae found that London was not quite how she remembered it. 'You have so many Yanks down here!' she remarked in horror.

Living in Mansfield, Rae had only encountered US soldiers occasionally, but with two brothers in the Army she had picked up their prejudice against the GIs. Relations between

British and American soldiers were often tense, not least because of the Tommies' belief that the Yanks were stealing their women. When one GI asked for a pint of beer 'as fast as the British got out of Dunkirk', a group of Tommies threw him in the nearest river, shouting, 'Is that how the Yanks swam at Pearl Harbor?'

Before Rae had joined the ATS, her brother Bill had told her, 'I never want to see you in uniform, or dating a Yank.' She had already gone against his first decree, but she had no intention of breaking the second.

When Rae and Mary stopped for a drink in a pub, they made sure to choose a table in a quiet corner, where they could talk without being interrupted. But they had not been there long before a couple of GIs sauntered over.

'Hey, baby,' said one. 'Do you want to see my place back home in Florida?'

He took out a photograph of a palatial beach-front property. Rae could tell immediately that it was a hotel.

'Oh, lovely,' she replied. 'I've got one just like that myself!'

The men were not discouraged, however, and were soon finding other subjects to brag about, including their country's claim to be a beacon of democracy.

'You Brits are stuck with your King, but we can tell our President to kiss our ass if we want to!' said the second GI.

'Don't you dare mess with royalty,' Rae said angrily.

'Hey, we came over here to help you win this war, don't forget,' the first young man retorted.

'Just a minute,' said Rae. 'We'd been at it for two years before you came along!'

The men could see their charms were not having the desired effect, and made a hasty exit.

Rae was annoyed enough already, but when she and Mary left the pub an hour later, insult was added to injury. A tipsy GI saw Rae's uniform and shouted, 'Oh, look, it's the ATS – the American Tail Supply!'

Rae had run out of patience with the Americans. She walked straight up to the man and socked him on the jaw.

Soon Rae found that it was impossible to avoid the Yanks in Mansfield too, thanks to the arrival of an American hospital division in nearby Sutton-in-Ashfield. On market day, she and her housemates headed into town and found the ancient square thronging with American uniforms.

They decided to go into the nearest pub to get away from the crowd, but it was even more packed inside. They jostled to the bar and eventually got a round of drinks. 'Where shall we go?' Eileen asked.

Rae could see three GIs at the end of the bar. 'This way,' she said, heading in the opposite direction. The girls were lucky to get to a table at the front of the pub just as the people sitting at it were leaving.

They had barely taken a sip of their drinks, however, before the three Yanks came over. Rae and Irene were at the end of the table, and to Rae's annoyance the men started trying to chat them up.

'Hey, baby, how about you and me get out of here?' one of them asked her. He was a tall, thick-set American at least ten years older than her, with short-cropped blond hair and small eyes. But if he had been Clark Gable, Rae still wouldn't have given him a second look. He was a Yank, and therefore not to be trusted.

'Get lost,' she told him.

He laughed. 'Oh, c'mon, don't be like that, sugar,' he said. 'Lemme buy you a drink.'

'No way,' she said, turning her back on him and trying to talk to her friends.

But the man seemed to be enjoying her ripostes, and to her annoyance everything she said made him smile more. The GIs were used to rebuffs from English girls, and even had a nickname for their attempts to wear down resistance: the Battle of Britain.

Rae was furious – once again, the Yanks were ruining her day. As soon as she and her friends had finished their first drink they left as quickly as they could.

But the men were not so easily deterred. All the way back to the girls' billet on Layton Avenue, they followed them, calling, 'Oh, come on girls, we're lonely!'

'Just ignore them,' muttered Rae, relieved when they got back and could shut the door behind them.

Rae didn't give the men a second thought, but a couple of days later there was a knock on the door.

She went and opened it, only to find the big, thick-set American on the other side, smiling at her.

'Hey, baby, can I take you for a drink?' he asked.

'I'm not going anywhere with you,' Rae replied.

'Oh, c'mon, give me a chance,' he said, laughing. 'What's your name, sugar? I'm Raymond.'

'I'm not interested,' said Rae, and slammed the door.

A few days later, there was another knock. Once again, she opened the door to see the GI's big, grinning face looking down at her.

'I thought I told you to get lost!' she said, pushing the door shut.

Raymond stopped knocking for Rae, but when she left the house to go to the cinema the following Friday, there he was, hanging around on the pavement.

'I don't believe it!' said Rae angrily. She turned on her heel and marched straight back into the house before he had a chance to speak to her.

After several weeks, Rae's admirer still hadn't given up, and he had become a regular fixture outside her billet. 'There's your boyfriend again!' the girls teased whenever they spied him from behind the curtains.

'Why don't you just put him out of his misery and go out with him?' suggested Helen. It was clear he wasn't going anywhere until he got what he wanted.

The next time Rae saw him, she was heading to the cinema again.

'Hey, wanna go to the movies?' he asked her, smiling. Rae sighed. She couldn't be bothered to go through the whole rigmarole again. Nor did she want to miss the film. Maybe Helen was right and she should just put him out of his misery – then he would see he wasn't going to get anywhere with her and he wouldn't bother asking again.

'Well, I'm going anyway, so you might as well come along,' she said.

Raymond didn't need to hear any more. He was already by her side, his grin bigger than ever.

3

Margaret

Margaret Boyle finished typing the letter the American army sergeant had dictated to her, and proudly pulled it out of the brand-new Royal typewriter. She went into his office, laid it on his desk with a smile and returned to her seat. She was confident of her typing skills and felt sure she was doing well in her new job at the European Theater of Operations, United States Army (ETOUSA) headquarters in Mayfair.

But the sergeant, a plump man in his thirties with oily, slicked-back hair, was finding his English secretary rather frustrating. A few minutes later, he emerged holding the letter. 'Who is this?' he asked, pointing to the top of the letter, where Margaret had faithfully typed, 'Dear Bird.'

'Well, that's the man you're writing to, isn't it?' Margaret replied. 'Bird.'

'I said Bud!' he exclaimed. 'B.U.D.'

'Well, I'm sorry,' responded Margaret, 'but I simply *can't* understand your accent.'

The sergeant went away grumbling, but she didn't care – her eyes were on the other officers who milled around the headquarters. All the best, most ambitious young men the Americans had were here, and none had failed to notice the pretty new secretary, with her tall, slim figure and blonde hair pinned up in luscious curls on top of her head.

Margaret was making the most of it, having been starved of male company for years. Since her teens she had been living in the depths of the Irish countryside, where her mother had dragged her and her three sisters after running away from their father, a major in the Royal Artillery.

For as long as Margaret could remember, her parents had endured a tempestuous relationship. She had witnessed the terrible rows that Mrs Boyle provoked with her husband, always for the most spurious of reasons. Sometimes she would vent her frustration by hitting her daughter, or stabbing her with knitting needles. Margaret had learned to obey when told to pull down her sleeves, to hide the telltale marks left by these attacks.

Her parents' final showdown had come when Major Boyle was posted in India, where Mrs Boyle had invented an affair between her husband and their nineteen-year-old nanny Elfreda. Using all her theatrical talents, she had played the part of the spurned wife to perfection, dramatically sailing off from Bombay vowing that he would never see his children again.

She had chosen rural Ireland as her new home, since it had the advantage of putting the sea between herself and her relations in England, enabling her to reign over her daughters without any outside interference. There, she subjected them to a primitive life in a crumbling old mansion, where they had no electricity and had to cook on an open fire in the hallway.

With her children a captive audience, Mrs Boyle – a creative if unbalanced woman – invented strange plays, which she performed to them in the evenings. She continued to fly into irrational tempers, and took to beating Margaret with a broom as well as her fists.

When Margaret turned eighteen, Major Boyle had arrived unexpectedly, offering to take her back to England with him. She was overjoyed to be rescued from her mad mother, and left before she had a chance to stop her.

Once she was safely in England, Margaret wrote to her mother, asking for her clothes to be forwarded. There was no reply, but a trunk soon arrived. Inside it were Margaret's clothes – all cut to shreds.

Major Boyle was stationed near his hometown of Canterbury, in charge of the Boche Buster – a large railway gun capable of firing across the Channel. But having pulled a few strings among his army contacts, he had managed to get his daughter her coveted job at the ETOUSA headquarters, arranging for her to stay with some family friends called the Steadhams in Holland Park.

In London, Margaret had quickly discovered the effect she had on men, and had been using it to its full advantage, enjoying dates with a string of Americans. But it was one young second lieutenant that she particularly looked out for. Taylor Drysdale was a tall, athletic man in his late twenties with the chiselled looks of a movie star, and all the girls in the office swooned whenever he walked by. 'They say he was an Olympic swimmer before the war,' a young secretary called Grace whispered to Margaret as he passed by in the corridor one day. 'Isn't he an Adonis?'

Margaret had to admit he was quite possibly the best-looking man she had ever seen in her life, and she secretly determined to make him hers.

The next time Taylor swaggered towards her, she absent-mindedly dropped her handkerchief on the floor, causing him to stop and retrieve it for her. 'Oh, thank you so much,' she said. 'How silly of me.'

She looked up at him through her lashes and he smiled knowingly. Soon Margaret was the envy of all the girls in the office, having secured a date with the adored Taylor.

That Saturday they dined at the Savoy, which had become a regular hangout for American officers. The hotel had to comply with the blackout like everywhere else, so its revolving doors had been painted dark blue, and it was protected with sandbags. Restaurant meals, which were off-ration, had recently been capped by the government at five shillings, but luxury foods served in the top hotels were not subject to regulation.

Sitting opposite the gorgeous Taylor, enjoying a plate of caviar, Margaret was aware of the admiring glances that the two of them drew from around the room. He really was astonishingly good-looking – and, as she soon realised, intelligent as well. He had Master's degrees in mathematics and nuclear physics and had been chosen for a special electronics training group in the signal corps, where he was currently developing radio navigation charts to increase the safety of long-distance aircraft shipments. He was also an accomplished athlete, and had competed in the controversial 1936 Olympics in Germany, coming fourth in the 100-metre backstroke and narrowly missing out on a medal. Margaret was convinced she would never meet a more perfect man, and by the end of the meal she was utterly in love with him.

Soon Margaret was spending several nights a week at Taylor's flat in Chelsea. In order for her comings and goings not to be reported back to her father, she moved out of the Steadhams' house and rented a room of her own.

Up until now she had been a social butterfly, enjoying the attention of various beaus. But suddenly she found herself totally obsessed with one man and one man alone. She thought about Taylor all the time, and was in a constant state of agitation at work, worrying about when her next date with him would be. There was only one way to rid herself of her malady, she decided – to make sure that Taylor stayed hers forever. She had to get him to marry her.

First, Margaret started making little jokes about wartime weddings and how everyone was rushing to the altar, but Taylor merely laughed good-naturedly. Then one morning, when they were lying in each other's arms, she felt so overcome with passion that she could contain her feelings no longer. 'Oh, Taylor, I love you so much,' she gushed, looking up at his perfect face. 'I do hope we'll be married soon.'

To her horror, Taylor only laughed, just as he had at her other comments. He got out of bed and dressed, keeping his back to her. Margaret felt sick to her stomach and bitterly regretted what she had said.

She got up and dressed too, and then Taylor offered to walk her to the Tube. All the way there, she did her best to keep up a stream of light-hearted conversation to cover her embarrassment.

When they reached the station, Taylor turned to her. 'Margaret, you're a great girl, and we've had a good time together,' he said, 'but I'm not looking for something serious. Maybe it's best we don't see each other any more.'

Struggling to fight back the tears, Margaret hurried away from him to the platform and jumped onto a train just as it was about to leave the station. Once the doors were shut, she started crying desperately into the same handkerchief she had used to get Taylor's attention in the first place.

An older lady a few seats over looked at her in sympathy. 'Your boyfriend gone off to fight has he, dear?' she said.

'No,' replied Margaret. '*He's* absolutely fine.'

Over the next few weeks at work, Margaret was determined not to look as if Taylor's rejection had crushed her, and she put more effort into her appearance than ever. She found she both dreaded and at the same time longed to bump into him in the corridor, and when she occasionally did, she said hello brightly. She hoped that her cheery disposition would convince him she had been unfazed by his rejection and he would ask her to go out with him again. Perhaps if she had more time with him, she could make him fall in love with her.

But in her heart she knew her plan was doomed to failure. 'A man that beautiful can't be tied down,' sighed her workmate Grace.

For the first time since she had left Ireland, Margaret felt lonely. The life that had seemed so exciting to her a few weeks before now seemed empty, and as she came back alone to her rented room each night, she started to wonder if she wasn't just as isolated here, surrounded by millions of people in London, as she had been living in the middle of nowhere in Ireland. Who did she really have in her life? A mad mother who had abused her, a father whom she adored but who had often been absent thanks to his military career, and a widowed grand-mother in Canterbury who couldn't possibly understand what she was going through.

On Christmas day, 1942, having no one to celebrate with, Margaret volunteered to stay on at work. At lunchtime, she headed to the Maison Lyons restaurant at Marble Arch. Normally, she loved to sit amid its ornate decor and potted palms, listening to the little orchestra play. But that day, as she sat having Christmas dinner surrounded by empty tables, she had never felt so alone. She wondered what Taylor was doing, and the thought of him made her eyes prick with tears.

After lunch Margaret hurried back to work, and as she came in she found a dark, wavy-haired American captain waiting outside the sergeant's office.

'Hello,' she said. 'Can I help you?' She felt his eyes go over her figure. She was wearing her tightest skirt and jacket that day, and she knew they showed it off to perfection.

'I have an appointment at one,' he told her, in the sing-song accent of the American South, 'but I see your boss has found something more interesting to do. Can't say I blame him.'

'Can I get you a cup of coffee while you're waiting?' she asked.

'Would it be troubling you too much to ask for a cup of tea?' he replied. Seeing her surprise, he added, 'I got used to drinking it when I was in the Canadian Army.'

'What were you doing with the Canadians?' Margaret asked.

The man told her how, frustrated by America's neutrality at the outbreak of war, he, along with other men from his native Georgia, had gone up to Ottawa to join the Canadian Active Service Force. 'They're more British than the British,' he said. 'Tea five times a day, and every house and car has the words "There'll always be an England" in the window!'

Margaret laughed, for a moment forgetting her misery over Taylor Drysdale. Her boss soon came back from lunch, and the captain disappeared into his office. But on his way out, he stopped at Margaret's desk again.

'Would you do me the honour of accompanying me to dinner Wednesday night?' he asked.

Margaret was about to say no. Since Taylor, she had lost all interest in other men, and while the captain was perfectly pleasant-looking, he was no tall, chiselled Adonis. He was of medium height, and although he had very dark, striking brown eyes, they were set in quite a large face, and there was a scar across his nose.

But she liked his manners, which were those of a Southern gentleman and made him seem rather old-fashioned, even though he couldn't have been more than thirty. Then she had a thought that made up her mind: if she went out with the captain and Taylor got to hear of it, he might feel jealous and try to get her back.

'Certainly,' she said, with a winning smile.

The following week she accompanied Captain Lawrence McCaskill Rambo to Kettner's restaurant in Soho. It was a glamorous place, with mirrored, panelled walls and a pianist tinkling away in the corner, and Margaret felt a stab of longing as she thought how good she and Taylor would have looked there together.

Lawrence was the perfect gentleman, however, pulling out her chair and ordering for them both. As they ate he regaled her with stories about his time in the Canadian forces. 'They told us you can't get seasick in a hammock, because it rolls with the ship,' he said. 'Well, I can tell you, it's an outrageous lie! Three of the men were hanging so far over the rails being sick that their false teeth are now sitting on the Atlantic seabed!'

Margaret learned how, after arriving in Britain, Lawrence had been sent to the Scottish highlands with the Forestry Corps. 'Now, this is a Georgia boy who thought thirty degrees was a cold day,' he said, shivering at the memory.

'So, how did you end up in the American Army?' she asked him.

'Well, when Uncle Sam finally decided to join the war, I was shipped back to America,' he told her. 'I was so darn angry I threw my papers overboard before we got into New York, hoping they'd send me back to England. Sure enough they did, but when I arrived they wouldn't let me off here either. I went back and forth across that ocean six times!'

Margaret was soon in tears of laughter. The captain was clearly quite a storyteller, and he certainly seemed to be enjoying himself, laughing loudly at the end of each tale, even though he hadn't had a drop of wine. What he lacked in looks he made up for in confidence and charisma, and she felt she could listen to him talk all night. Afterwards, she went back with him to his flat in Kensington and did her best to lose herself in his embrace, trying to block out thoughts of her previous boyfriend.

The next day at the office, however, she made sure to tell Grace all about her date with Captain Rambo, counting on her to spread the news around the office. Margaret hoped it wouldn't be long until it reached Taylor's ears.

In the meantime, Lawrence proved to be a welcome distraction from her broken heart. His job was in purchasing and contracting, and he was constantly going back and forth between ETOUSA HQ and Whitehall to liaise about equipment that would eventually be needed for the invasion of Europe. As a result he came into her office all the time, asking her out on many more dates over the following weeks.

She soon learned that he came from an old land-owning family in Blakely, Georgia, where his late father had been the judge of the city court. She couldn't help being impressed by this, and by the fact that he was university educated. He also turned out to be a book lover like herself, and soon started lending her novels.

But despite all the time Margaret was spending with Lawrence, Taylor still hadn't made any attempt to win her back. She decided the only way forward was to contact him herself, so one evening after work she called him at his flat.

'Oh, hi, Margaret,' he said, sounding surprised. 'How are you?'

'I'm very well,' she replied. She chatted for a little while, and then dropped in nonchalantly, 'I've been dating a captain in the Engineer Service, Captain Rambo. Perhaps you know him?'

'No, I don't think so,' Taylor replied, unconcerned. 'Well, I've gotta go. See ya.'

After she hung up, Margaret felt almost as wretched as she had done when Taylor had thrown her over. He clearly wasn't the slightest bit jealous, and all she had done was embarrass herself again.

When Lawrence called later asking if she was free, she ran to him. She didn't want to be alone that night, and it felt good to be in the arms of a man who she knew really wanted her.

The following week, Margaret was surprised to find she had missed her period. She put it down to the distress caused by Taylor and forgot all about it. But a month later, still it hadn't come, so she made an appointment with a doctor.

'I'm afraid to say you're pregnant,' he told her.

'How is that possible?' Margaret cried. 'I used the cap.'

'Oh, those things don't always work,' he replied.

Margaret couldn't believe it. She rushed out of the doctor's surgery and hurried home as quickly as she could, afraid she might burst into tears in the street. Once in the house she ran up to her room and locked the door behind her, before collapsing on the bed and crying bitterly into her pillow.

Margaret felt beside herself with fear and regret. She had only really gone out with Lawrence to make Taylor jealous, and now not only had her plan failed, but it had backfired in the worst way imaginable. To give birth to an illegitimate baby would utterly ruin her, and her family would never get over it.

The next day was a Sunday, and Margaret spent the whole day locked in her room. The landlady came and knocked on the door, worried about her. 'I'm all right – just a slight cold,' Margaret called out. But inside the room she was in hell. She hadn't eaten for twenty-four hours and she had been crying all night long. To make matters worse she was feeling nauseous, and wasn't sure if it was the pregnancy or her dread of it that was making her want to vomit.

Once again she felt how alone she was in the world. If only she had a normal mother, perhaps she could have turned to her and confessed what had happened. But she hadn't had any contact with Mrs Boyle since she had left Ireland. The thought of her military father finding out about the pregnancy filled her with dread. Margaret knew abortions were illegal, and that backstreet abortionists were often little better than butchers. If she was going to find a solution to this problem, she would have to find it for herself.

She went to the cupboard, took out a wire coat hanger and untwisted it. Then she lay down on the bed, took a deep breath to steady her sobbing and inserted the hook.

4

Gwendolyn

In July 1943 the US Army took over the port of Southampton, putting the docks under the control of their 14th Port Transportation Corps, who would handle the huge influx of cargo necessary for the invasion of Europe. Before long, the city had become the chief supply centre for the Americans in Britain.

One local girl had a perfect vantage point from which to study the American officers as they zoomed in and out of the forecourt of the grand, red-bricked Polygon Hotel, where they were billeted. Gwendolyn Rowe counted herself lucky, at seventeen, to have scored a job as a shorthand typist at the Chamber of Commerce just opposite the hotel, where she and her female colleagues watched the new arrivals with great interest. When she cycled into work, her glossy black hair streaming in the wind, she always drew calls of, 'Hey, baby – slow down for me!' But she responded with a curt 'I'm *not* your baby.'

Watching from afar was one thing, but Gwen's first real encounter with an American soldier had been something of an embarrassment. A young GI, slouching along her road with his hands in his pockets, had made her almost jump out of her skin by suddenly pulling out a small box and waving it in her face. 'Hey, want some talc, miss?' he asked.

Gwen was infuriated. What did he think she was – a charity case? 'No, I do not,' she snapped. 'I don't take presents from strangers.'

The young man's face fell. 'Sorry, miss, didn't mean to cause no harm,' he said.

Gwen's mother Mrs Rowe, a forthright Scottish lady with raven hair just like her daughter's, had witnessed the scene from the doorway of their house on Padwell Road. As soon as Gwen reached the doorstep, she reprimanded her: 'Those men are here to help us. You go back at once and say thank you.'

Gwen let out an irritated sigh, and went after the young man. 'Sorry,' she said, as she caught up with him. 'I didn't mean to be rude.'

'No problem, miss,' he replied with a smile, pushing the talcum powder into her hand. When she got the gift home, Gwen was secretly thrilled. Rose scented and luxurious, it was the most wonderful thing she had been given in four years of rationing.

Gwen and the girls at the Chamber of Commerce found that American officers were frequently coming in to ask them for local information, and it was sometimes difficult to know whether their enquiries were genuine. The Americans seemed particularly keen to solicit local information from Gwen, although so far none of them had actually asked her out – perhaps because, being very slender, she looked younger than her seventeen years. But one day, as she was going into work, a jeep screeched to a halt beside her. The driver called out 'Hey, sugar!' and Gwen, turning to give a smart reply, was caught speechless.

There, with one foot on the dashboard and a large cigar hanging languidly from the corner of his mouth, was a stunningly attractive GI with sparkling brown eyes and exotic good looks. 'What you doing tonight, baby?' he asked.

'Um, I don't know,' replied Gwen, flustered.

He laughed. 'Come to the dance at the Polygon with me. What's your name, sugar?'

'Gwen.'

'I'm Ed. See you at eight, Gwen.'

His beautiful face zoomed off with a big smile on it.

That evening Gwen peddled home from work faster than she ever had before. A date at the Polygon would require a sophisticated outfit, and she knew there was only one dress that would be up to the task: her emerald-green one. Handmade by her mother from curtain material, since dress fabric was rationed, she knew the colour complimented her dark eyes and jet-black hair.

With relief she found the dress hanging up pressed and immaculate in the cupboard. After bathing in the regulation five inches of water and dousing herself in her rose-scented talc, she put it on – and immediately felt like a princess. Unfortunately, with no carriage and horses to transport her, she would have to make do with her bike to get her to the hotel, so she hitched up the dress with safety pins and rode off.

When Gwen arrived at the Polygon, she stowed her bike out of sight and walked through the grand revolving doors. The hotel had long been frequented by passengers from the grand ocean liners that came in and out of Southampton, including many from the fateful *Titanic*. Its elegant dinner dances were legendary, and had continued throughout the war, providing American officers with an upmarket setting in which to entertain the local female population.

As Gwen entered the room, Ed stood up to greet her and she felt giddy at the sight of him. 'Just stand still for a moment,' he said, looking her up and down. 'My, that is such a beautiful dress. And you have such pretty eyes.'

Gwen smiled. Clearly the green dress was having the intended effect.

Sitting opposite Ed, she found herself hardly able to eat her dinner – he was just too distracting, and she was trying too hard to be sophisticated. But it was dancing in his arms that she was really looking forward to.

When the resident band struck up, Gwen and Ed moved onto the dance floor, and as she spun around the room with him she felt as if she were in a fairy tale.

The musicians took a break, and Gwen caught Ed looking at her again. 'My, you really do look beautiful in that dress,' he said, lighting a cigarette. 'But I can't see you again.'

Gwen was confused. 'Why not?' she demanded.

'Because', said Ed, drawing slowly on his cigarette, 'I'm thirty years old. And you're just a child.'

Gwen felt indignation rising in her. 'I can handle it,' she said. Then, grabbing at a phrase she had heard some of the GIs use, she added, 'I've been around the block a few times.'

'I'm not sure you know what that means,' Ed laughed.

'Of course I do,' Gwen said, crossly.

'All right then,' he replied. 'Do you want to come upstairs and show me?'

Gwen was horrified. 'Oh *no*,' she blurted out.

Suddenly, she felt very young indeed, despite the green dress. It wasn't long before she was peddling as fast as she could back to Padwell Road.

Despite the unsuccessful date with Ed, the glamour and elegance of the Polygon Hotel had taken hold of Gwen, and now she couldn't stay away from it. Some of the girls from work went to the dinner dances every Saturday night, and she started going with them. It required her mother's expert sewing skills to keep Gwen in suitable outfits for these nights out, often pulling apart her own old dresses and turning them into skirts with a more fashionable cut for her daughter. After the humiliating experience with Ed, Gwen was determined to look as sophisticated as possible on the dance floor.

She had also made a decision: she would no longer go by the name Gwen. Her family might have called her by the nickname for as long as she could remember, but she had decided that Lyn sounded much more grown up. The girls at work soon adapted to the change, but her mother, despite repeated reminders, still insisted on calling her Gwen.

One Friday morning, Lyn was daydreaming about the weekend to come when an American ensign came into the Chamber of Commerce. 'Do you know where I could get some invisible mending done?' the man asked. His enquiry struck her as falling into the spurious category, but nevertheless she did her best to advise him.

Afterwards, he lingered, his brown eyes gazing at Lyn. It was only then that she noticed how deep they were, and what beautiful tanned skin he had. Like Ed, he had something exotic about him that elevated him beyond the brashness of the usual Yanks, but his eyes seemed clearer and more open in their gaze than Ed's had.

'Say, miss,' he said. 'Would you like to have tea with me?'

He must be at least in his mid-thirties, Lyn thought, impressed, and agreed to his request.

The next day, she met the GI, whose name was Russ, at a little tea room. As they sat down, he put his hat on the table and Lyn caught sight of a photograph tucked inside the rim.

'Who's this?' she said, pulling the picture out. The woman in the photo was a beauty, with tumbling dark curls and a flower in her hair.

'Oh, that's my wife,' Russ said, sounding wistful.

'You're married?' Lyn asked, shocked. 'Why are you having tea with me then?'

'Because I trust you, and I think you trust me,' he replied. 'And I think we could be friends.'

As he poured the tea, Russ poured out his heart about his beloved Larina. They were both of Mexican origin, he told Lyn, and she was a singer in a mariachi band.

Their life together in Florida, surrounded by sunshine and orange trees, sounded idyllic, and the tear in his eye as he spoke of her was very affecting. By the time she had swallowed the last of her tea, Lyn was so impressed by Russ's apparent devotion to his wife that she felt overcome with warmth towards him.

Soon she and Russ were meeting regularly. As he stared into her eyes, talking about another woman, Lyn found herself squeezing his hand in consolation, her heart overcome with feeling. But she couldn't help wishing it was she, not Larina, who was the lucky recipient of his idolisation.

'You know,' he said one day, 'if you lived in the US you would never date a man like me.'

'You mean because you're married?' asked Lyn.

'No, because I'm a Mexican.'

Lyn thought this the most ridiculous thing she had ever heard.

'It's true,' Russ continued mournfully. 'American girls don't date Mexicans.' He smiled sadly at her.

'I would!' Lyn felt like saying, but she managed to stop herself.

After a while Mrs Rowe noticed that Lyn wasn't going out on the town as much as she once had. 'Have you met someone special?' she asked.

'Not really,' Lyn replied, 'we're just friends. He's married and he really misses his wife.'

'Well,' said her mother, 'why don't you invite him home for tea?' She knew that all Americans loved to be invited into British homes, and local families were actively encouraged to host them.

When Lyn passed on the invitation, Russ accepted immediately.

On the appointed day, he arrived at Padwell Road, his black hair combed back and greased even more than usual. Just as they were all about to take their seats in the front room, Russ said, 'Mr and Mrs Rowe, I must tell you that I am married. But I would never hurt Lyn for anything – we are just friends.'

'Well, Russ,' said Lyn's father, 'we appreciate your honesty.'

Mrs Rowe enjoyed having a new visitor to the house, and loved listening to Russ's tales of Florida and the beautiful wife waiting there for him as much as her daughter did. He was soon a regular dinner guest, and he told the Rowes tearfully, 'I feel like you're my family now.'

Lyn's parents seemed blissfully unaware, however, that their generosity was encouraging their daughter's hopeless crush all the more. The fact that Russ was unavailable only made her longing for him stronger, and she wondered if he felt the same about her. There had been signs that he did, Lyn thought, but despite her confident front she was woefully inexperienced with men, so it was difficult to know if they meant anything. When her parents were out of the room, and he rubbed his foot against hers, saying wistfully, 'This is what Larina and I used to do,' surely he was simply thinking of his wife?

As they said goodbye at the door after dinner one warm evening, he brushed her hair back from her face with his hand. 'You know, it would be very easy for us to get involved,' he said.

If he tries to kiss me now, thought Lyn, I *am* going to kiss him back. She looked up into his eyes.

'But', continued Russ suddenly, 'I'm not going to do that. Goodnight!'

'Goodnight,' mumbled Lyn. She closed the door and ran to the window to watch him disappear into the darkness of the blackout.

Once again, she thought, Russ had proved himself the most honourable of men – which only made poor Lyn adore him all the more. While the girls around her were having fun dating the GIs, her love life was in limbo.

5

Sylvia

Sylvia's first GI date, Andy, who had been such a hit with her mother, was soon posted elsewhere. But there was no shortage of keen young men at the American Red Cross club where she volunteered, and she soon had so many dates that she rarely had a night to herself. Among those who took a liking to her was a swaggering Texan called Wally Benson, who liked to impress her with talk of his life back home. 'My dad's got a real big ranch,' he told Sylvia, who listened wide-eyed.

'What's it like being a cowboy?' she asked.

'Oh, you know, like it looks in the movies,' he replied vaguely. 'Texas is so big you could fit this little country inside it four times over! I'd like to show it to you someday…'

Wally often came into the club, and repeated his wish to take Sylvia back to Texas with him. 'Hey, baby, how about you and me get hitched, and when this war's over you can come live on the ranch with me?' he asked one day.

Sylvia didn't know what to say, so she gave an embarrassed giggle and hurried back into the kitchen. 'I think Wally just asked me to marry him!' she told one of the other volunteers.

'Oh, they're just after a bit of hanky-panky when they say that,' the other girl replied. 'It doesn't mean anything.' She knew that in war a man was likely to seize his pleasures where he could, not knowing what tomorrow might bring.

Sylvia soon began to accumulate marriage proposals at the rate of about one a week. Since she always thought the best of people, she preferred to believe it was a little bit of permanence and security the men were looking for, in the midst of so much uncertainty. But she learned to bat away the proposals all the same.

Wally continued to be a regular visitor to the club, however, and when he had some leave coming up he asked if he could come and visit her and her family in Woolwich. Sylvia's mother was all for the idea, and Wally duly turned up, bringing with him a bottle of expensive perfume for Sylvia. She felt like a movie star when she put it on, and walked back and forth for the sheer pleasure of wafting the divine scent around.

Mrs Bradley insisted on the two of them joining her and her husband at the pub, and while Sylvia stuck to her usual shandies, her mother became increasingly tipsy. She was on top form, and had Wally laughing at everything she said.

On the way home they were still having a good giggle when Mrs Bradley said, 'Oh, I'm going to wet meself laughing if I don't find a loo.' At the top of the street was an empty air-raid shelter, and they waited as Mrs Bradley ran in to use the toilet. They chuckled as they heard strains of 'Swanee' coming out of the shelter, as she sang away merrily to herself on the toilet. Then suddenly there was a screech of 'Oh my Gawd!' and a flustered Mrs Bradley came racing out, followed by a homeless man waving a stick and shouting, 'Can't you be quiet? I'm trying to get some sleep in here!'

The sight of Mrs Bradley hitching up her skirts and legging it up the road had them all in stitches again, and even

Sylvia's usually reserved father had to clutch his belly with laughter.

Wally was transferred soon after, but he wrote to Sylvia, 'I can still hear your mother's voice in my head, singing "Swanee" on the "loo". I don't think I'll ever forget that evening.'

Sylvia read the letter aloud to her mother, who was tickled pink at her conquest.

After that, Mrs Bradley even began bringing home soldiers for her daughter herself. 'This is Frank Dunphy,' she announced when she got home one evening, introducing an English soldier quite a bit older than Sylvia. Frank accompanied the Bradleys to the pub, and after that took Sylvia to the pictures a few times. She didn't mind – since he was older than her, it felt a bit like having a big brother around. Frank came from Nottingham, and one day he mentioned that he had some leave coming up and was planning to go back and visit his mum. 'Would you like to come with me?' he asked.

Sylvia had never been to Nottingham before, and thought it might be fun to see a new place. 'All right then, why not?' she replied.

They took the train up that weekend, and had a pleasant time with Frank's mother, who seemed very pleased to meet Sylvia. 'Your mum's nice,' she said, once they were back on the train.

'Oh, I'm so glad you liked her,' replied Frank, 'because when we're married I thought we could –'

'When we're what?' asked Sylvia in surprise.

'When we're married. We are getting married, aren't we?'

Sylvia thought back to Mrs Dunphy's eagerness to meet her, and it suddenly dawned on her that the whole trip had been arranged with very different intentions to those she had imagined.

'Frank, you're like my big brother,' she told him, feeling terrible as she saw the disappointment on his face. 'I like you and all that, but I can't marry you.'

'Well,' Frank replied, 'I'm going to keep on trying.'

Unfortunately, they were only halfway back to London, and Sylvia had to endure the rest of the awkward train ride with him.

When Frank was sent to Africa, he wrote to Sylvia constantly, and to her surprise so did one of his friends, Tom, whom she had met only briefly in London through Frank. She now had several soldier pen pals and kept up the correspondence religiously, feeling she couldn't let the boys down in their hour of need.

So far, Sylvia had enjoyed her dates, but most of the men she had gone out with she regarded, like Frank, as little more than brothers. One day, however, a young sailor walked into the Red Cross club who changed all that.

She spotted Carl Russell immediately. With his flame-red hair he was hard to miss, and he was clearly the comedian of his group, doing all the talking as his fellow sailors laughed at his jokes. He didn't look much older than her – around eighteen or nineteen – and he had a big smile that made her feel warm all over.

Sylvia was used to being watched as she went about her work, but this time, it was she who was looking on longingly. After a while Carl noticed her and came over. 'Would you like to go out with me?' he asked, confidently.

'Oh, yes,' she replied, blushing at the idea that he had guessed her thought.

'You know what I'd like to do?' he said. 'I'd like to visit one of your English tea rooms. I've never done that before!'

Sylvia knew there was a Lyons Corner House close to Charing Cross station, where she took the train home every day, so she suggested they go there. As she sat drinking tea with 'Red', as his friends called him, he told her about his hometown of Boston.

'So, do they drink tea where you come from?' asked Sylvia. She had noticed at the American Red Cross club the men always seemed to drink coffee.

'Oh, sure,' replied Carl, smiling. 'We had a pretty famous tea party in Boston in 1773!'

Carl was just a regular sailor, but he was from a wealthy background, and lived in the exclusive Beacon Hill district. Sylvia knew a rich Englishman would be unlikely to take her out to tea, but the Americans were oblivious to distinctions of English social class and treated all girls they liked equally. Carl seemed fascinated to hear all about her life in Woolwich and her job at the Piccadilly Hotel. He was intelligent and lively, and Sylvia couldn't help feeling she was having a much more interesting time with him than she had with her previous dates.

When he kissed her goodbye at the station she felt tingly all over, and as she rode the train back to Woolwich she couldn't stop smiling.

Carl was a cultured young man, and the next time they met up he insisted on taking her to the National Gallery in Trafalgar Square. Sylvia had never been to a gallery before, but she didn't want to seem unsophisticated, so she agreed to go.

The experience proved to be something of a disappointment, however. The gallery had been hit several times in the

Blitz – in one case killing seven people – and its paintings had been evacuated to secret locations in Wales and Gloucestershire to keep them safe. Its rooms were all empty, except for a special reinforced chamber that was showing a single 'Picture of the Month' – in this case, Velázquez's *The Rokeby Venus*.

Sylvia was rather shocked at the sight of the lady's pink, bare buttocks, but Carl seemed to be transfixed. 'Isn't she beautiful?' he sighed.

'I suppose so,' Sylvia replied.

Carl turned to her. 'But not as beautiful as you,' he said.

Sylvia's dates with Carl quickly became the highlight of her week, and she always felt a rush of excitement when she spotted his red hair out of the window of the Piccadilly Hotel, as he waited for her after work. But the ritual visit to Woolwich beckoned, so that Mrs Bradley could meet him. This time Sylvia found herself unusually anxious that her mother should like her date, but to her relief they hit it off immediately.

At the end of the evening they were sitting in the living room, when Mrs Bradley announced, 'Well, I'm off to bed. Don't stay up too long, now.'

As soon as she was gone, Sylvia slipped onto Carl's lap and they started kissing. After about ten minutes, she had to jump off hurriedly as Mrs Bradley bustled back into the room.

'I forgot to bank the fire,' she said, walking over to the fireplace.

'You just did that!' Sylvia said.

'Oh, yes,' her mother muttered. 'So I did.'

She bustled out again, and Sylvia sidled back up to Carl. No sooner had they resumed kissing than her mother came barging into the room for a second time.

'Did I lock the back door?' she enquired of her daughter.

'I don't know, Mum,' Sylvia said, trying to suppress her frustration. 'Did you?'

'I'll just go and look,' said Mrs Bradley, and off she went.

Ten minutes later, Mrs Bradley came downstairs again, telling them loudly that she was going out the back to use the loo. Clearly there was going to be no privacy this evening, so Carl soon left.

Mrs Bradley's tactics had got the desired result, but as she lay in bed that night her mind was still not at rest. For the first time, she had seen her daughter truly smitten, and she knew that no umbrella could protect her Sylvie once she had given her heart.

One day, after Sylvia and Carl had been dating a month, he came into the Washington Club while she was on her shift. At the sight of his red hair, her heart skipped a beat, and she immediately put down the plates she was taking to the kitchen and rushed over to greet him.

But the look on his normally cheery face told her he was not there for fun. 'I've come to say goodbye,' he said. 'I'm being sent away for training. They won't tell us where we're going, but I'll be gone a while.'

Sylvia couldn't believe it. She had only just found a GI she really liked, and after a few short weeks together now he was to be snatched away.

Tears ran down her face as Carl gave her a final, lingering kiss. 'Don't forget to write me,' he said, as he turned to leave. 'And have a pot of tea ready for me when I come back!'

Sylvia nodded, too upset to reply.

6

Rae

Having waited outside her billet week after week, Rae's GI admirer had finally worn down her resistance and got the date he wanted. After this small encouragement Raymond's unannounced arrivals continued with the same frequency, and she got into the habit of letting him accompany her to the movies. It wasn't much more than that – a habit – and she always made sure to walk off briskly at the end of the night before he had a chance to linger on the doorstep.

But one night, Raymond confronted her. 'Rae, do you know how many times we've been out now?'

'I haven't been keeping count,' she retorted.

'Well, it's been five dates, and you've never given me a good-night kiss!'

Rae couldn't help laughing at his hang-dog expression. 'Oh, go on then,' she said. An eighteen-year-old tomboy, she had never been kissed before. Why not get it over and done with?

At six foot two, Raymond had to lean over quite some way, but he took her in his arms and kissed her passionately. Rae found it a strange and not particularly pleasant experience.

However, after that there was no point pretending they weren't a couple. 'Why don't you invite him round for Sunday lunch?' suggested her housemate, Irene, who had also started dating a GI. Having an American at the table always guaranteed a better meal, since their food was shipped in from the States.

Raymond was a cook at a nearby US general hospital, and before the meal he made sure to sneak out some tins of turkey meat. The ATS girls were ecstatic when he turned up with this bounty, and devoured their turkey on toast. He also brought them glossy American magazines, which they kept under their mattresses.

Raymond was soon being invited to join them on nights out, and although he wasn't a dancer he was happy to stand at the bar and watch Rae dance. Her friends joked that he didn't seem to be able to take his eyes off her, and she could see they had quickly taken to his easy-going personality. Among his own friends in the US Army, Raymond was nicknamed 'Hap', because he seemed so happy all the time. The two of them quickly acquired a new moniker: Big Ray and Little Rae.

Rae liked it that Raymond was tall and manly – she would never have been able to date a puny guy – and the fact that he was ten years older than herself, and in the Army like her own poor dad had been, made him feel a little like a father figure. She also found his persistence reassuring. 'I love you, Rae,' he told her over and over again, and although she never said it back, each time she felt a little fonder of him.

Raymond always made sure to walk Rae home at the end of an evening, stopping along the way for fish and chips – a delicacy unheard of in America – and as they strolled back to her billet he would tell her all about his life in Pennsylvania. He came from a small community called Hackett, not far from Pittsburgh, and like the rest of his family he had worked in the local coal mine since he left school. To Rae, who had grown up in London, coal-mining was an alien world, but she was pleased that he was from an ordinary, hard-working family like her own. She remembered the bragging Yank who had shown her a picture of a hotel in Florida and claimed it was his house, and appreciated Raymond's honesty about his humble background.

But while Raymond was winning over Rae and her friends, there was another group of people who she knew would be less easy to convince: her family. Given her brothers' dislike of the GIs, she had so far kept the relationship a secret.

She knew that her mother had recently put paid to her sister Mary's relationship with her boyfriend Bob. Having got a 'funny feeling' that he was married, Mrs Burton had taken her tallest son round to confront him. When Bob admitted that her suspicions were correct, she had told him, 'You stay away from my daughter. Here's my son, and I've got two more just like him, so don't you even try to come near us!'

As the weeks and months went by, Big Ray and Little Rae grew closer and closer, but she continued to put off mentioning him whenever she wrote to her mother. In any case, Mrs Burton had more pressing worries. After her 'funny feeling' about Mary's boyfriend had turned out to be correct, she had begun to trust her intuition more and more. Now it was telling her that her own husband wasn't being faithful.

During his long shifts with the military police, guarding 'vulnerable points', Rae's stepfather had been eyeing up his own target, a much younger woman in the ATS. When the girl had taken him home to meet her parents, they had been surprised to meet a man their own age. But they liked Mr Burton and willingly gave him their daughter's hand in marriage, little knowing that he already had a wife and family.

'He's being tried for bigamy,' Rae's distraught mother wrote to her, 'at the Old Bailey.'

Rae was furious. She got leave to return to London for the court case, and made sure she was there to hold her mother's hand as they watched the man who had been a father to her for more than a decade stand in the dock. Mr Burton argued that he had only married his mistress because she had fallen pregnant, and with a good character witness from his officer he avoided jail. But Rae's mother refused to give him the satisfaction of a divorce, and he and his ATS girl lived out the rest of their days unmarried.

Back in Mansfield, Big Ray and Little Rae's weekly dates continued, always followed by a visit to the fish-and-chip shop. One day, they were sitting in the pub when Raymond drew something out of his pocket.

'Would you accept this?' he asked her.

He was holding a large gold ring with five stones in it. Five stones meant five words: Will You Be My Wife?

Rae was completely taken aback. Marriage had never crossed her mind in their months of dating, and she'd had no thoughts of the future whatsoever. What was the point, when no one knew how long the war would rumble on – or what the eventual outcome would be? She and Raymond could both be dead by tomorrow.

But she liked him, and all she knew at this point in time was that she wanted to carry on being with him.

'Yes,' she said, a little surprised at herself.

Now that they were engaged, there was no way Rae could continue to keep the relationship a secret, so finally she wrote to her mother. An anxious reply came back: 'Are you sure you know what you're doing?'

There was only one way to convince Mrs Burton. The following month, they took a train to London so that Raymond could meet her, as well as Rae's sister Mary. Rae just hoped her mother's intuition didn't give her another 'funny feeling'.

Raymond came armed with several tins of turkey and some much-coveted butter. To Rae's relief her mother seemed to like him, although she did repeat the question, 'Are you sure you know what you're doing?' as soon as he left the room.

But throughout dinner Rae noticed that her sister seemed a little quiet, and as she helped her take the plates out to the kitchen she asked her what was on her mind.

'I'm just not sure about him, Rae,' she said. 'I don't know why.'

Rae soon discovered that family introductions were only the first hurdle. The US Army was not keen on its soldiers marrying while on duty abroad, and the process of obtaining permission to wed was an elaborate one. A commanding officer had to approve the application, and write a letter to the civil or church authority who would conduct the marriage, having interviewed the GI in question. The potential bride was also subject to questioning, usually by an army chaplain, and was required to provide character references. The Army did its best to dissuade prospective brides, who were often accused of using marriage as a ticket to a more prosperous country. Meanwhile, checks were made into any dependants of the GI in the US, to ensure that the husband could afford to keep his new wife. Unsurprisingly, the process often took many months, but any GI caught violating the Army's strict procedures was subject to a court martial.

Rae set about accumulating the necessary paperwork for her marriage to go through smoothly. Her captain provided a character reference, and even agreed to walk her down the aisle. Rae's housemate Eileen, the colonel's chauffeur, and Nancy, a girl from the storage depot, were to be bridesmaids.

But despite all their work, Rae and Raymond were told it would take at least six months for the Army to process their application. In a war, that seemed as bad as six years. Then there was worse news: Rae received notice that she was being transferred to a workshop in Buntingford, more than a hundred miles away.

That was the last straw. Raymond went straight to his commanding officer. 'I need special permission to get married quickly,' he said.

The CO looked at him knowingly. 'Is your girlfriend pregnant?' he asked. That was normally the reason for such requests.

'No!' laughed Raymond. 'She's just being transferred.'

'I'll see what I can do,' said the other man.

The wedding was brought forward by three months, giving them just enough time to wed before Rae had to leave, although that meant it would have to take place in chilly January.

Rae intended to be married in her army uniform, just like Raymond. But he thought there might be something he could do to prevent her wearing the regulation thick cotton ATS stockings on their wedding day. 'I bought you this,' he said the next time he visited her, handing her a little box. Inside was a pair of silk stockings, with seams up the back.

'I can't wear these – they're not regulation!' she said.

'Rae, just take them,' Raymond pleaded.

The fourth of January 1944 was a cold day, but there was a clear sky and no sign of rain. Entering the church, Rae could see all her ATS friends, as well as some of her male colleagues from the workshop and army friends of Raymond's. His best man was another cook called Chet, who lived in a town near Raymond's home in Pennsylvania. As Rae reached the altar, Raymond smiled with relief to see that she had forsaken her thick regulation stockings and was wearing the silk ones he had given her.

After the ceremony they went straight in to sign the register. Then the little group went to the pub for a few celebratory drinks, before heading to the couple's favourite restaurant for the wedding feast: the local fish-and-chip shop.

The next morning, they took a train down to London for their honeymoon. Rae enjoyed giving her new husband a guided tour of her city – she showed him the Houses of Parliament, pointed out the Tower of London and took him to Hyde Park to hear the ranting men on their upturned fruit boxes at Speakers' Corner. On their way out of the park Rae paid a visit to the underground public toilet, while Raymond waited for her up on the pavement.

When she came back up the stairs, he was standing where she'd left him, but next to him was a busty redhead, one of the 'Piccadilly Commandos' who plied their trade in the West End. Since the arrival of the Americans these prostitutes now swarmed the area around Piccadilly, Leicester Square and Park Lane, making the most of the rich pickings. At night they lined the streets around the American Red Cross club on Rainbow Corner, shining torches on their ankles to attract the soldiers, and carried out their business in shop doorways.

The girl was clearly propositioning Raymond, but as soon as she saw Rae she quickly walked off.

'You better not leave me alone round here!' Raymond joked, putting his arm around his wife.

Back in Mansfield, it was only a matter of days before the new Mr and Mrs Raymond Wessel were parted, as Rae left for her 100-mile journey to Buntingford. She was leaving behind not only her husband, but the girls who had become like family to her: Eileen, Nancy, Irene and Helen. Rae knew she would miss her life in Mansfield terribly.

After the relative luxury of her previous billet, Buntingford brought a return to life in a Nissen hut, and the camp was muddy and cold. Rae had been sent to a Central Command workshop, much bigger than the one she was used to, and once again she was the only female welder. But this time there was no messing around with odd jobs – the Allies were gearing up for D-Day and her role was to seal over any holes in the hundreds of tanks that came in. Since many were being modi-fied as amphibious vehicles, to be launched into the sea a couple of miles off shore, it was essential that they should be buoyant.

Rae threw herself into the work, glad to be finally making a significant contribution to the war effort, but the pressure to get the tanks out quickly was intense. One day, when she had finished working on a tank, she jumped down from the top to save time, instead of waiting for a ladder, and immediately felt a pain in her abdomen. Thinking that she must have pulled a muscle, she got on with her work, trying her best to ignore her discomfort.

But by the end of the day the pain still hadn't gone, and after a night on her hard wooden bed it was even worse. The accident also seemed to have brought on her period, and the cramps added to her misery.

Rae struggled on with her work, but after two more days she was in agony. She woke up with a fever, and the pain in her abdomen was so severe that she couldn't move.

A medical officer came to her bedside and examined her. 'Rae,' he said quietly, 'did you know you were pregnant?'

Rae shook her head. She was too dumbfounded to speak.

'I'm afraid you're having a miscarriage,' the man informed her.

Rae was shocked. She and Raymond had spent so little intimate time together that the possibility of her being pregnant hadn't even crossed her mind. She had been clambering over tanks for the last six weeks. If only she had known.

Minutes later, Rae was in an ambulance speeding to Bishop's Stortford Hospital. As she lay in the back of the vehicle, every bump and pothole it went over brought her fresh agony.

By the time she got to hospital, it was clear Rae had haemorrhaged badly. For three days she was so delirious that she couldn't speak. But in her more lucid moments, lying in her hospital bed 100 miles away from her new husband, she felt utterly miserable.

When she was finally discharged, Rae was given two weeks' sick leave, but to her dismay she was not allowed to go up to Mansfield to see Raymond because of the distance. The only place she could go was back to her mother's in London.

It was a relief to be with family again, but the person she really longed to see was Raymond. Rae had kept him at arm's length when they first met, but now she found she desperately wanted him around. Fortunately, since they were married, he was able to put in a request for her to be stationed closer to him.

Rae was hoping she might be sent back to Mansfield where her friends were, and looked forward to returning to her old, happy life. But it was not to be. The best the Army could do was a post twenty miles south in Chilwell, a suburb of Nottingham. Reluctantly, Rae packed her bags and headed to the depot, which was the largest in the Royal Army Ordnance Corps.

At least Raymond could now visit her every weekend. The miscarriage had made her feel more connected to him, and it was good to have his big strong arms around her again.

But the reunion was short-lived, and soon Raymond was sent away to Wales for training, more than 200 miles away. Rae knew all too well what he was training for. D-Day was looming and his hospital unit would be required to deal with the inevitable casualties on the far shore. Raymond was going into the battlefield, and Rae had no way of knowing if he would ever come back.

7

Margaret

'Margaret Joy Boyle, will you take Captain Lawrence McCaskill Rambo to be your husband? Will you love him, comfort him, honour and protect him, and, forsaking all others, be faithful to him as long as you both shall live?'

'I will.'

As she said the words, Margaret just hoped that the skirt suit she was wearing was doing a convincing job of hiding her pregnancy. She was now five months along, but thankfully it wasn't showing too much.

Her attempt at aborting the baby had failed, and she had been left with no option but to tell Lawrence everything. To his credit, he had proved a Southern gentleman in deed as well as manner, and had immediately said he loved her and wanted to marry her. She knew she was lucky – many GIs who got their girlfriends pregnant simply put in for a transfer and were never heard of again, and the army hierarchy was adept at blocking women from tracking down errant fathers.

Margaret and Lawrence had waited until after her twenty-first birthday in October 1943, so that no explanation had to be given to her parents. Not that either of them had come to the wedding. Margaret had written to her mother in Ireland but received no reply, and her father was once again overseas with the Army. Her grandmother had come up to London from Canterbury for the service. Sitting in the front pew of St Mary Abbots in Kensington she looked on disapprovingly. She couldn't understand why her granddaughter had decided to marry an American of all people.

With so few guests at the ceremony there was no reception to speak of, and Margaret and Lawrence went back to the flat he had rented for them in Pembridge Villas, Notting Hill.

Margaret knew she wasn't in love with her new husband, but by force of will she had put her old boyfriend, Taylor Drysdale, out of her head and was trying her best to focus on Lawrence instead. There were certainly things to recommend him. They had a love of books in common, and he was intelligent and charismatic. He was a decent man, and hadn't deserted her.

Moreover, he had told her that his family in Georgia owned a lot of land, so she gathered that the Rambos were wealthy. His descriptions of growing up in a beautiful white Greek Revival mansion sounded like something from *Gone with the Wind*, and Margaret began to look forward to one day going to Georgia.

Once she was married, Margaret left her job at the ETOUSA headquarters and spent most of her time sitting at home reading novels. One day in December, when she was only seven and a half months pregnant, she felt a warm liquid trickle down her leg. She looked down and to her horror realised that her waters were breaking.

She heaved herself up, walked as quickly as she could to the phone in the hall and called an ambulance. As she was rushed to Hammersmith Hospital, she was struck by the bitter irony of her situation. Trying to get rid of the pregnancy, alone in her room, had been the darkest hour of her life. Yet now, just when she was beginning to be hopeful about her future with Lawrence, she stood to lose the child.

By the time she arrived, there was nothing the doctors could do to stop the baby from coming, even though it was still in a breech position. The labour took twenty agonising hours and Margaret did her best to breathe through the waves of pain, hoping and praying that the child would survive despite being six weeks premature.

Just as the baby was finally coming, the doctor shouted, 'Quick! She's breathing in.'

The breathing reflex had kicked in while the child's head was still in the birth canal, and she was inhaling mucus. If it went on too long she would be brain-damaged.

The doctors managed to extricate her and the cord was hastily cut before she was rushed out of the room.

'What's happening?' asked Margaret, so weak after almost a day in labour that she could hardly speak.

'Don't worry, Mrs Rambo. They just need to clear her tubes,' the midwife said, patting her hand.

News soon came that baby Rosamund was now breathing normally, but the doctors couldn't say what effect those first few minutes without oxygen might have had.

'I want to hold her,' Margaret sobbed. But Rosamund was so tiny, at just three pounds three ounces, that she had to be kept in an incubator, and Margaret was not able to see her until the next day. Even then, she wasn't allowed to pick her up.

Margaret was sent home, but she had to leave Rosamund behind, and since the baby was too small to breast-feed she had to express milk for her and take it to the hospital every day.

Eventually, Margaret was allowed to take the baby home, but she felt that the separation of the first few weeks had made it hard for her to bond with Rosamund, and even harder for Lawrence to do so.

He seemed distracted and fretful, and explained that he was under immense pressure at work. He was helping to plan the equipment needed for D-Day, and was coming home later and later from the office. Margaret worried about the long hours he was putting in, and knew that having a screaming baby in the house wasn't helping. Sometimes he didn't come back until eleven or twelve at night, having gone for a drink after work, which he said was the only way he could unwind at the end of the day. He would often wake in the night and lie there tossing and turning until morning.

He also seemed to be anxious about money. When bills arrived they sent him into a fit of anxiety, and he scratched out endless sums on pieces of paper, then screwed them up and threw them into the bin. 'Don't you worry your pretty head about it, my dear,' he told Margaret, when she asked him if something was wrong.

One day Lawrence arrived home late again, clearly already more than tipsy. He was carrying a bottle of whisky and went straight to the kitchen and poured himself a large glassful. Margaret watched in surprise as he knocked it back, then immediately poured himself another one and knocked that back too, as if it was no stronger than water.

'Lawrence, are you sure that's a good idea?' she asked, concerned.

He turned to her, his familiar features contorted into a furious scowl and his dark-brown eyes flashing with anger. 'Don't you go telling me what to do!' he shouted.

The baby started to cry and Margaret rushed from the room to comfort her. As she soothed the child she could feel her heart racing with fear. The man who had just spoken to her seemed like a completely different person to the husband she knew.

When the baby calmed down, Margaret crept into bed, hoping that by now Lawrence had drunk enough to fall asleep in his chair.

The next morning when he went off to work he looked a little worse for wear, but acted as if nothing had happened. He kissed her goodbye as usual and went on his way. The previous night's behaviour must have been an aberration, she told herself, and she tried to put it out of her mind.

The following night Margaret was already asleep when Lawrence came in, and they didn't have a chance to talk. But on Friday, he once again returned home tipsy and produced a bottle of whisky from his pocket. He seemed to barely notice her as he set about pouring himself a large drink.

Margaret felt instantly nervous. 'Have you had any supper?' she asked, and when he didn't reply she quickly went to make him some food, hoping it might sober him up.

But in the meantime he had drunk half the bottle. The wild, furious look was back in his eyes, and once again he seemed transformed into a completely different person. The Southern gentleman was gone and in his place was someone she didn't recognise.

'I don't want that!' he slurred, as she put the food in front of him. He shoved the plate away, sending it crashing onto the floor.

Margaret didn't stay to see what he would do next. She ran into the bedroom, and this time she locked the door. From under the covers, she could hear crashing and banging noises, and dreaded to think what he was doing.

In the morning, Margaret was woken by a gentle knocking on the door. When she opened it, there her husband stood, his brown eyes full of grief. 'I'm so sorry, Margaret,' he said. 'I don't know what came over me last night. I'm under so much pressure at work, I just can't think straight.'

He looked overcome with shame and regret, and she couldn't help feeling sorry for him. 'It's all right,' she said, shakily. 'But Lawrence, please don't bring whisky back to the house again.'

'No, of course not,' he agreed. 'Margaret, you are the finest wife a man could have.' He kissed her goodbye, gave her an adoring look, and then he was gone.

When she went into the kitchen, she saw that he had cleared up the broken plate and food, but in the living room she found that the electric heater had been smashed to pieces. So that was what the crashing and banging had been. She shuddered to think of him in such a violent rage.

Margaret couldn't help feeling angry towards the Army, who were clearly putting her husband under such terrible stress that he was buckling. She was worried he might have some kind of collapse.

The next few nights Lawrence came home earlier and did not bring any whisky with him. Margaret was relieved, but she was still worried about him, since he seemed anxious and again wasn't sleeping well.

One day Lawrence came home and announced, 'I've found somewhere much better for us to live. We're moving immediately.'

'But don't we have to give notice on our flat?' she asked him.

'I've arranged all that,' he told her. 'Just pack our things and we can go there now.'

Margaret was surprised, but she hoped that a change of scene might help her husband. She did as he said and followed him to an address in Rabbit Row, half a mile away.

When they arrived, she found it was a small mews street that had been badly bombed earlier in the war. But she didn't want to complain, so she got on with the unpacking.

The new flat didn't seem to do anything to lighten the considerable load Lawrence was carrying, however. One day, while putting away some laundry, Margaret discovered two empty whisky bottles in his sock drawer.

Worse, a letter arrived addressed to her from their previous landlady, Mrs Campion, demanding payment for the electricity, phone and cleaning bills, as well as the cost of the smashed electrical fire. The woman said she had spoken to Captain Rambo several times about the bills, and he had promised to pay them, but she had received nothing. So that's why we had to leave in such a hurry, thought Margaret.

She decided she would speak to Lawrence that night, and planned out in her head what she was going to say: that he needed to tell his superiors his workload was too large, that he needed a break and that she would help him keep on top of the bills. She just hoped that Lawrence would come home sober and at a reasonable hour.

That afternoon, there was a knock at the door and Margaret went to answer it. She found an American military policeman waiting outside. 'Mrs Rambo?' he asked.

'Yes.'

'Ma'am, I need you to pack a bag and come with me. Your husband has been arrested.'

'What for?' Margaret asked, horrified.

'I understand he's been running up bad debts, ma'am. He's being held in a US Army hospital in Lichfield.'

'Why, what's wrong with him?'

'Suspected alcohol poisoning, ma'am. They're drying him out before he can be court-martialled. I'm here to take you and the child up to Lichfield.'

Margaret couldn't believe what she was hearing. In a daze she went back into the flat to pack her bag, and then she and Rosamund left with the military policeman.

In the car up to Staffordshire, she felt too humiliated to ask any more questions. What on earth would her father, a respected major in the British Army, think if he knew his daughter's husband was being court-martialled? She had married Lawrence to save her family from shame, but now he was bringing it upon them anyway.

While Lawrence was being treated, Margaret passed the time in Lichfield at the nearby Red Cross centre, where, to keep her mind off things, she volunteered to type letters for US servicemen, while Rosamund stayed in a day nursery. After a while, she was allowed to visit her husband, and was relieved to find him sitting up in bed looking rested and returned to his old self. 'Lawrence, I've been so worried about you,' she told him.

'I'm sorry to worry you, my dear,' he said, stroking her hair lovingly. 'I got myself into a terrible mess, with all the stress of the war and the hospital bills we had for Rosamund. When I explain everything to the court they'll understand.'

'Can we go home now?' she asked.

'I'm being sent to another hospital for some tests,' he said. 'Routine procedure before a trial.'

Margaret nodded. On her way out she stopped the doctor and asked where Lawrence was going. 'He's being transferred to the 96th General Hospital near Worcester for observation,' he told her. 'They have specialist psychiatric facilities there.'

'But why?' asked Margaret. 'There's nothing wrong with him, is there?'

'We have to determine whether he's responsible for his actions,' the man told her. 'That requires a neuro-psychiatric examination.'

Before long, Lawrence was passed fit to stand trial, and once he was released from the hospital, he was taken to London for the court martial. Margaret had been called as a witness, and she travelled down separately. Her mind was in turmoil – as well as worrying about Lawrence's impending trial, she had just learned from a doctor that she was pregnant again.

On the day of the court martial, Margaret felt sick with shame as she watched the first witness take the stand – a Miss G. M. Blayney from the American Red Cross club on Charles Street, Mayfair. 'That's Captain Rambo, over there,' she said, pointing to Lawrence, who looked down at the floor. 'I recall cashing a cheque for him on 24 January.'

The young woman was presented with the cheque. 'Yes, that's it,' she said. 'I took it from him and gave him ten pounds cash for it.'

The cheque had been returned from the bank marked 'insufficient funds'.

'Thank you, Miss Blayney,' the judge said.

Next, a Mrs Gwendolen Sommerville was called from the Red Cross's Jules Club. 'I cashed a check for Captain Rambo on 15 January for ten pounds,' she said. 'There's an entry in our club's cheque registry.'

Again, there had been no money in Lawrence's bank account.

One after another, women from the Red Cross clubs stood up to testify that Lawrence had obtained cash from them with cheques that were returned marked 'insufficient funds' or 'no account'. Twelve times he had pulled the same trick – at the Duchess Club, the Reindeer Club, the Nurses Club, the Washington Club, Rainbow Corner – all the most famous GI hangouts in central London. In total, he had swindled them out of £103.

Margaret was appalled. Of all the institutions to steal from, to target the Red Cross seemed beyond the pale.

Lawrence's bank manager, Mr Wigmore, from Barclays Bank on Oxford Street, told how Lawrence had been overdrawn for a year, by sums of as much as £96. 'I was constantly in touch with Captain Rambo by means of personal interviews, telephone calls and letters, and was continually pressing him to repay the money he owed the bank,' he told the court.

No wonder Lawrence had seemed distracted and fretful all the time, thought Margaret.

To her surprise, her own bank manager from Lloyds was also called to testify. He identified seven of the cheques written to the Red Cross and told the court: 'These cheques were taken from a book issued to a customer who was then named Miss Boyle.'

Margaret gasped. He had stolen *her* chequebook to carry out his fraud!

Next, their old landlady, Mrs Campion, testified about the unpaid bills and the cost of the smashed electrical fire that they had left behind at 58 Pembridge Villas. 'Captain Rambo assured me the money had been sent, but I never received anything and the amount is still due,' she said. 'I also wrote to Captain Rambo's wife.' As she spoke she caught Margaret's eye.

Margaret felt her cheeks go red. She wondered if the whole court thought she had known of her husband's crimes and had been in on them.

Luigi Martini, head waiter at Kettner's, the restaurant where she and Lawrence had gone for their very first date, was next to point at him across the courtroom. 'That is the gentleman I served,' he said, in a thick Italian accent. 'His food and drink bill came to five pounds, sixteen shillings and sixpence, and he gave me a cheque.' Once again it was from Margaret's chequebook, and had been returned marked 'no account'.

Finally, it was Margaret's turn to speak. She took the stand shakily and was sworn in, and was asked to explain her relationship with Lawrence.

'I met Lawrence Rambo on 25 December 1942, and we married in October 1943,' she told the court. 'Our daughter was born in December.'

'What did you know of his financial situation?'

She hesitated. 'I knew that his financial troubles were worrying him, because he couldn't sleep and he drank too much.'

'And how did he seem to you in his state of mind?'

'He was restless and nervous,' she said. Then, fighting back a sob, she added, 'He seemed to be a different man from the one I knew.'

'Thank you, Mrs Rambo. That will be all.'

She returned gratefully to her seat.

Lawrence had failed to enter a plea in response to the charges, and Margaret wondered what on earth he was going to say to explain himself.

As he took the stand, he looked contrite and his brown eyes glittered as if he might be about to cry. He read from a written statement, admitting all the charges against him and throwing himself on the leniency of the court. Lawrence explained that during his years in the Canadian Army earlier in the war, he had fallen into drinking heavily and spending more than he earned. He had got his family to send him money several times from his bank account in Georgia. When he left the States, there had been $2,000 in the account, but now it was all gone.

'I have never been a particularly good manager of money matters, and I can now see very clearly that I simply weakened under the strain of three years of living under conditions of excess drinking and both domestic and money troubles, and although it was very wrong and very foolish, I began to default on debts,' he said. 'It was then that I cashed the cheques listed against me in the charges in this case.

'I have made a terrible mistake during the past several months, and I fully realise it. I do not know whether my nerves were affected, or what happened to my judgement, but I can thoroughly understand how it must appear to anyone who has not experienced the pressure caused by my personal finances.

'Unfortunately for me and for my family, I have a wife and a four-month-old baby who will suffer more than I will. I hope that some punishment can be assessed against me that will enable me to remain in the Army so that I may immediately have a chance to begin paying off the money represented by these cheques, so that my wife and daughter will not be made to suffer for what I have done.

'I appeal to the mercy of the court, but I stand ready to meet whatever sentence it adjudges against me with a humble and contrite heart, and regardless of the sentence, with a firm resolution that I shall never again give way to the temptation that put me in such difficulties.'

It was a moving speech, and Lawrence seemed genuinely regretful. Despite her shock and anger over what he had done, Margaret couldn't help feeling sorry for him as she thought of the mental anguish he had been going through.

Nevertheless, the judge decided not to grant his request to save his job. Lawrence was found guilty, and sentenced to be dismissed from the Army. He was to be repatriated as soon as possible.

'I'm sorry, I'm so sorry,' he told Margaret at the end of the trial. 'Can you forgive me? I told the judge I would never give way again, and I meant it. I'll never touch another drop of alcohol. If you come with me to Georgia we can start afresh – as a family. Promise me you'll follow me to America. Promise me.'

Margaret had no idea what to do. How could she trust Lawrence's words after what he had done? But then, what kind of life would she have if she stayed behind? She had no one in England to support her, and now with another baby on the way, who knew what would become of her? She didn't want to end up like her mother, raising her children alone, and she couldn't bear the thought of telling her father that her marriage had ended in failure.

Lawrence's dark eyes looked at her earnestly. Maybe he just wasn't cut out for this war, she thought. Back in Georgia, with his family around him, things would be different. She had to hope so.

'All right then, I promise,' she said.

8

Gwendolyn

Early one morning towards the end of May 1944, Lyn woke to a rumbling noise outside her window. She leaped out of bed and flung open the curtains.

In the street below, an endless column of American tanks trundled along at a glacial speed, while dozens of jeeps were parked up on the pavement.

One was sitting right in Lyn's front garden, and when she went out to investigate, the driver smiled at her. 'Want a doughnut?' he asked, gesturing to a Red Cross van up the street.

'Yes, please,' she replied.

The man went and fetched a couple of doughnuts, handing one to Lyn. She had never tried this particular American delicacy before, and the moist, sugary dough tasted like heaven.

She learned that the young man's name was Eugene Gidcombe – 'from Hermiston, Oregon, ma'am' – and that he was passing through the town on his way to a staging area further down the coast.

From the build-up of troops and vehicles in Southampton it was obvious that the long-awaited D-Day was imminent, although officially the plans remained top-secret. Lyn knew that Eugene would soon be fighting in France.

'Are you scared?' she asked him.

'Of what?'

'Going to war.'

'Yes, ma'am. Were you scared when the Germans bombed Southampton?'

'Not really,' Lyn replied honestly.

Eugene laughed. 'Hey, do all limey girls talk funny like you?'

'You're the ones who talk funny!' Lyn replied.

They sat chatting for a while, until the time came for him to move on. 'Can you do something for me?' he asked her.

'Of course,' Lyn said.

'Scratch your name on the side of my jeep. It'll give me something to remind me of you when I'm on the other side.'

Eugene offered her a pocketknife and she carved a shaky 'Lyn' on the side of the vehicle. He took down her address and promised to write to her.

Lyn waved goodbye to Eugene and he went on his way, but she found that every new jeep that stopped outside her door contained a young man equally eager for a little conversation before he went off to face the war. Soon Lyn had given out her address to half a dozen GIs, all of them promising to write.

As the vehicles trundled out of Southampton, she wondered if she would hear from any of them again.

On the morning of 6 June, the sky above Southampton was filled with planes heading towards the Continent. Meanwhile, a body of men and machines comparable in size to the city of Birmingham was making its way across the Channel.

Lyn sat glued to the wireless, desperate for news of the invasion. At 8 a.m., the BBC announced that paratroopers had landed in France overnight, and just after 10 a.m. news broke that ground troops had landed in Normandy. A lump formed in Lyn's throat as she thought of Eugene and the other GIs who had pulled up outside her door.

On the first day of the invasion more than 4,000 Allied soldiers were killed, among them 2,500 Americans. Many never even made it ashore.

Over the next few weeks, Lyn was surprised to receive letters from all the GIs who had asked for her address. Eugene wrote most vividly, describing the liberation of Paris and the hordes of young French girls weeping and throwing flowers on his jeep.

For Lyn, the letters were a welcome distraction from thoughts of another GI. She was still struggling with her feelings for Russ, the charming Mexican-American who was so devoted to his wife. They had continued to spend tantalising yet chaste evenings together under the supervision of her parents, who believed they were doing their patriotic duty in welcoming a GI into their house.

One day, Russ surprised Lyn by presenting her with a gold bracelet. 'Could you take it to a jeweller's and have it inscribed?' he asked.

'Oh, yes,' Lyn replied excitedly. 'What should it say?'

'To Larina, from Russ,' he said wistfully.

Lyn hid her disappointment and dutifully took the bracelet to the shop. She watched as the words were carved into the metal, wishing the bracelet bore her name instead of Larina's.

As more and more Americans arrived in Southampton after D-Day, the city was soon even busier than it had been before. Over 60 per cent of all American personnel and equipment shipped to the Continent came through the town.

The Polygon Hotel, where the American officers stayed, was busier than ever, and Lyn and her workmates were there every

Saturday night. One evening, they were eating dinner before the dancing began when she heard a commotion by the entrance.

'I'm sorry,' the maître d' was saying, 'but it would disturb our clientele.'

Standing behind him was a group of men in RAF uniform, their faces severely disfigured by burns, like those of many pilots who had survived the Battle of Britain.

Lyn's heart went out to them. Her older siblings, Bunty and Ron, were in the Air Force, so she felt a natural sympathy towards the men.

But the maître d' was resolute, and the group reluctantly shuffled away.

As they left, a young American lieutenant stood up from his table and followed after them. He didn't look much like the typical GI Joe – he was slim, dark and delicate looking – but something about him caught Lyn's attention.

'You should be ashamed,' he told the maître d' on his way out.

A few minutes later he was back, but there was no sign of the disfigured young airmen.

'Excuse me,' Lyn said as he passed her table. 'Wouldn't they come back?'

'No,' the American replied. 'And to be honest I don't blame them.' He returned to his table just long enough to pay for his food, before leaving.

Lyn went back to her dinner, but all through the rest of the evening she couldn't help thinking of the airmen, and how disgusting the maître d's behaviour was.

On Monday morning, Lyn was cycling to work at the Chamber of Commerce when she caught sight of the American lieutenant. 'Hello!' she called, jumping down from her bike. 'I just wanted to thank you for what you did at the hotel on Saturday.'

'Well, I thought it was a low blow,' he said. 'Those guys were willing to give their lives for their country, and to be treated that way…'

'I couldn't believe it either,' Lyn agreed. 'Are you going to file a complaint?'

'I'd love to, but I can't. We've got enough issues between Yanks and Brits as it is.'

'Well, you did what you could,' she told him, as she hopped back on her bike and rode off.

The next day, Lyn saw the GI again on her way into work, and again she stopped to speak to him.

'Morning,' he said politely, giving her a smile. Lyn noticed that he had never called her 'baby' or 'sugar'.

'Morning,' she replied. 'I just realised I never found out your name. I'm Lyn.'

'Ben Patrino,' he said.

Lyn learned that Ben was from California, that he was Italian-American – she thought the Italian part sounded very romantic – and that he supervised the black troops who loaded and unloaded the cargo in the Port Company.

In the days that followed, the two of them bumped into each other regularly and Lyn found herself looking forward to it, although somehow she never got round to mentioning her new friend to Russ. Ben might not have had the Mexican ensign's easy charm, but the more Lyn saw of him the more she liked him. He was polite and softly spoken, so different from most GIs she had met.

After several more brief encounters, Ben finally got up the courage to ask Lyn out to the movies. She found herself saying yes, and only afterwards thought of Russ with a jolt. But then, why shouldn't she go out on a date? Russ was allowed to spend time with her despite having a wife in Florida.

When Lyn arrived home that afternoon, her mother told her she had just missed a visit from Russ. 'He's left something for you on the mantelpiece,' she said.

Lyn rushed into the front room to find a crisp white envelope waiting for her, and ripped it open impatiently. Inside, Russ explained that he was being transferred away from Southampton. 'To my little English girl-friend,' he wrote, 'I pray that someday you will find what I have – the happiness of a loving and peaceful marriage.'

He had included a photograph of himself, looking intensely at the camera, and signed it, 'To Lyn, without you I would have been lost.'

Lyn held the letter to her heart. She felt choked at the thought of never seeing Russ again and filled with disappointment that their romance had come to its inevitable, unsatisfying end.

In a desultory mood, she put the letter back on the mantelpiece and went up to change for her date with Ben. She couldn't believe she had missed the chance to say goodbye to Russ.

When she met up with Ben outside the cinema, he beamed at her. 'You look beautiful,' he said, taking her hand and leading her inside.

'Thanks,' Lyn replied a little weakly.

It was a relief to take her seat in the darkened cinema and focus on the screen, rather than having to make conversation. As the film played out in front of her, Lyn's mind kept drifting back to her dates with the Mexican ensign, to the way he had looked into her eyes and played footsie with her under the table. After a while, she realised she had no idea what was happening in the film. At least Ben seemed to be enjoying it, though – and he hadn't even made a move to kiss her.

'Would you like some food?' he asked her afterwards. 'We could see if the Polygon's still serving.'

It was already getting late, and all Lyn really wanted was to go home and read Russ's letter again, but now Ben had mentioned it she was pretty hungry. 'All right,' she replied politely. 'That would be nice.'

Unfortunately, with a clientele made up almost exclusively of Americans, the Polygon had begun serving dinner early, and all they could offer Ben and Lyn was sardines on toast. As they ate, he told her about his former job as a book-keeper, and about his family back in California – how his dad would sit out on the porch at night playing the banjo and every Friday his mom would throw open their doors to the whole neighbourhood.

'Your family sounds lovely,' Lyn said, in between mouthfuls of toast.

'You're quite a chowhound!' Ben laughed. 'You know, you would love my mom's homemade pizza.'

'What's pizza?' Lyn asked.

Ben's jaw dropped. 'You never had pizza? Boy, you Brits are really missing out.'

'Well, I bet you've never had a good English roast,' Lyn responded. She told Ben about the wonderful meals her mother used to make every Sunday before rationing started, with roast beef, Yorkshire puddings, Brussels sprouts and roast potatoes.

The more they laughed and shared stories together, the more Lyn found she was enjoying herself. She was surprised to find she hadn't thought about Russ for a while.

At the end of the night, Ben walked Lyn home. He made no attempt to kiss her, but he held her hand. It felt good, Lyn realised – and unpressured.

'Goodnight then,' she told Ben, as they reached her front door. 'I had a nice evening.'

'Goodnight, Lyn,' he replied, squeezing her hand.

Inside, Lyn went straight to the mantelpiece and picked up Russ's letter. But this time she didn't open the envelope, or look at the photograph. Instead, she took it straight upstairs to her bedroom and shut it away in a drawer.

On her next date with Ben, Lyn gave him her undivided attention – and he gave her his unqualified devotion. It was clear that he was smitten, and at times he would drift off from talking and simply gaze at her.

At first, it made Lyn feel a little uncomfortable. 'What is it?' she asked, as Ben sat staring at her in silence.

'Boy, you really don't know how cute you are,' he replied. After that, Lyn decided that she rather liked it.

Soon, Ben and Lyn were seeing each other every evening. He treated her like royalty, always taking her coat for her, pulling out her chair at the table and bringing her chocolates and flowers. He persisted in calling her his 'chowhound' whenever he saw her stuffing her face, which always made her laugh.

When Ben and Lyn went to the pictures together they would stroll back home afterwards through Watts Park. It was on one of these walks that Lyn saw another side of Ben's character that raised him even further in her estimation.

'Wait here a minute,' Ben told her suddenly, guiding her to sit down on a bench before rushing over to a mixed group of black and white GIs.

Lyn could hear the men were arguing, and it sounded nasty. 'Get back in the gutter where you belong,' one of the white men shouted angrily. 'Uppity nigger,' another said.

Since the black GIs had first arrived in Britain two years earlier, racial incidents like these had grown common. Some had spilled over into violence, with knife fights, murders and even castrations of black soldiers. In one town a group of GIs from the South regularly went out 'nigger hunting', boasting of the black soldiers that they had killed. Since the Americans were subject to US Army law and beyond the control of the British police, such crimes were easily swept under the carpet.

But Ben was loyal to the black soldiers who served under him, and would always do his best to protect them. From the safety of her bench, Lyn watched as he waded right into the group. He was not a physically imposing man, but he had a quiet authority.

Lyn strained to hear what Ben was saying, but she couldn't make it out. Evidently it had the desired effect, though. As fired-up and angry as the young white men had become, soon they began to disperse. The black GIs thanked Ben and then went off in the other direction.

'I'm sorry about that,' Ben told Lyn, rushing back to the bench.

But she didn't mind. Once again she felt stirred by Ben's strength of purpose and decency.

As they continued to date, Lyn saw a string of similar encounters from her vantage point on the bench in the park. Each time Ben somehow managed to step in and diffuse the situation before a single blow was even landed.

'I like the way you stand up for your men,' she told him. 'A lot of Yanks don't give them a chance.'

'I didn't either, to begin with,' he admitted. 'When I first heard they were putting me in charge of Negroes, I was down in the dumps for a week. I thought they smelled bad, they were lazy, I didn't want anything to do with them. But those were my orders so I figured I just had to swallow it. Then I started to realise that some of them weren't so bad after all. You ask me now, I'd say they're the best group of guys I ever met.'

Lyn took Ben's hand and squeezed it tightly. She thought of Russ, the man she had previously thought was so perfect. Somehow, she couldn't imagine having the same conversation with him.

After Lyn had been dating Ben for several weeks, her parents insisted on meeting him. Mrs Rowe was keen to make a good impression, and having heard about the legendary Italian love of pasta, had blown most of her week's rations on tins of Heinz spaghetti in tomato sauce.

Ben smiled politely as Lyn's mother doled the sticky red gloop onto a piece of toast in front of him.

'Well, eat up everyone,' she said.

Ben took a hearty mouthful and made appreciative noises. But after a while Lyn noticed that he seemed more interested in the toast than the spaghetti, and once that was gone the rest merely moved around his plate.

'What's the matter?' asked Lyn. 'You're not eating.'

'I'm not that hungry is all,' Ben replied tactfully.

'Don't you like the spaghetti?' Mrs Rowe asked anxiously.

'Oh, yeah, it's real good,' Ben replied.

'Then why aren't you eating it?' Lyn demanded.

There was a silence until Ben spoke again. He turned to Mrs Rowe and said, 'To be honest, ma'am, I've never eaten spaghetti out of a tin.'

'That's all right,' she laughed. 'You don't have to eat it.'

But Lyn was incensed. 'I knew Americans were rude, but I never thought you would insult my mother like that!' she declared.

'Don't be silly, Gwen,' Mrs Rowe replied. 'I like a man who's not a phoney. I wish all Americans were as honest as he is.'

Lyn leaped from her chair and stormed upstairs to her bedroom. 'You'll need a firm hand with that one,' she heard her father tell Ben as she went.

When, after twenty minutes, no one had come up after her, Lyn became curious and crept back downstairs. She was surprised to see that Ben and her parents were getting on brilliantly. Her dad was fascinated to hear all about Ben's black troops, and observed that down the pub the black GIs always seemed more courteous than the white ones. For his part, Ben laughed at all of Mr Rowe's jokes, while Mrs Rowe was evidently taken with Lyn's new young man too.

Watching Ben's easy relationship with her parents, Lyn's anger at him dissipated. Somehow, despite the spaghetti incident, everything seemed to be going really well.

One evening, before the city was swallowed up by the blackout, Lyn and Ben were strolling through Watts Park. Everywhere she looked, she could see girls just like her, walking and laughing with their GI boyfriends. This was how it was meant to be, she thought: a guy, who liked a girl, who liked him back – not the tortured longing that she had endured with Russ. It was simple, really. Why had it taken her so long to realise?

'Want to go sit on "our" bench?' asked Ben, pointing out the one that Lyn had sat on so many times watching him sort out fights between the black and white soldiers.

'As long as you promise to sit with me this time,' she joked.

They sat down together and Ben pulled her close. 'Lyn,' he whispered. 'You know I'm head over heels in love with you. I'll never love anyone else as long as I live.'

It was the most romantic thing Lyn had ever heard – and coming from Ben she knew that it was true.

'Here,' he said, 'there's something I want you to have.'

Lyn watched as he reached inside his shirt and took off a little beaded chain with a crucifix on it. He pressed it into her hand. 'I want you to wear this,' he said. 'It's my mom's – she gave it to me the day I went away.'

'But Ben, I can't take this,' said Lyn. 'Your mother will be hurt if she finds out you don't have it any more.'

Ben shook his head. 'No,' he said. 'She'll understand when I tell her I gave it to you.'

When Lyn got home that evening there was another letter waiting for her on the mantelpiece, this time from Eugene. She had continued to correspond with the young GI throughout his time in Europe, and still thought of him often, sitting outside her house in his jeep.

Eugene wrote that he would soon be coming home on leave and would like to see her again. 'There's a question that I really want to ask you,' he said.

Lyn didn't hesitate. She took a pen and paper and drafted a quick but friendly reply. She told him she was sorry, and she wished him all the best in his life, but she was now with someone else – and it was serious.

9

Sylvia

Sylvia had corresponded with her GI boyfriend Carl all throughout his training for D-Day. The cheerful red-headed young man had eclipsed all the previous men she had dated, American or English, and she had fallen for him with all her heart. It seemed that Carl had felt the same way about her – several times he had mentioned the sights that he wanted to show her in his hometown of Boston, and she had begun to look forward to one day following him to America.

Then Carl had written to let her know that he would be travelling to Normandy on an LST – a large boat capable of transporting tanks – and that he would write again as soon as he could. But in the weeks after D-Day no letter had come, and when Sylvia tried writing to him, her envelope came back marked 'UNDELIVERABLE'. Much as she didn't want to admit it, she knew in her heart what that meant – Carl was one of the many who hadn't made it.

As Sylvia sat holding the crumpled envelope, which she herself had carefully inscribed with her boyfriend's name only a few weeks earlier, the tears streamed down her face.

Her mother came over to comfort her. 'There, there, love,' she whispered.

Mrs Bradley knew exactly how her daughter felt. She had suffered a similar loss in the First World War, before she had met Sylvia's father. She had told her family humorous stories of her dalliances with Australian soldiers stationed in Britain, but it hadn't all been mere fun and flirtation. One man in particular had made a more meaningful impression, and she had been ready to cross the ocean to be with him – then his letters, just like Carl's, had dried up, leaving her with the same inevitable, bleak conclusion that Sylvia now faced.

Mrs Bradley hugged her daughter tight. 'What do I do now, Mum?' Sylvia asked her through her tears.

'Only one thing you can do, love,' her mother replied. 'Get back on your feet and keep going.'

While soldiers were being killed every day on the Continent, life on the home front was far from safe. Since the Normandy landings, the Nazis had begun using two devastating new weapons. The V-1, or 'doodlebug', was a pilotless plane that would fall from the sky when its engine cut out, causing a ton-weight warhead to explode on impact. Even more terrifying was the V-2 rocket, which travelled at nearly five times the speed of sound. The only warning it gave was a sonic boom as it dropped from 30,000 feet, and it could destroy a whole row of terraced houses.

Every Sunday, at their home in Woolwich, Mrs Bradley threw open the windows so that the whole family could hear the band playing in the church parade at the chapel of the Royal Artillery. But one week the drums and brass were silent.

'I can't hear the band this morning,' Sylvia told her mother.

'No, love,' Mrs Bradley replied. 'I think one of them doodle-bugs got the chapel. The band won't be playing any more.'

'Oh,' Sylvia replied quietly. From then on, Sunday mornings passed in silence.

Sylvia was doing her best to throw herself into her work at the Piccadilly Hotel and the Red Cross club. On her commute 'Up West' every morning she had made friends with a group of young women who always caught the same train – the 8.10 from Woolwich to Charing Cross. There was a local girl by the name of Olive Kelsey who Sylvia had been to the pictures with a few times, a young married woman called Vera whose parents owned the local pet shop, and two other girls whose company and gossip she always enjoyed. Chatting away with the little group had become one of the rituals of Sylvia's day. They had all agreed to meet in the carriage at the back of the train every morning, to make sure they would always find each other and that everyone would get a seat.

One day, however, Sylvia was running late – so late, in fact, that she almost missed the train altogether. Dashing down the steps to the platform just as it was about to leave, she hopped onto the first carriage, disappointed that she wouldn't get to sit with her friends.

The train was just beginning to pull out of the station when Sylvia heard a deafening thunderclap. The glass window by her side shattered and a shard of glass nicked her right cheek, as she heard a second, deafening noise – the sound of a V-2 rocket exploding behind her. The train carriage shook, and Sylvia heard a buzzing in her ears, followed by some more indistinct noises of crashing and crunching. The train's brakes screeched as the driver brought it to a halt, and she noticed that all the doors had been blown open.

All around her was pandemonium. Her fellow passengers stumbled about, some of them screaming in panic, and those who had sat nearer the windows were badly cut and bleeding. Sylvia reached up to her own face, where the shard of glass had caught her. Her fingers came down red with blood, so she took a hanky from her bag and held it up to her cheek.

The conductor rushed down the carriage to check whether anyone was seriously hurt. Mostly their injuries seemed fairly superficial, but they were in a frantic state and he struggled to restore calm.

Sylvia ran over to where one of the doors had blown open. Leaning her head out, she could see the carriage behind, with its windows shattered just like her one. But where were the carriages beyond that? She was sure there had been four of them when she boarded the train.

Then she saw the remaining carriages, laid on their sides across the track, ripped open by the blast. The back carriage looked like little more than a pile of debris. From amid the mess of wood and metal a human arm protruded, but it wasn't moving. She knew it was the carriage that Olive, Vera and the others would have been sitting in. It was only because she had been running late that she was not lying among the wreckage too.

In a daze she went back to her seat and sat down again. Before long, the conductor ushered the passengers off the train, and walked them along the track to a waiting area. The glimpse Sylvia had caught of that dead arm kept playing over and over in her mind, and she felt sick to her stomach.

After about forty minutes, the conductor returned with news. 'We're going to uncouple the train and send the front two carriages on to Charing Cross,' he said.

The dazed group of passengers boarded the train again, and it continued to Charing Cross. There, Sylvia boarded a bus to Piccadilly as usual, but she felt strangely detached, as if none of the morning's events were real. Still holding the handkerchief up to her face, she wandered up the spiral staircase to the billing office.

Miss Frank accosted her on her way in. 'What time do you call this, young lady?' she barked angrily. 'Don't you know you're two and a half hours late?'

As she heard the harsh words, something in Sylvia snapped and she collapsed to the floor sobbing. The handkerchief fell from her face, and Miss Frank saw the bright-red gash across it. 'Sylvia! What's happened?' she asked, crouching down by her side.

'A V-2 hit the train,' Sylvia sobbed. The image of the dead arm came into her head again.

'Someone run down to the hotel bar and fetch some brandy,' Miss Frank shouted. Sylvia's friend Peggy left the room, returning a few minutes later with a glass of Armagnac, which she put up to Sylvia's lips. As she sipped the drink, Sylvia began to feel a little calmer.

'That's better,' Miss Frank said soothingly. 'Now, let's get you home. You can't work today.'

Sylvia was vaguely aware of being led back downstairs to the street and put into a black cab.

Back in Woolwich she staggered up to her front door. She was fumbling to find her key when her mother threw the door open. 'Oh thank God, you're alive!' she cried, pulling Sylvia into a hug.

Since the V-2 had struck, Mrs Bradley had been having the worst morning of her life. She had heard the noise from the house and had rushed up the hill to the local butcher, who had a good view, to find out what had happened. When he told her the rocket had struck a train leaving just after eight, she had been beside herself with worry. She was sure it must have been Sylvia's train, and was convinced that she had been killed.

The two women stood on the doorstep, holding each other close for several minutes, both sobbing. Then Mrs Bradley brought her daughter inside the house and gently led her up to bed. Exhaustion caught up with Sylvia, and before long she had drifted into a deep sleep, her mother sitting anxiously by her bedside.

For the next few days Sylvia was unable to get up, too shaken by her experience to face the world and barely aware of the days passing by. After a while she began to develop carbuncles under her armpits, which the doctor said were caused by the trauma of the bombing.

One day, after about a week, her mother knocked on the bedroom door. 'You've got a visitor, love,' she said. She ushered in Sylvia's friend Vera from the train.

Sylvia gasped – she could hardly believe her eyes. 'Vera!' she said. 'I thought you were dead!'

Remarkably, Vera had survived the attack with only cuts and grazes, and she told Sylvia that two of the other girls had also been very lucky – they were in hospital, but had avoided any serious injuries. But Olive Kelsey had not been so fortunate – she had been sitting by the window when the rocket fell, and had died instantly.

Knowing that she should have been in the carriage with the other girls, Sylvia felt a tremendous sense of guilt. She was glad that Vera and the other two had recovered so well, but the thought of Olive dying just feet away from them haunted her, and she couldn't shake the image of the arm she had seen poking out of the rubble.

Slowly, the carbuncles went down and Sylvia began to regain her strength. She started spending more of the day out of bed, even going for short walks down to the river. Mrs Bradley could see she was beginning to think about returning to work.

'Don't go back, Sylv,' she pleaded. 'It's too dangerous. You don't know what trains might be hit next.'

'I could be somewhere else and the same thing could happen, Mum,' Sylvia replied. She loved her jobs at the hotel and the Red Cross club – they were her social life – and she didn't want to give them up.

'All right then, love,' her mother replied reluctantly.

That first morning getting back onto the 8.10 to Charing Cross was the hardest thing Sylvia had ever done. Her stomach was doing somersaults and her heart was racing as she stepped up from the platform, and she spent the whole journey feeling like she was about to throw up. But she managed to get into work on time, and as the weeks and months passed, bit by bit the morning journey became easier.

Every day as she boarded the train, she remembered what her mum had told her when Carl had died: 'You just have to get back on your feet, and keep going.'

10

Margaret

Margaret stood on the deck of the RMS *Mauretania* and watched England fade into the distance. It was four months since her husband had been kicked out of the American Army for defrauding the Red Cross and failing to pay his debts, and he had been repatriated shortly afterwards. In his letters to her since then he had repeated his promise that if she followed him to America they could start afresh and he would never touch another drop of alcohol. His apologies seemed heartfelt and sincere, and Margaret hoped that once he was away from the stress and strain of the war things would be easier.

As the wife of an officer, Margaret had been entitled to transportation by the Army, which had requisitioned Cunard's great ocean liners to carry troops from America to the theatres of operation and had spaces onboard on their return journeys. But the voyage was top secret – the passengers' bags were marked with a code number rather than their destination, and the brides had been instructed to tell no one at home when they were travelling, for fear of a U-boat attack. On some voyages, brides found the secrecy meant that even the crew didn't know who they were and assumed they must be prostitutes brought onboard for the officers.

Margaret soon learned that as well as taking British war brides to New York, the *Mauretania* was bringing German prisoners of war to Canada. 'Do not attempt to communicate with the prisoners,' the war brides had been told sternly when they boarded. But they watched with interest as the Germans were allowed up on deck once a day to take the air, and could hear them singing German folksongs at the tops of their voices down in the hold.

'Sounds like they're pretty happy down there,' Margaret's cabin-mate said. 'I bet they can't believe their luck, going to Canada!' Like Margaret, the woman had a baby with her, and though their cabin was clean and pleasant, it was hard to get any sleep with both infants crying at night.

Margaret was suffering from morning sickness, and combined with the motion of the boat she felt queasy almost all the time. To add to her discomfort, on the first day onboard the women all made the mistake of overeating at dinner. After years of rationing they were unable to control themselves at the sight of the tables laden with bowls of fruit – a rare treat in England – and the enormous portions of steak and potatoes. The children onboard, meanwhile, gorged themselves on sweets and chocolates, and soon the whole deck the GI brides were on smelled of sick. Luckily the plush carpets that had once lined the floors had been removed when the *Mauretania* had been requisitioned.

The ship had also been robbed of other luxury trappings, including its silver, crystal and china, which were now languishing in a warehouse. Tiers of canvas bunks had been installed in the first-class cabins in order to squeeze in as many troops as possible in rooms where once only one or two well-heeled guests had stayed, while the ship had been painted a dull battle grey and fitted with armaments. German U-boats still lurked in the waters, and it had to zigzag to avoid being targeted, setting a new course every few minutes.

Its grand restaurants had been turned into mess hall cafeterias, with narrow tables that could seat large numbers of troops at a time. But even these attempts at wartime economy couldn't mask the *Mauretania*'s beauty. The ship wasn't as big as the *Queen Mary* or *Queen Elizabeth*, but when it had been built just before the war it had been the largest vessel ever constructed in Britain for the newly combined Cunard White Star Line, and had been intended to bring glamour to the Atlantic crossings. It still had its exquisite chandeliers, grand staircases and glittering ballroom, and Margaret enjoyed simply wandering around gazing at them.

Among the *Mauretania*'s passengers was the well-known bandleader Spike Jones, who was being transported home after having entertained the American troops in Europe. He and his band performed in the ballroom every night of the voyage, but with young babies to look after, Margaret and her cabin-mate usually retired early.

During the day, Margaret did her best to get up on deck as much as possible to assuage her seasickness. Staring out across the endless miles of ocean, she was reminded how cut adrift she had always felt in her life. Some brides might feel the ache of homesickness, but she had never had a real home to miss.

Thankfully, the *Mauretania* was one of the faster Cunard vessels, and after just seven days at sea they approached New York. Margaret rushed up on deck with the other war brides to catch a glimpse of the Statue of Liberty. Some of the women were moved to tears by the sight of it, and it gave Margaret a rush of hope for the new life she was embarking on.

One woman, however, was incredulous. 'You mean it's *green?*' she exclaimed. Having only ever seen the statue in black-and-white photographs, she had assumed it was silver.

When the *Mauretania* pulled into Pier 86, those brides who were being met by their husbands were allowed to disembark. Lawrence had told Margaret he would meet her in New York and then take her by train to Arlington, in Southwest Georgia, where he was staying with his sister Ellen.

Margaret and the other brides waited to have their documents stamped and to undergo a medical check. Standing in line pregnant, with little Rosamund in a carrycot, she felt exhausted. Army transportation had not yet taken account of the needs of war brides and their children, and there was nowhere she could change the baby, who cried pathetically as she got wetter and wetter.

It was well into the evening by the time they got through, and representatives from the Red Cross were waiting to link them up with their husbands. Some had come to the port to meet their wives, while other women were being taken away in cars by the Red Cross to go to their husbands' addresses.

Margaret scanned the faces of the men, but she couldn't see Lawrence anywhere.

'Are you sure he didn't expect you to go to him?' a Red Cross girl asked her, after she had waited for about half an hour with no sign of her husband.

'I don't think so,' Margaret replied. 'He said in his letter he would be waiting for me.'

'Do you have the address where he's staying?' the girl asked her.

Margaret produced Lawrence's latest letter from her bag, which gave the name of the hotel. 'Let me drive you there,' said the girl.

Margaret was too tired to argue, so she climbed into the Red Cross car, doing her best to soothe Rosamund as she started crying again.

'Any sights in New York you'd like to see?' the girl asked, cheerily.

Margaret felt like asking whether she would want to go sightseeing if she had spent seven days at sea and had a baby crying to be changed, but she merely shook her head.

'This is the one,' the girl said eventually, as she pulled up in front of a rather seedy looking hotel.

She picked up the luggage while Margaret took the carrycot. The receptionist gave Margaret a key to her husband's room, and they travelled up in the lift.

When they arrived, the Red Cross girl knocked on the door but there was no reply. Margaret put the key into the lock and pushed the door open.

'Hello?' she called. 'Lawrence?'

Margaret flicked the light switch, and at last she saw her husband. He was passed out on the bed, an empty glass in his hand, and on the bedside table was a half-finished bottle of Scotch.

When they stepped off the train at Arlington, Margaret felt for a moment as if she was in a completely different country. It was Saturday, and the town was so busy that it was almost impossible to walk down the street – and almost every face she saw was black.

'Welcome to the South!' Lawrence said.

He was back to his funny, charming self and was doing his best to smooth things over between them. He had pointedly avoided alcohol in the train's dining car throughout the long journey, and Margaret just hoped that now she was here he would keep his promise not to drink any more.

The heat was unbearable, even though it was late in the day, and the smell of cooked fish rising from stalls set up in the street was overwhelming. In between the crowds, carts drawn by mules moved slowly along the uneven roads, which Margaret noticed had not been paved. She felt as if she had stepped back in time by a hundred years.

They made their way down Cedar Street, a road along the railway line that divided grand houses owned by white families on one side of the tracks from the main black residential area on the other.

Lawrence's sister Ellen and her husband Jack Cowart lived in a beautiful white wooden house with balustrades and columns and a large front porch. As Margaret opened the gate in the white picket fence and walked into the front garden, two blond-haired boys ran past shooting BB guns. 'Those are my nephews, Lawrence and Jack,' Lawrence told her.

Ellen emerged on the porch. She had short red hair and was wearing a dark patterned dress and elegant little heels. Her husband, following her, was a tall lanky man with an open, honest face.

'Why, *Margaret!*' Ellen cried, with a strong Southern lilt, her arms outstretched. 'You are just as pretty as Lawrence led us to believe. Welcome to Arlington, my dear!' She embraced her and kissed her on the cheek.

Jack Cowart also greeted Margaret warmly, although she noticed he was slightly cooler in welcoming her husband.

'This here's my daughter, Jane,' Ellen said, as a slim girl of around thirteen with a shoulder-length brown bob came onto the porch, 'and I'm sure Rosamund will have a friend in baby Daniel.'

A black nanny appeared with a little a boy who wasn't much older than Margaret's own child, and offered to take Rosamund.

'Y'all must be hungry,' Ellen said, leading them into the house. They crossed a large hallway with hardwood floors and went into a pine-panelled dining room with an enormous table. 'I hope you like chicken because I've been busy frying up a whole heap,' she told Margaret. 'It's just about the only meat we've had since the war started.'

Margaret had never heard of frying chicken before, but did her best to keep an open mind as it was brought onto the table, along with rice, broccoli, sweet corn and bread and butter. She was relieved to see there was no alcohol.

To her surprise, the family picked up the chicken drumsticks in their hands and began tearing at the meat with their teeth. Margaret tried to pick at hers daintily with a knife and fork.

'No need to stand on ceremony round here,' Jack Cowart told her, smiling.

Seeing everyone turn to look at her, Margaret picked up the drumstick hesitantly and took a bite.

'That's it!' said Jack approvingly.

'Lawrence tells me you're quite a reader,' Ellen said. 'Help yourself to any books you like in the house.'

'Thank you,' Margaret replied.

'Oh, my sister's got a real library,' Lawrence said. 'She's always giving books to the help.'

'I think it's important,' Ellen replied. 'It's a chance for them to educate themselves.'

Margaret asked them how the war was affecting life in Georgia. She knew the family had around 2,000 acres of plantations, including several hundred that had belonged to Lawrence's late mother.

'With young black men going off to war there's been a pretty bad labour shortage,' Jack told her. The Cowarts' sons, who weren't yet in their teens, had been helping with the cotton picking.

'Industry's having a fine time out of this war, but we farmers are struggling more than ever,' Ellen said bitterly. 'Very few of us are turning a profit these days. You won't find a more helpless, discouraged group of people in all of America.'

Margaret learned that most of the farming was still done with mules and Jack owned the only tractor in the county. She was shocked – when Lawrence had talked about his family owning plantations she had assumed that meant they were wealthy, but it seemed she was wrong. Despite the nice house and acres of land, money was a constant source of worry for the Cowarts, and their bill at the grocery store had been known to go unpaid for months.

She also discovered that being a 'landowner' didn't stop Jack from having to get his hands dirty. On Monday morning, he and his sons were up at 5 a.m., going out in their pick-up truck to collect the farm hands and head out to help with picking the peanut crop. It was back-breaking work, and the boys were sent off with handfuls of salt pills to counteract the effect of sweating under the hot sun. They came home at lunchtime for their main meal of the day, but then stayed out again until almost midnight.

While the men were out at work, Margaret and Ellen sat on the porch, drinking iced tea and chatting. Margaret felt she had found a true soulmate in her new sister-in-law, who was intelligent and kind, just like her brother in his better moments. But she was taken aback by a comment she made about Lawrence. 'He's always been able to charm his way out of anything – just like he did when they let him resign from the Army,' said Ellen.

'Let him resign?' Margaret said, confused.

'Yes, after he had the argument with the General and threw him down the stairs.'

Margaret realised Lawrence had told his family a tall story about why he had come back to America. But she didn't have the heart to tell Ellen about him defrauding the Red Cross.

Later, they went into town to run some errands. Margaret was surprised to discover that, as they walked along the pavement, black people stepped out of their way and into the gutter in deference to them.

Arlington was in the grip of segregation – there was a 'colored' school and a white school, a 'colored' church and a white church, and even the water fountains were marked as separate. Ellen told her that in the cinema, black people had to sit upstairs, unless they were a nanny accompanying a white child.

'It's as if there are two separate towns in the same place!' Margaret exclaimed.

Meanwhile, although slavery was a thing of the past, the black workers on the plantations seemed to live the same life as their forefathers, living in board houses on small plots of land without plumbing or electricity. Ellen's husband Jack was more forward-thinking than most, and whenever one of the sharecroppers needed new clothes for their children or had to see a doctor, he would pay for them.

Over lunch, Jack told Margaret of his disgust at the way crimes within the black community were treated with little interest by the white justice system – when an employee of theirs had had her throat slit by her jealous husband, the man had escaped jail. Yet if a black man committed a crime against a white person all hell would break loose, and lynchings were still taking place in the region.

Because Jack was a respected member of the community, when disputes flared up people would often send for him to sort them out. Late one Saturday afternoon, the family were all home when a man came to the door asking for Jack to come and talk down Billy, one of the local farmers. Billy had got a mob together who were threatening violence against a white girl and a black man who had slept together.

The girl, Lila, came from one of the white sharecropper families, who lived in similar conditions to the black share-croppers but were looked down on as 'white trash' and accused of being less clean than their black counterparts. Lila was only thirteen, but like many of the girls she was already married, and her husband was quite a bit older than her. He had been approached by a local black man who wanted to sleep with Lila in return for payment. The husband had agreed, and had sold his young wife.

In such a small town the arrangement hadn't stayed a secret for long, and soon Billy had got a group of white folks together, outraged not at Lila's husband, but at her and the black man for having had interracial sex.

When Jack arrived, the mob had been whipped up into a frenzy by Billy, who had clearly had one too many beers. Jack went straight up to him and, drawing himself up to his full six feet two inches, told him, 'You better shut your mouth and go home right now, if you know what's good for you. And take your buddies with you.'

Being publically admonished by Jack Cowart was enough to make Billy back down. Cursing under his breath, he left, and the mob began to disperse.

The sheriff had now arrived and was about to take Lila and the black man to the county jail. Jack knew there was a good chance he would throw the pair out on the side of the road, shoot them and claim they had been trying to run away.

'If these two people don't get to the jail alive, you'll have me to answer to,' he warned him.

As a result of Jack's actions, Lila and the black man were neither lynched nor shot that day – even if they were later convicted of miscegenation and sent to the state penitentiary.

Margaret was beginning to realise that her in-laws were pretty special people. But after a while she discovered that Jack had one, rather familiar, flaw. Walking past the kitchen one day she saw him take a brown paper bag out of a cupboard under the sink, quickly pour himself a large whisky, knock it back and hurriedly put both the glass and bottle away again. Margaret was shocked. She had been led to believe that alcohol was shunned by the good Christians of Arlington. There weren't even any bars in the town for the white men.

It wasn't long before she started to suspect that Lawrence had discovered the secret stash too. He began staying up late, coming to bed after she had gone to sleep, and not emerging in the morning until ten or eleven o'clock. When he did, he seemed on edge, as if his nerves were jangled, and any loud noise hurt his head. But when she questioned him about it he claimed it was just the heat.

The children in the house were learning to avoid Uncle Lawrence in the mornings. One day, when young Lawrence Cowart was making a lot of noise, his uncle hissed at him, 'Listen boy – if you don't be quiet I'm going to twist your head off, put it on the table and watch you wiggle on the floor!' The child made a hasty exit.

While Jack seemed to be able to manage his drinking and still go out and do a long day's work, Lawrence increasingly just hung around the house and wasn't helping on the plantation. Margaret had thought that once he was back in America, surrounded by his family, he wouldn't need to reach for a drink, but now she began to worry that he was slipping back into his old ways.

She decided to talk to her sister-in-law. 'Have you known Lawrence to drink before?' she asked her.

'Oh my dear child,' Ellen said, giving her a pitying look, 'he's been tied to the bottle since his student days.'

She told Margaret that their late mother had gone up to the University of Georgia to try and straighten Lawrence out, but to no avail. He had been kicked out of the university for his wild antics. She also told her that the prominent scar across Lawrence's nose was the result of a drink-driving accident when he was in his early twenties, in which he had gone through the windscreen.

'As soon as I heard he was getting married I was worried,' Ellen said, shaking her head. 'I foresaw there would be problems for Lawrence's wife.'

Margaret had a sinking feeling. During his court case in England, Lawrence had blamed his drinking on the stresses and strains of his war jobs, yet now she realised the problem had started long before. What was more, it seemed entrenched in the culture of the South. As well as Ellen's husband Jack, she discovered it was an open secret that numerous men in the family and the community had drinking problems, or worse. One uncle had such a serious addiction to morphine that his wife had locked him in a room to go cold turkey, and his howls could be heard for miles around. When he was finally released, his iron bedstead had been twisted like spaghetti. Even the doctor in neighbouring Edison was an addict, and had got several of his patients hooked on drugs.

Margaret began to feel that if Lawrence was to have any chance of staying on the straight and narrow, they would have to leave Georgia, and soon. But she was torn: she loved Ellen and the Cowarts, and they had been so kind to her. She had felt more of a sense of family and community here than she had anywhere else.

But one day, she overheard a conversation that convinced her the time had come for them to go.

'He's always taking advantage of you,' Jack was telling his wife. 'You don't hear from him for years, but as soon as he's in trouble and needs money he shows up again!'

Margaret didn't need to be told who they were talking about.

Much as she hated the thought of upping sticks again when she was now heavily pregnant, she urged her husband to look for work elsewhere. Since Lawrence had squandered his inheritance, and they weren't getting any payments from the Army due to his dismissal, the only way they could stand on their own two feet was if he got a job.

Luckily, Lawrence announced that one of his old army contacts had offered him a position as a buyer at the Goodyear Tire & Rubber Company headquarters in Akron, Ohio. Many Southerners were flocking to the industrial northeast for jobs, and Akron – famous for its tyre companies – was booming thanks to the war.

Margaret was pleased, and with that weight off her mind she was able to enjoy a goodbye dinner with the Cowarts before leaving for their new home. Relations might be strained between her and Lawrence, but looking around the table at the faces of the people who had made her feel so welcome in America, she felt she couldn't have married into a better family.

11

Rae

With the war on the Continent now well underway, there was plenty of work to do at Chilwell Depot, where damaged vehicles were brought in for repairs before being sent back to the front. Rae had been shocked to learn of the number of amphibious tanks that had sunk on D-Day, despite all she and her colleagues had done to render them waterproof. But while many of those were now rusting underwater off the Normandy coast, new battle-scarred vehicles were arriving every day for repairs, and the men and women at Chilwell were busier than ever.

While her colleagues would replace broken tank tread or install new guns, Rae was responsible for repairing small holes and gashes in the metal with her welding torch. It could be a gruesome responsibility given the kind of action the vehicles had seen in France. As the muddy tank tracks warmed up, they would release the sickening smell of dried blood.

One day, a tank came into the depot that all the male welders seemed keen to avoid. Rae decided to investigate, climbing the ladder onto the top of the vehicle and looking down into it.

Immediately, she was hit by an odour even worse than those she had got used to, and soon she saw why. The inside of the tank was bloodied, and lying on the floor was a pair of human fingers that had obviously been ripped off at the knuckle.

Rae gagged as she stared at the bloodied stumps, and covered her mouth to avoid breathing in any more of the terrible smell. But there was work to be done, whatever the unpleasant conditions. She climbed down to fetch her welding torch, steeled herself for a moment, and then returned to get on with repairing the tank.

The months of waiting since Raymond had been sent to France had been difficult for Rae. She had volunteered to go to the Continent herself in one of the REME's (Royal Electrical and Mechanical Engineers') mobile workshops, which were sent out on D-Day plus five, but her mother had refused to sign the papers. 'I've enough children overseas with the Army,' she had told Rae firmly.

Rae understood her mother's anxiety, but she found it hard staying put in England while her husband was in France. Since Raymond's hospital unit had arrived in Cherbourg, Rae had heard from him only occasionally, and she was gripped by any news she could get hold of about how the war was going. She kept as busy as she could with her work, but dark thoughts and worries never went away completely.

The Normandy landings had been only the start of the American war on the Continent. In September 1944, tens of thousands of Allied airborne troops dropped into Holland as part of Operation Market Garden, which aimed to end the war before Christmas by capturing bridges on the border with Germany. It was the first major defeat for the Allies since D-Day, and proved that victory over Germany wouldn't be easy.

Even greater American losses occurred three months later at the Battle of the Bulge – the final German offensive of the war. During six weeks of bitter fighting in freezing conditions the Americans lost 19,000 men, their worst death count in the entire war.

Rae's husband Raymond was sent to the 'Bulge' – named for the shape the Germans had created in the American line – along with some medics from his hospital in Cherbourg. She was shocked to read in his letters how, short of reinforcements, the Army had given him and the other cooks rifles and sent them up to the front lines.

The Allies' eventual success at the Battle of the Bulge was decisive, and a German victory now seemed all but impossible. But with GIs continuing to die every day, the waiting didn't get any easier.

Meanwhile, Londoners were still suffering the 'flying bomb war'. One V-2 rocket fell close to Rae's family home in Neasden, ripping a corner off the local school and reducing several houses to rubble. Her sister Mary rushed to join the neighbours in the search for survivors, with one local resident foremost in her mind – her friend Lil, whose house had been opposite the school.

Mary found Lil's mum, who told her Lil was missing, and together they began searching the rubble, calling out her name at the tops of their lungs. Finally, they received a response from beneath a huge mound of fallen masonry. 'I'm all right, Mum,' came Lil's muffled reply. Furiously they raced to pull away the piles of bricks and rubble, until the voice grew clearer and more distinct. 'I'm all right, Mum, I'm all right,' Lil kept calling. But when they finally got her out, she died in her mother's arms.

There was no time for Mary to stop and mourn her friend, however – other people were still desperately searching for their loved ones and needed help. One family had been looking for their eighteen-month-old baby for hours, but the child seemed to have completely disappeared. Every so often, they would stop and listen quietly for the faintest hint of crying, but they heard nothing. Mary joined in the search, but however many bricks they turned up and however hard they looked, there was no sign of the child.

Towards dawn, Mary happened to look up from the rubble, and saw a sight overhead that would haunt her for the rest of her life. There, in the branches of a tree, was the little baby, hanging by its nightgown, limp and silent.

Something in Mary changed at that moment. The next morning she went along to the local recruiting office and volunteered for the ATS, just as her sister had done before her.

While Rae was proud of the decision that Mary had taken, she felt more and more worried about their mother. First Mrs Burton's husband had left her for a woman half her age and now she was all alone, in a city where bombs continued to fall. Reading her mum's letters at her billet in Chilwell, Rae was alarmed. They were fearful and bleak, but frustratingly there was little Rae could do since her leave had been cut to a five-mile radius.

Eventually, Rae decided to risk the consequences and go AWOL. There was nothing she could do to help her husband serving on the Continent, but she could at least give her mum some support down in London. One Friday after work, she hopped on a train at Nottingham station, keeping an eye out for any military police who might ask awkward questions, and turned up in Neasden unannounced.

Her mother was delighted to see her, but asked immediately, 'When do you have to go back?'

Rae hugged her tightly. 'Not for a couple of days, Mum,' she told her, not mentioning the fact that she wasn't supposed to be there at all.

Rae found that in some ways she needed the visit as much as her mum did. She had been lonely up in Chilwell ever since Raymond had left for Europe, and it felt good to be with family again. Her presence seemed to lift Mrs Burton's spirits too, and by Sunday evening they were both feeling better.

On Monday morning, Rae got up early to pack her things. Her mother had already left for her shift at the factory where she worked, a mile or so up the road, and Rae was planning to drop in and say goodbye to her on her way to the station. As she packed her bag, she heard a chugging noise coming from outside and looked out of the window. There in the distance was the menacing outline of a doodlebug passing over houses opposite. Then suddenly the noise stopped. Rae knew what that meant – the flying bomb was about to fall.

She ran away from the window and down the stairs. Halfway down the staircase to the landing, Rae heard the explosion of the doodlebug outside. The shock made her stumble and she fell down the rest of the steps, scraping the skin off her knees and hitting the side of her face against the wall at the bottom.

Dazed, she scrambled to stand up again, the noise of the bomb still echoing in her ears, and ran back up to the front bedroom to inspect the damage. Remarkably the windows had not been shattered, but the street outside was a scene of mayhem as people ran about in panic.

Rae took her bag and went downstairs and into the street. There were wardens dashing past in the direction of the bomb-site round the corner in Dog Lane, and Rae could see smoke rising into the sky.

She rushed up to the North Circular Road and headed for the shelter opposite her mum's factory, sure that she would find her there.

When she arrived, Mrs Burton was already inside. 'Thank God you're all right!' she cried. 'I was worried about you.'

She saw Rae's grazed legs and sore eye. 'What happened?'

'Oh, nothing, I just fell over,' said Rae. She had been so preoccupied that it wasn't until now that she felt the pain from the fall.

The inhabitants of the shelter waited patiently for the all-clear signal – a green flag flown by a spotter on the roof of a building opposite – and then began to pour into the factory yard. It was a working day and they were expected back at their production lines.

But just as the last of them were leaving the shelter, the man on the roof dropped his green flag and put up a yellow one, indicating that another doodlebug was on its way. The men and women turned and began to file back in again. Then the yellow flag was replaced with a red one, signalling imminent danger.

The bodies pushing and shoving began to grow more frantic. 'Come on, hurry up!' someone shouted, 'There's a bomb about to fall out here!' Rae felt herself being shoved this way and that, and she and her mother were separated from one another. 'Mum!' she shouted, and saw Mrs Burton looking around for her. Then in the confusion, Mrs Burton lost her footing and Rae saw her fall over. The woman behind her tripped over her and also fell to the floor, and as the people behind them carried on surging forward, both of them began to be trampled on. Rae heard her mother screaming frantically.

'Stop!' Rae shouted. 'My mum's under there!' She pushed and shoved her way towards her, elbowing people out of the way. A warden got there first and hauled Mrs Burton up by the back of her dress, which was dirty with footprints. She had always taught her children not to swear, but at that moment she emitted the most ear-aching string of expletives Rae had ever heard.

She was silenced by the sound of the doodlebug exploding outside.

Everyone held their breath for a moment, until they realised they were safe. The bomb had fallen nearby, but not close enough to do them any damage. Ray hugged her mother tightly, shaken by the ordeal.

'Well, at least it didn't hit us, that's the main thing,' Mrs Burton said. Rae could feel her trembling.

Once the green flag went up again, everyone filed out of the shelter. Rae felt terrible leaving her mother, but she knew she had to get back before anyone noticed she had gone AWOL.

'I'm really sorry, but I've got to go now, Mum,' she said.

'All right, love,' her mother said sadly. She squeezed her hand, and Rae watched her head back into the factory.

As Rae sat on the train back to Nottingham, troubled by the morning's events and now sporting a black eye from her fall, she felt far from reassured about her mother's wellbeing.

Fortunately, the threat from the skies was only temporary, and as the advancing Allied armies in Europe overran the V-1 and V-2 launch sites, the flying bomb war came to an end. It was only a matter of time until the ground war followed suit.

But for Rae, waiting it out from the relative safety of Nottingham, the suspense was unbearable. Her mind kept fixating on one question: who will be the last man to die? Day by day, the Allied forces in Europe grew closer to Berlin, but still the Germans were putting up resistance, and still British and American men were being killed. Rae felt like she wanted to scream, 'Get it over with!'

One day, some of the other ATS girls were surprised to find her sitting on her bunk, sobbing her heart out. Rae wasn't normally one for tears, but the suspense had proved too much for her.

'What's happened?' they asked, worried that she had received some bad news.

'Nothing,' she replied. 'I just don't think I can take any more of this.'

12

Sylvia

On 12 April 1945 President Roosevelt died suddenly of a stroke, and at the Washington Club, where Sylvia volunteered, the Stars and Stripes flew at half-mast. But even this tragedy couldn't dent the belief among the Americans and their allies that victory was now within reach. The Germans were fighting a defensive war, falling further and further back within their own country as the Americans and Russians moved in. A more positive mood pervaded all over London.

Sylvia was feeling more like her old self again. She still thought of Carl Russell now and then, and worried about Wally, Frank, Tom and all the others in her own personal pen-pal club. But as she collected the plates and glasses at the Red Cross club, she sang along to the jukebox at the top of her voice.

One evening, Sylvia had just come out of the kitchen with a cloth to wipe down the tables when Issy Bonn's 'There! I've Said It Again' came on. Since it was an English song, she really belted out the number, causing a young GI sitting with his back to her reading the paper to turn around in surprise. 'Holy smokes, you really have a voice!' he remarked.

Sylvia stopped singing, instantly self-conscious.

'Do you always sing like that?' he asked.

'Oh, well, when the jukebox is on I usually sing along,' she said shyly.

'What's your name? And what are you doing here?' he asked her, putting down his paper.

'My name's Sylvia,' she replied. 'I work at the Piccadilly Hotel and I just come down here after work to volunteer.'

'Well, Sylvia, my name's Bob. And I think you could really go somewhere with that voice,' he said. There was a twinkle in his hazel eyes that made her giggle involuntarily.

The man stuck around until Sylvia returned to the kitchen to start washing the dishes, and then he stood up to go. She glanced over as he was leaving and saw him put his hat on at a jaunty angle over his dark, wavy hair, which gave him an impish air. He cast her a last look and then he was gone.

Three days later, Sylvia was chatting away with Peggy at the Piccadilly Hotel when their manageress marched in and told her there was a call for her.

'For me?' she asked. She didn't know anyone back in Woolwich who owned a phone.

Sylvia followed Miss Frank to the phone, took the receiver and hesitantly said, 'Hello?'

'Hello, Sylvia!' a cheerful man's voice replied.

'Who is this?' Sylvia asked.

'It's Bob. Don't you remember? I said I liked your voice at the Red Cross club.'

The image of the dark-haired young man with the twinkle in his eye popped into Sylvia's head.

'I'm coming to meet you after work today and we're going for tea,' he continued. 'Meet me in front of the hotel. Bye!'

The line went dead, and Sylvia looked up to see the annoyed face of Miss Frank, who had been listening to every word.

'Sylvia, personal calls aren't allowed in the office!' she reprimanded her.

'Sorry, Miss,' Sylvia faltered, 'I didn't even give him the
number.'

Miss Frank looked unconvinced, and Sylvia scurried back to
her desk.

Sylvia clocked out at 5.30 p.m. that day as usual, and found
Bob waiting outside the Piccadilly's grand entrance, his hat
cocked impishly to one side as before. As soon as she saw him
her heart beat a little faster, and she was surprised to find she
had butterflies in her stomach.

'At last!' Bob said, as if they had arranged a time and she was
running terribly late. 'Come on!'

He took her by the arm.

'Where are we going?' she asked, giggling.

'Do you like scones? Of course you do. So do I!'

Like her previous boyfriend Carl, Bob took her to a nearby
Lyons Corner House. Why were Americans so keen to go to tea
rooms? Sylvia wondered.

She was pleased to discover that Bob genuinely did like tea.
He ordered a large pot, along with two scones, and although
they came with only a measly amount of jam and no cream, he
devoured them hungrily.

'I'm not a fan of all your British food,' he told her, seeing her
smile at him. 'Fish and chips – now what do you want to eat
that stuff for?'

He had the twinkle in his eye again. Sylvia giggled. 'Well,
what do you eat?'

'We eat hamburgers and hotdogs. Much more sophisticated.'

'Why do you call it a hotdog?' she retorted. 'It's just a blinking sausage!'

'Why do you call it a blinking sausage when it can't blink?'

They traded quips over the tea cups, laughing until Sylvia's tummy was so sore she could hardly breathe. Bob was a third-generation Irish-American, and if he hadn't kissed the Blarney Stone himself, someone in his family clearly had. He certainly had the gift of the gab.

Between the banter, Sylvia learned that Bob had been called up the day after his eighteenth birthday and that he had fought in the bloody Battle of the Bulge. He had recently been sent back to England with a shoulder injury he had sustained in the lead up to the Battle of Remagen, for which he had been awarded the Purple Heart that now adorned his uniform.

She also learned that he came from a place called Baltimore, which she had never heard of. 'It's where "The Star-Spangled Banner" was written,' he told her proudly. 'We whooped the British there in 1814!'

As she listened to his descriptions of his hometown, with its beautiful downtown, big shops and historic harbour, Sylvia had a picture in her head of a glamorous modern city, not unlike the ones she had seen in the movies, where every American girl seemed to live in a swanky apartment and drive her own car.

As on most of her dates, Sylvia let Bob do the majority of the talking. He was so funny, and knew so much about history, that listening to him was a joy. She was so absorbed that she completely lost track of time, and suddenly realised with a jolt that three hours had flown by. Her mother would be worrying about her.

'I've got to catch me train!' she exclaimed. Bob paid up and they ran to Charing Cross station. There was only time for him to give Sylvia a quick peck on the cheek before she boarded her train.

The following Tuesday, when she arrived for her shift at the Washington Club, Bob was already waiting for her. As she saw him, her heart instantly began to beat a little faster again.

'Hi, shortstuff!' he called. It was a fitting description, since Sylvia was the smallest of all the Red Cross volunteers, but she pulled a face nonetheless.

'Oh, I'm sorry,' he said, affecting a soppy tone. 'How about "babycakes"?'

'That's not much better,' she giggled. Then she noticed there was something different about him. He was wearing the uniform of a military policeman.

'I've been promoted,' he told her. 'They need me patrolling the streets to make sure our boys behave themselves.'

The MP headquarters were further along Piccadilly, opposite Green Park, and patrolling the area as hundreds of GIs swarmed into town every night to have a good time was no mean feat. But it meant Bob would be based in London for the foreseeable future – and close to the Washington Club. That evening, as Sylvia went about her work, he grabbed the chance to talk to her whenever he could, paying her compliments, cracking jokes and keeping her smiling. After a while he even took to following her about the room, not content with waiting for snatched moments of conversation.

On her Thursday shift, there he was again at the same table, and once again he seemed to fix all his attention on her. All night none of the other GIs got a chance to talk to Sylvia, but she didn't mind – she hardly noticed they were there.

That weekend Bob had two days' leave and he told her he wanted them to spend it together. Sylvia knew she couldn't arrange any more dates until her mum had met Bob and had a chance to vet him, so it was agreed that he would come to Woolwich and stay overnight on the sofa.

Before he took the train from Charing Cross, Bob made sure to make a visit to the Army Post Exchange, and turned up at St Mary Street loaded with gifts. On his arrival, Sylvia's younger sisters watched in fascination as he took out his various presents with the air of a magician, transfixing all the family.

'This is what soldiers eat,' he told Audrey and Enid, handing them a couple of Hershey bars. 'And this is what little girls in America eat.' He gave them two lollipops with chocolate toffee centres, which they handled like precious treasure.

For Mr Bradley, there was pipe tobacco and for Sylvia there was liquid shampoo in a bottle – a novelty after the packets of powdered shampoo she usually bought from Woolworth's.

Then he turned to Mrs Bradley. 'This, ma'am, is for you,' he said, handing her the biggest bar of soap any of them had ever seen, with the evocative name Cashmere Bouquet.

'It's blinking huge!' Mrs Bradley said, marvelling at the oval bar and turning it over in her hands.

'Yes, ma'am. Everything's bigger in America,' Bob said, with a cheeky grin.

'Big isn't always best, Bob,' Mrs Bradley retorted. She laughed heartily at her joke and Bob joined in as if it was the most hilarious thing in the world.

But Bob's crowning glory was yet to come. From each of his pockets he produced four perfect hen's eggs – the equivalent of two months' rations – which he had somehow managed to carry all the way on the train from Charing Cross without breaking.

'What did you do – stand up all the way?' Sylvia asked, giggling at the thought of him jiggling around on the train with his pockets full of eggs.

'Pretty much!' Bob replied.

'Well, Bob, being poor little English people we're not so well stocked here,' Mrs Bradley told him. 'I'm afraid we're out of meat rations, so if you want your Sunday lunch tomorrow you're going to have to catch it yourself.'

''Scuse me, ma'am?' Bob said.

Mrs Bradley pointed to the back yard. 'We used to keep chickens out there, but all that's left is an old duck who's had his day,' she told him. 'Maybe you and Mr Bradley can finish him off.'

'No, not Ducky!' Sylvia's sisters protested. The bird was two years old, and they had come to regard it almost as a pet. But Mrs Bradley couldn't bring herself to send an American soldier away hungry, so Ducky was for the chop.

But first, Bob and Mr Bradley would have to catch him. Perhaps it was Bob's uniform that warned Ducky he was there on a mission, or perhaps it was the hungry look in Mr Bradley's eye, but whatever it was the bird instantly ran quacking to the other end of the garden. 'Run, Ducky!' Sylvia's sisters called, cheering the bird on. But Mr Bradley had managed to run at him from the side and wrestled him to the floor. 'Hold him fast, Bob,' he said as he took a knife from Mrs Bradley and went to cut its neck. The blade was halfway across when the duck put up one last fight for freedom. It managed to wriggle out of Bob's grasp and went careering up the garden again, its head half hanging off, veering all over the place like a drunkard.

Finally Bob managed to pin the creature down again, Mr Bradley finished the job and Ducky was laid to rest once and for all. Mrs Bradley took the bird to hang it up overnight, and Sylvia and Bob were at last allowed to go off and enjoy their day together. It had been quite a baptism of fire for Bob, but Sylvia admired him even more, having seen how well he handled it.

That day, Sylvia gave Bob a tour of the area, telling him about the devastating raids they had suffered during the Blitz. She took him up to the Royal Artillery Barracks for a stroll on the common, then down to the river for a ride on the ferry across to North Woolwich and a walk around Royal Victoria Gardens. She had brought other GIs to Woolwich before, but she felt especially proud to be seen out and about with Bob. He took a lively interest in all that they saw and seemed fascinated by everything she had to say, all the while keeping her laughing and giggling with little witty asides and jokes. Sylvia had never felt such an attraction to anybody – even poor Carl Russell.

On the way back they walked through the little park next to St Mary's Church and into the graveyard, where Bob was fascinated by the ancient tombstones and went around reading all the inscriptions.

'There's one here from the seventeenth century!' he said, astonished.

'Yeah – we've got proper history here,' Sylvia quipped.

Bob turned to her and, out of the blue, took her in his arms and kissed her properly for the first time. They might be in the middle of a graveyard, but to Sylvia it was the most romantic moment of her life.

The next day, they sat down for the much-anticipated Sunday lunch. Mrs Bradley had spent all morning making beautiful Yorkshire puddings, roast potatoes, carrots and gravy to accompany Ducky, who had been roasted in the oven. Mr Bradley carved the meat, Mrs Bradley served up the veggies and then they all went to tuck in.

'How do you like a traditional English Sunday roast, Bob?' Mrs Bradley asked.

'Um, it's very nice,' said Bob, chewing hard.

Mrs Bradley took her first bite of duck and her face darkened. The meat was impossibly tough. She removed the piece into her napkin and took another bite. Again she was unable to chew it. She looked around the table and saw the faces of her husband and three daughters, all of whom were struggling to eat what was in front of them.

'This darn duck's like boiled leather!' she exclaimed, putting her napkin down.

The others followed suit, relieved not to have to persevere any longer.

'That duck's had the last laugh after all!' her husband said.

Over the following weeks, whenever Bob had time off from racing around the West End in his jeep wielding a truncheon, he and Sylvia spent their time together. He was a regular presence at the Washington Club during Sylvia's shifts on Tuesdays and Thursdays, and he spent all his leave at the Bradleys', always turning up with new gifts for all the family. Knowing his love of history, Sylvia took him out to Kent, to visit the village of Eynsford, where she knew he would love the sixteenth-century pub and eleventh-century church. Anything built more than 100 years ago was 'ancient' to the Americans, and Bob couldn't get enough of walking around graveyards, marvelling at engravings that were so faded by time and weather that they were almost illegible.

Sylvia loved his enthusiasm, and the humour and fun he injected into even the most mundane outings. Every time she saw him he seemed to have become more handsome, and on the days they were apart he was all she could think about. She felt she had never met a more wonderful man, and was almost sick with love for him. When he told her he was in love with her too, she was over the moon. Sylvia had always been one to sing along with the jukebox, but now she was so happy that she sang all the time, whether it was on or not.

As April rolled into May, world events were also taking a happy turn. Hitler took his own life on 30 April 1945, and by the early hours of 7 May General Jodl had signed the unconditional surrender of all German forces. The news was broadcast in Germany and picked up by the BBC and the British papers before an official announcement could be made.

The girls in the billing office of the Piccadilly Hotel heard the news from an excited waiter, who ran up the spiral staircase and burst into the room shouting, 'The war's over! The war's over!'

But their manageress, Miss Frank, wasn't about to let her employees leave early. Sylvia, Peggy and the others would have to wait until the end of the normal working day before they were free to celebrate.

When Sylvia finally left for the day there seemed to be Union Jacks everywhere. Selfridges had been doing a roaring trade in flags for several weeks now, and they were being put to good use, while some people had taken out their old ones from the Coronation of 1937. Bonfires were being lit in Piccadilly, and when she got to Trafalgar Square it was teeming with people. The hat sellers were out in force, flogging 'Montgomery's berets' at a bob each – two bob with feathers. Everyone was laughing and smiling, people were singing and dancing, and some overexcited souls had even jumped into the fountains. On the train home, commuters who normally never spoke to each other were suddenly chatting away as if they had been friends for years. It was as if they had all been holding their breath for six years, thought Sylvia, and they had finally been able to breathe out again.

Bob was on duty all that week, but back in Woolwich the end of the war in Europe was celebrated with a big party at the playground round the corner from Sylvia's house. Mums, dads, children and grandparents all sang and danced together, most of them fuelled by little more than euphoria and a few ginger-beer shandies – although a couple of the granddads had started early and were already two sheets to the wind.

Sylvia's neighbour, Mr Chalk, brought his accordion, and as he played 'Knees Up Mother Brown' everyone danced in a circle. Mrs Bradley pushed her daughter into the centre. 'Pick them knees up, Sylv!' she shouted.

Sylvia did as she was told, dancing and singing away so loudly that by the end of the night she had lost her voice completely.

13

Gwendolyn

As impromptu street parties began to spring up all over Britain, Lyn and Ben were snuggled up together in the cinema, totally unaware of the excitement that was fast spreading around the country. They were watching *A Song to Remember*, the story of the nineteenth-century composer Frédéric Chopin and his lover George Sand.

Suddenly the lights went up, the door flew open and the cinema manager came running breathlessly down the aisle. 'Ladies and gentlemen, the war is over!' he announced.

The audience burst into a spontaneous round of applause. But even on such a momentous occasion most people decided to stay until the end of the film.

Afterwards, however, it was time to celebrate. The Polygon Hotel was marking the occasion in the way it knew best – with a dance – and Lyn wasn't going to miss out on the biggest ball of the year. When they arrived the hotel was swarming with people, and for once elegance went out of the window as elated American officers drank themselves silly, jitterbugging with abandon. Bottles of beer were shaken vigorously and sprayed around like champagne. 'My mother's going to kill me if I go home smelling of beer!' cried Lyn, as the pretty dress she was wearing got soaked.

The mention of Mrs Rowe reminded Ben that Lyn's curfew was 10 p.m., even if the war was over. As they walked home she couldn't stop humming the Chopin polonaise from the movie, which now seemed to sum up the victorious sentiment of the night. Ben was always the more reserved of the two, but now he was quieter than ever. Unlike Lyn, he was thinking beyond the current celebrations and worrying what the end of the war in Europe might mean for them.

As they neared their usual bench in Watts Park, he suggested they sit for a moment. 'What's wrong?' asked Lyn. 'Aren't you pleased the war's over?'

'Lyn,' he said quietly, 'I want you to come to California.'

'What do you mean?' she asked, still so elated that she wasn't really concentrating.

'I mean,' he said, 'will you marry me?'

Lyn couldn't believe what a wonderful night it was turning out to be – first the war had ended and now the man she loved had proposed to her. 'Yes, please!' she said, and Ben scooped her into his arms and gave an uncharacteristic 'Whoop!'

Ben would have to ask her parents' permission before any engagement was confirmed, so Lyn couldn't mention her news to her family. But she was more than happy to run up to bed and clutch her happy secret to her chest in solitude. As she lay down to sleep she had visions of herself in an exquisite long, white wedding dress. She played the scene through in her head – the perfect gown, the crowds of admiring onlookers, the wedding banquet, the romantic honeymoon.

Then she suddenly wondered what came next. She remembered with a jolt what Ben had said just before he had asked her to marry him: 'I want you to come to California.' She had been so carried away that she had completely forgotten that part.

Lyn was always one for adventure, and as a child she had longed to join the rich passengers who used to leave Southampton on the liners heading for exotic places. But the passengers had always come home again afterwards.

Instead of spending the night dreaming of her white wedding, Lyn was soon tossing and turning, unable to sleep.

In the morning, she ran to the corner shop and used their phone to call Ben at the Polygon. At the first sound of his voice she blurted out: 'I don't think I can do this!'

'Lyn,' Ben said, sounding confused, 'what are you talking about?'

'I don't think I can marry you,' she said, a lump forming in her throat.

'Why?'

'I just don't think I can go that far away from home,' she said. 'What if I don't like it there? What if things go wrong? What if you can't find a job?'

'Don't worry,' he interrupted. 'We'll do the best we can.'

'But if things didn't work out,' she insisted, 'would we come back to England?'

'Lyn,' he said gently, 'I can't promise you that.'

It wasn't what she wanted to hear, but it was a reminder of his honesty.

'Look, will you come here and meet me for tea?' Ben asked.

'Okay,' Lyn agreed.

'I love you, chowhound.'

Lyn laughed, despite the tears forming. 'I love you too.'

When she arrived at the hotel, Ben was already waiting for her. He jumped out of his chair and hugged her tight. 'I'm so glad you came,' he said. He looked like he hadn't had a good night's sleep either. While everyone else had been celebrating the night before, some of the black GIs had been busy setting fire to taxi cabs and committing other acts of vandalism around Southampton. Ben knew they were furious at having to go back to America, to be treated as second-class citizens once again as if, despite the war, nothing had really changed. In a way, he couldn't blame them.

Ben got Lyn a cup of tea and sat back down again. 'Guess what?' he said.

'What?' Lyn asked hopefully. Maybe Ben had decided they could live in England after all.

'I got orders,' he said. 'I'm being shipped out soon.'

'Where are you going?' asked Lyn, looking up in panic.

'They won't tell us, but probably Japan.'

It was the word she had been hoping he wouldn't say. The war with Germany might be over, but the Japanese had still not surrendered, and while people were celebrating all over Europe the Americans were still embroiled in the increasingly bloody Battle of Okinawa. Many US ships had already been destroyed by kamikaze pilots, and thousands of men had been lost.

Ben reached for her hand. 'I don't want to leave without being married to you,' he said.

Lyn felt utterly overwhelmed. Now she had to consider not only the prospect of moving to another continent, but the fact that Ben was about to be sent to the most dangerous place on earth, and that she might never see him again.

'Please don't think I'm rude, but I have to go,' she said. 'I need to go home and think about everything.'

All day Lyn struggled with herself. She was devastated at the thought of Ben leaving the country, and of not knowing when they would see each other again. But she didn't want to rush into a marriage that might commit her to a lifetime away from everyone and everything she knew and loved.

Another sleepless night passed for Lyn, and when she woke in the morning she knew she had to make up her mind. The worst thing would be if Ben was suddenly taken away from her, before they had a chance to resolve things.

Back she went to the telephone at the corner shop. 'I've made up my mind,' she told him.

'Which way?' he asked anxiously.

'I think...' Lyn paused, knowing that what she said next would change the course of her life forever. 'I think I want to marry you.'

Ben let out an enormous sigh of relief. 'That's pretty good news!' he said. She could hear he was choked, and it revealed the torture he had gone through waiting for her reply. But now that she had given it, she felt no regret. Her heart had always told her she should be with Ben, and once she had stopped listening to her fears, she had been able to hear it.

Once Ben had got a yes out of Lyn for the second time, he wasn't going to risk another change of heart, so he came straight round to Padwell Road to speak to her parents. Mr and Mrs Rowe were upstairs in their bedroom. 'Maybe we shouldn't bother them now,' she said.

'No!' said Ben, unusually insistent. He took her hand and led her upstairs, holding onto the handrail to steady his nerves.

As soon as Mr and Mrs Rowe saw them in the doorway, they knew instantly why they were there.

'May I have Gwen's hand in marriage?' Ben asked, careful to use the name that Lyn's parents knew her by.

'Will you be staying here in England?' asked Mrs Rowe.

'No, ma'am,' said Ben. 'We'll be going to California.'

Mrs Rowe nodded. It was the answer she had feared, but like her daughter she appreciated Ben's honesty.

'Well, Ben,' said Lyn's father, 'if it was anyone else but you, we would say no. But we know you'll take good care of Gwen.'

The long wait for the marriage application to be processed began. Since Ben's CO, Shady Lane, was fond of the couple, he did his best to move things along as swiftly as possible, but knowing her fiancé could be sent to Japan at any moment made the days go by agonisingly slowly for Lyn.

Even after the fall of Okinawa, the Japanese stubbornly refused to capitulate, determined to fight to the last man standing and take as many Americans as possible down with them. Then, on 6 August, everything changed. An atom bomb, the product of many years of top-secret planning, devastated the city of Hiroshima. Three days later, Nagasaki was flattened. The following week, Japan offered an unconditional surrender.

On 14 August 1945, the end of the war was announced by the new Prime Minister, Clement Atlee, on the BBC's midnight bulletin. Church bells began ringing all around the country, bonfires were lit and revellers partied in the streets. In London, people leaped into the fountains of Trafalgar Square and fireworks filled the sky. In Paris, a conga line of GIs spontaneously snaked from the Red Cross club to the Place de l'Opéra and back. In Times Square, a sailor embraced a woman in an impromptu kiss that would come to transfix the world.

But for Lyn, lying awake in bed in Southampton, there was one thing that mattered most about the good news: Ben was safe from being sent to Japan.

Although the war he had come to fight was now over, Ben was told he would be required to stay on in Southampton at least until Christmas. Lyn was relieved – now that the Army had finally given permission for them to marry, it would give her time to plan that dream wedding she had fantasised about.

But she found that it wasn't going to be easy, even in peacetime. Rationing was still tight, and there simply wouldn't be enough food for a large group of people. Apart from a couple of co-workers, it would just be her mum and dad, and her siblings Bunty and Ron, if they could get leave from the forces. Some wedding banquet, Lyn thought.

Then there was the dress – or rather, the lack of it. Wedding dresses were almost impossible to get hold of, and many a wartime bride got married in a borrowed or rented dress – an option that Lyn flatly refused. A friend of the family offered her a dress made out of reclaimed parachute silk, but knowing that the material was often salvaged from German pilots who had been shot down, she couldn't bring herself to take it. In the end, with some donated ration coupons, she bought a knee-length blue dress. She borrowed a hat from a girl at work, and thankfully Ben's mother sent her a pair of nylon stockings with seams, so at least she wouldn't have to draw lines down the backs of her legs on her wedding day.

Soon Mrs Patrino was being called on to save the day again, as it had proved impossible to find gold wedding bands, let alone an engagement ring, in a town where many shops had been bombed out. Ben sent his mother the money and she picked out a beautiful wedding set – a diamond engagement ring and two gold bands – which she put in the post to her son.

Lyn waited patiently for the parcel to arrive. She couldn't wait to show off her engagement ring to the girls at work. But as the weeks went by there was no sign of it.

The rings were making their own little odyssey. First, they were returned to sender, since Ben was listed incorrectly as having been sent to Japan. Then his mother tried sending them again, and they mistakenly arrived in Cardiff, but the Army would not allow Ben to go and get them, so back they went again across the Atlantic.

'Has this fella of yours really got you a ring, or do you think he's just making it up?' asked one of the girls at work.

'You sure you know what you're doing, going to California with an Italian-American?' demanded another, meaningfully.

'Yes, I do,' snapped Lyn. 'He's a good man and I trust him.'

Lyn found herself increasingly spending time with girls who, like her, were dating GIs, rather than with her old friends from work. In particular, she became friendly with a girl called Jean, who was marrying another of the 14th Port officers. Lyn didn't like the term 'GI bride' – she felt many in Britain looked down on girls who they assumed were marrying for a ticket to prosperity. But she was beginning to feel that she and others like her had better club together.

Lyn's boss solved the problem of the wedding bands at least, with a couple of pot-metal rings that he had managed to acquire on the black market.

Meanwhile, since Ben was Italian-American, the wedding would have to be in a Catholic church. The priest at nearby St Edmund's agreed to marry them, but to Lyn's annoyance he would only do so if she pledged to bring up her future children as Catholic.

'I'll agree to marry you in the Catholic church,' Lyn told Ben, 'on the condition that we can have a fireworks display afterwards.'

'But how can we manage that?' Ben asked anxiously.

'Oh, I'll write to the King and Queen and say that I want fireworks on my wedding day,' she told him. The following morning, she went and booked the ceremony for 5 November. It had been six long years since the British had been able to celebrate Guy Fawkes Night, but this year fireworks would be permitted once again. If Lyn's wedding was not going to be what she had dreamed of, she would at least make sure it went off with a bang.

When the long-awaited day finally came, Lyn woke to the sound of children calling out 'Penny for the Guy!' as they carted their stuffed Guy Fawkes dummies down the street, many of which sported Hitler moustaches. She realised with a pang that this was the last time she would get to celebrate the British tradition.

Downstairs, Mrs Rowe was putting the finishing touches to the spread she was preparing, if it could be called that. She had done her best, given the limited means.

Lyn got dressed in her wedding outfit and looked at herself in the mirror. The blue dress didn't look so bad, and the little flowers on her borrowed hat matched the small pink, white and blue bouquet she had managed to obtain. She loved being able to look over her shoulder at the real seams running down her legs. 'You look beautiful, Gwen,' her mother said.

'You look beautiful, *Lyn*,' she reminded her. How was her mother ever going to cope with remembering her new surname too?

At the church, Ben stood nervously waiting for her. 'I'm still expecting that fireworks display,' she whispered to him, as she reached his side at the altar.

After the ceremony, she was surprised to see that all the neighbours were out in force and broke into spontaneous applause as the newlyweds arrived back at Padwell Road. Her mother's meagre wedding spread had multiplied into a hearty buffet thanks to those same neighbours, who had all pitched in. Instead of a tiny gathering in the Rowes' front room, the party spilled out onto the street as everyone celebrated the new Mr and Mrs Patrino. Miraculously, Lyn's spartan wedding had been transformed, loaves-and-fishes style, into a decent party.

The celebrations were well underway by the time the first fireworks began to explode overhead. Ben turned to his wife in surprise. 'But how did you…?'

'I told you,' shrugged Lyn, 'I asked the King and Queen.'

Lyn and Ben took the train down to London for their honeymoon. As they arrived at their hotel they heard a wireless playing in the bar. 'Does that tune sound familiar to you?' she asked him.

It was the Chopin polonaise from *A Song to Remember*, the film they had been watching when the war ended – the same night Ben had proposed. Words had been added by the lyricist Buddy Kaye, and the result, 'Till the End of Time', had become a hit for Perry Como.

Ben looked into Lyn's eyes. 'From now on, this is our song,' he told her solemnly. 'You and me together, till the end of time.'

When the happy couple returned to Southampton, the perfect bubble of their honeymoon burst abruptly. Ben was given notice to ship out in just forty-eight hours.

The number of GIs in the country had been dwindling ever since D-Day, and by the end of the war in Europe less than 250,000 remained. The operation to get the men home from the Continent was well underway, with 370 ships bringing an average of 3,000 men a day into New York. But Lyn had hoped that Ben would be around for a bit longer since he worked at the port in Southampton.

'I bet you'll be right behind me,' Ben told her, as they said a tearful goodbye on her doorstep.

'Well done, son,' her father said, clapping Ben on the back. 'You've done a great job here.'

'Thank you, sir,' said Ben, shaking his hand.

When Ben had gone, Lyn felt devastated. She went to see the only person she knew who would understand what she was going through – her GI bride friend Jean, whose own husband had also just shipped out.

'You're staying with me,' Jean told Lyn, opening the door to see a tear-stained face that matched her own.

That night, the two young brides cried together well into the early hours.

Like many GI brides, Lyn was now playing a waiting game. With hundreds of thousands of GIs still being shipped back to America, their brides were not the US Army's priority. Before the war had ended they had already changed the rules on army transportation of dependants, which had previously offered help only to wives of officers and high-ranking NCOs. The new rules meant that the number of war brides eligible for army transportation was huge – a growing list of 60,000 British women were now awaiting army transport, some of whom hadn't seen their husbands since before D-Day.

Many of the brides waited patiently, while others openly expressed their frustration at being turned into 'wallflower wives', as the American press had termed them. There were protests outside the US Embassy in Grosvenor Square, which was already receiving 500 visits from war brides daily, in addition to a further 1,000 letters of enquiry. In Bristol, a baby show was organised to help draw publicity to the cause, and when the recently widowed Eleanor Roosevelt visited London in November 1945, her hotel was besieged by an angry mob of brides and their babies, waving placards that read 'We Demand Ships' and 'We Want Our Dads'.

The tabloid press were not always sympathetic to the war brides' cause, but they did give it plenty of column inches. Meanwhile, in the House of Commons, the foreign secretary was asked how long the brides could expect to be kept waiting. He replied that it was a matter for the American authorities, not the British Government.

Eventually, the mounting pressure led to action in Washington. On 28 December, the American House of Congress passed Public Law 271: The War Brides Act, which offered non-quota immigration status to the wives of US servicemen, meaning that they could enter the country freely and without a visa. The cream of the trans-Atlantic fleet, the *Queen Mary* and the *Queen Elizabeth*, were among the ships that would be made available for war-bride transport.

A month after the passing of the War Brides Act, the SS *Argentina* set off from Southampton to New York. Operation War Bride had begun.

14

Margaret

It was almost 900 miles from Arlington, Georgia, to Akron, Ohio, where Lawrence was to take up his new job as buyer at the Goodyear Tire & Rubber Company headquarters. Akron was known as 'Rubber City', since it was dominated by four tyre companies: Goodyear, Firestone, Goodrich and General Tire, which all had headquarters there. While Arlington had been struggling, Akron was a city in its prime, with a fast-growing population and a bustling, modern downtown.

While Lawrence was busy sorting out their accommodation, Margaret wandered along Main Street with little Rosamund, watching the smartly dressed women in white gloves going shopping in the big department stores, O'Neil's and Polsky's. It was a shock to see paved streets full of cars again, and to be surrounded by neon shop signs and crowds of people. Margaret felt she'd returned to civilisation.

Lawrence soon returned in a company car that came with his new job. 'I've found us a great little place,' he told her. 'Hop in!' He was back to his old self and full of energy again, and she could see that encouraging him to make a fresh start had been the right decision.

After twenty-five minutes on the road, the view out of the window was becoming more and more rural, and after a while the houses had thinned out almost completely. Finally, on what was little more than a dirt track, they pulled up in front of a small summer house.

'Here we are! Like it?' Lawrence said.

He jumped out of the car and started unloading their bags. Margaret followed him slowly to the front door, speechless. So much for getting back to civilisation – they were in the middle of nowhere, in a place that didn't even have a street address.

But she tried to hide her disappointment. After all, she had pushed him to move north and take the job. If this was what it took to keep him away from his former life of drinking, she would have to put up with it.

The next morning Margaret got up early and made Lawrence's breakfast. She kissed him goodbye at the door as he set off happily for his first day of work, and felt for the first time in their marriage like a normal wife.

She went back into the house determined to do her best to make it spick and span. It clearly hadn't been much lived in, since it was only used as a holiday cabin by its owner, and there were cobwebs everywhere.

After doing what she could to clean it up, she took Rosamund for a walk. There were woods all around the house, but she remembered having seen a small farm shop on the drive over, and headed in what she hoped was the right direction. She passed out of the woods and through meadowland, and as she did so she was struck by how lush and green the area was. It looked very like the English countryside, and she felt her spirits lift.

The farm shop proved to be much further than it had seemed in the car, and by the time she got back home again she was exhausted. She put the baby down for a nap and waited for Lawrence to come home.

That evening she cooked him dinner and they chatted about the new life they were going to make for themselves. 'We won't be in this house long,' he promised her. 'As soon as I've saved up a bit of money we can move into town.' Margaret felt encouraged that their life in the sticks would only be temporary.

The next day, when Lawrence went to work, however, leaving her alone with Rosamund, she couldn't help feeling slightly at a loose end. In a cupboard in the bedroom she was relieved to find a radio, and managed to get a crackly signal for a local station. It wasn't particularly interesting, but until Lawrence came back it was the only adult conversation she would hear.

With no telephone, no means of transport and no other houses anywhere nearby, her days became monotonous. As her pregnancy progressed, walking any distance became difficult and she and Rosamund were almost housebound.

She desperately missed the company of Lawrence's sister Ellen and the rest of the family in Arlington, and though they wrote each other long letters, she felt increasingly lonely. She didn't want to burden Lawrence with how she was feeling, so she put on a brave face when he came home, trying her best to be a supportive wife.

It was hard enough waiting until six or seven for him to return, but after a while he began coming back later and later. One night, she smelled beer on his breath and realised he had been drinking. She felt immediately panicked, but he reassured her that she had no reason to worry.

'It's nothing, Margaret, just a few drinks after work,' he told her. 'In my department it's almost mandatory. I know my limits, and I have no intention of letting things go the way they did in England.'

He kissed her and she clung to him, relieved. Here in the countryside she was acutely aware that he was all she and Rosamund had in the world. The only people she knew in America were hundreds of miles away, and she had no one else to turn to. The radio had become her constant companion now, but even so there were days when she felt almost mad with loneliness.

When her due date was approaching, Lawrence took Margaret to the home of a colleague and his wife, who lived near Akron City Hospital. She left Rosamund with them and went in to be induced.

Once the contractions started, she was left alone in a room on the second-floor maternity wing, with a little bell next to the bed to ring for assistance. The waves of pain became stronger much more quickly than they had in her first labour, and Margaret rang the bell.

A nurse in a white starched uniform and cap came in. 'Yes?' she enquired.

'My contractions are getting very strong,' Margaret told her. 'Do you have anything for the pain?'

'No. Just breathe through them,' the woman told her, and walked out.

Margaret struggled on for what seemed like at least an hour, but she was almost beside herself with agony. Despite the nurse's brusque response last time, she decided to risk ringing the bell again.

After a few minutes no one had arrived, so she rang it a third time, and then a fourth. She began to panic. Had they forgotten that she was there? Desperately, she began calling out, but still no one came.

Margaret had felt so lonely ever since she came to Akron, and now, in her hour of need, she was alone again. The realisation of her utter isolation made her cry bitterly, and all she could do was grip the bars of the bed as she tried to bear the pain for hour after hour without anyone to support or comfort her.

As it grew late, the lights suddenly went out and Margaret found herself in complete darkness. She heard shouts and footsteps running along the corridor outside, and rang her bell furiously.

The lights flickered back on and eventually a nurse came and told Margaret that there had been a power cut in the city, but there was nothing to worry about.

'Please, don't leave me,' Margaret gasped, and seeing how far along she was, the nurse summoned a midwife. Baby Maeve was delivered not long afterwards and taken upstairs to the infants' ward.

The next morning, Margaret was woken by pains in her stomach and when she put her hand to it she felt extremely tender. She didn't remember feeling this way when Rosamund was born, but thought perhaps going through labour a second time had taken its toll on her body.

A nurse came in and told her that the doctor would be coming on his rounds shortly to give her a post-natal check-up. Margaret nodded. She was beginning to feel almost giddy with the pain and she was having hot and cold flushes.

Finally, the doctor arrived. 'How are we doing today, Mrs Rambo?' he asked.

'I'm having awful pains in my stomach,' she told him. 'Is that normal?'

The man frowned, and started to examine her. As he did so,

to Margaret's embarrassment, a huge gush of pus came out of her.

'Nurse!' he shouted, summoning one of the sisters. 'Take this woman's temperature.'

The nurse did so and told him it was 103 degrees.

'My God,' he said. 'It's puerperal fever.'

Margaret was terrified. She knew the disease was often fatal.

The fever was making her shiver uncontrollably and she felt increasingly woozy. Another doctor was called and Margaret struggled to focus on what they were saying.

They seemed to be arguing over whether or not to give her a new drug. 'But can you have an adverse reaction to it?' the second doctor was asking nervously. The other was arguing for administering the drug. 'It's the best chance of saving her,' he insisted.

In the end they seemed to reach a decision, and the nurse brought in a needle and syringe.

'We're going to give you something called penicillin, Margaret,' the doctor told her. 'It's rare as hen's teeth.'

The doctors kept a close eye on their patient after that, anxious to see whether the new 'miracle drug' would live up to its name.

Within four hours of the injection Margaret's temperature had dropped considerably, and by the end of the day it was back to normal.

A couple of days later she was allowed to go home. 'Well, Mrs Rambo,' said the doctor who had first seen her. 'It seems we've saved your life here!'

'Thank you,' Margaret said quietly. But the whole experience in the hospital, from the hours left alone in a room without pain relief to the power cut and the life-threatening fever, had been so terrifying that she didn't feel grateful – only desperate to get out of there.

First, however, she would have to pay the bill. 'Hasn't my husband been in to see to it?' she asked. But she was informed that Mr Rambo had not been seen.

'The bill needs paying before you leave,' she was told.

Margaret handed over all the money she had, but it wasn't anywhere near enough. 'I'm sorry, but that's all I have,' she told them. 'I'll ask my husband for the rest when I see him.'

The wife of Lawrence's colleague came to collect her, and she hurried out of the hospital shame-faced, clutching baby Maeve to her. She was shocked that Lawrence could have left her in hospital all alone, with no way of paying the bill.

Back at the other couple's house Lawrence was waiting for her, and was thrilled to see baby Maeve. Margaret felt too embarrassed to bring up the issue of the unpaid bill, but once they were on their own in the summer house, she confronted him about it.

'I told them to send the bill on to me,' he said angrily. 'I can't believe they demanded the money from you, after all you've been through. I'm so sorry, my dear.'

He sounded so adamant that Margaret didn't question him further, but she couldn't help thinking of all those unpaid bills back in England.

15

Sylvia

Sylvia had been dating her military policeman Bob for more than six months, but every time she saw him her heart still raced just as it had on their first dates. They went dancing together at the Hammersmith Palais, took day trips into the countryside and spent weekends at the Bradleys' in Woolwich, going down the pub with her parents – who had become almost as fond of him as she was. Now she knew what people meant when they said they were 'love sick' – she felt she was in a state of almost feverish passion, and every kind attention, every generous gift and every joke he told just made her love him more.

Since their first kiss in the graveyard of St Mary's Church, Sylvia and Bob had come back to visit it often. He still loved to read the ancient tombstones, marvelling at their age and inventing funny stories about the lives of the people buried there. One day, after strolling around the gravestones, they took a seat on a bench beneath a beautiful statue of a lion. Bob had been fascinated when Sylvia had told him about the man it commemorated – a nineteenth-century coal porter turned bare-knuckle boxer, known as the 'Black Diamond', who had become a world champion.

It was November and starting to turn chilly, and as they sat in the windy graveyard, Bob pulled Sylvia close and put his coat around her. Sylvia didn't mind the gloomy setting – she was glowing inwardly, happy just to be close to him. It was there, underneath the proud lion, that Bob asked her to marry him.

When they got back to St Mary Street, Sylvia could see from her parents' faces that Bob had already told them his intentions. 'Off to the pub, then,' Sylvia's mother said. 'We've got something to celebrate!'

But beneath her smile, Mrs Bradley was struggling. She wanted more than anything for Sylvia to be happy, but at the same time the thought of her eldest daughter going to the other side of the world, where she could no longer protect her, filled her with fear. 'I hope you know what you're doing, Sylvie,' she said, when Bob was out of earshot. 'It's a very big step.'

But her worried remarks couldn't pierce Sylvia's bubble. Sylvia had no thoughts beyond the fact that the man she adored wanted her to be his wife, and anyway Bob had promised her that when they did finally move to the States, he would bring her home to England on regular visits.

In the pub, Mr Bradley bought his daughter her first ever glass of wine. The alcohol burned Sylvia's throat and turned her face bright red, but she drank it nonetheless, feeling very grown up.

'To Sylvie and Bob,' her dad said. 'Good luck – and I hope all your troubles are little ones!'

Sylvia began excitedly planning the wedding, while her mother put her skills as a seamstress to good use making a beautiful wedding dress, giving up her own clothing coupons to buy the satin, taffeta and material for the veil.

But one night, four weeks after the engagement, Sylvia turned up for her shift at the Washington Club to find Bob waiting there with a concerned look on his face.

'What's wrong?' she asked him.

'Babycakes, I've got something to tell you,' he said gently. 'I'm being sent back to the US next week.'

Sylvia was stunned. 'But what about the wedding?' she asked.

'Don't worry, we'll still get married,' Bob said. 'It may take longer than we planned, and it might have to be in America, but it will happen.'

Sylvia felt as if the rug had been pulled out from under her. While all the other GI brides were getting ready to sail across the Atlantic to join their husbands, she had, quite literally, missed the boat. The War Brides Act did not cover fiancées, and since Sylvia would not be eligible for free travel courtesy of the Army, she and Bob would have to fund her trip themselves.

'I know it's a lot of money, but if we both start saving, hopefully we can get it together within a year,' he said.

Bob had two days' leave before he had to travel to Southampton to await embarkation. He and Sylvia spent their last afternoon together going to the pictures in Woolwich, but she found it impossible to pay attention to the movie. All she could think about was the fact that Bob was leaving.

Afterwards they stopped in the local pub so Bob could say goodbye to Mr and Mrs Bradley, and then Sylvia went to see him off at the station. They held each other tight for a long time, and Sylvia closed her eyes, wishing that the hug would never end. 'It won't be long until we see each other again,' Bob told her.

Sylvia was too choked up to reply. As she watched the love of her life walk away, she felt crushed.

Christmas of 1945 was a lonely one for Sylvia, and although she did her best to be cheerful for her younger sisters, she felt like a part of her was missing.

In the new year she carried on going to work at the Piccadilly Hotel as before, but around her everything was changing. Bit by bit the foreign uniforms were disappearing from the streets, and it seemed as if London was emptying out. Many younger British men were glad to see the Yanks go, relieved that the competition had finally been removed, but families like Sylvia's, who had got to know the GIs personally, felt bereft. The Americans had made the Brits more relaxed and less reserved than they had been before the war, and their happy-go-lucky, laid-back attitude had been appreciated. 'I miss chatting to all those Yanks you brought home,' said Mrs Bradley mournfully. She might have been wary of the GIs to begin with, but in the end Sylvia's various boyfriends had proven to be an opportunity for her to relive her youth.

At work things weren't the same either. Peggy had got a job nearer to her home in Battersea, so Sylvia no longer had her best friend in the office. Worst of all, the Red Cross clubs were beginning to close. When Rainbow Corner had first opened in 1942, the key had been thrown away to demonstrate its intention to be open twenty-four hours a day, but now a new key had had to be made to lock the doors. It closed with a 'GI's jamboree' and a visit from Eleanor Roosevelt, who announced, 'This club has proved we can work together. More than 80 per cent of the people working here were

British, and they worked with our American staff and made this club what it was and what it will always be in the hearts of our servicemen – a wonderful success.' But now those English volunteers were no longer needed, and Sylvia had to say a sad farewell to the Washington Club, which had been her social life for so long.

Meanwhile, she wrote to Bob all the time. Although he wrote back, it was only a couple of times a month, and she couldn't help wishing he would write more. She lived for his letters, and loved to hear about his life in America. He had got a job in the post office, he said, just like his father, and he painted a happy picture of going for picnics and playing cards at Chesapeake Bay with his family.

The weeks turned into months as Sylvia worked and saved to get the money for her boat trip. It seemed that the rest of the country was beginning to move on from the war, but her life was on hold.

One day, Sylvia rushed to pick up the post as usual, and to her delight found a letter from Bob. She ran up to her room to read it in private, sat down on her bed and tore open the envelope. As she pulled out the letter, to her surprise something else fell out: a Pan Am ticket from London to New York.

'Hey, shortstuff!' Bob wrote. 'I won $1,000 in a craps game and I'm sending you an airline ticket to come marry me!'

Sylvia gaped at the words in astonishment. 'Mum!' she shouted, running full pelt down the stairs. 'Guess what? Bob's sent me an aeroplane ticket to America!'

'An aeroplane?' Mrs Bradley replied incredulously. 'Is that safe?'

They had never met anyone who had travelled on a passenger plane, and Sylvia suddenly felt a little fear mingled in with her excitement. But she told herself that at least she wouldn't have to endure a week at sea before she could be reunited with Bob.

On her last day at the Piccadilly Hotel, the girls in the billing office all gave Sylvia goodbye presents – a little address book, lace handkerchiefs with her initials on them, a cake server in a little box and a few clothing coupons they had saved. Even her manageress, Miss Franks, had bought her a big box of fruit jellies. Sylvia was touched, and as she went home on the train for the last time, she knew she was going to miss her life at the hotel.

The next day, she used the coupons to buy a brand-new tweed skirt suit, which she planned to wear on the aeroplane so that she could turn up at Bob's in style. In the evening, her parents took her to see her Auntie Lil in Forest Hill, who had organised a surprise party for her. Her mum and aunt had spent hours making mini sausage rolls, finger sandwiches and a cake. Her grandpa led the party in games of pass the orange and blow the feather, and Auntie Lil played the piano as everyone sang along. By the end of the night, Sylvia was worn out with singing and laughing.

The day before she was meant to leave, Sylvia was surprised to receive a visit from one of her old pen pals. It was Tom, whose friend Frank had taken her to Nottingham to meet his mum, thinking they were going to get married. His time serving in the North African desert seemed to have aged him, she noticed.

'Hello, Tom,' Sylvia said. 'What brings you here?'

'I wanted to ask you something,' he said awkwardly. 'Will you do me the honour of being my wife?'

'What?' Sylvia gasped. Could it be that yet again she had unwittingly given a man the impression that she was interested in marrying him? She had seen her letter-writing as a patriotic activity – was she now going to receive a stream of proposals as all the men returned home?

'I want to marry you,' Tom insisted.

'I'm sorry, Tom, but I'm leaving for America tomorrow to marry someone else!' Sylvia said.

Tom looked at her mournfully with his big brown eyes. He reminded Sylvia of a spaniel. 'Oh, so I'm too late!' he said bitterly.

Mrs Bradley bustled into the hall. 'Well, since you've come all the way from Nottingham, you must stay,' she said. For the rest of the day Sylvia went about preparing for her journey, trying to ignore the reproachful looks Tom shot her.

The next morning, Sylvia came downstairs in her new tweed suit, with her suitcase and a fur coat, and she and her parents got ready to go to the airport. 'Can I come along?' Tom asked her mother. 'I'd like to see Sylvia off.' Mrs Bradley couldn't bring herself to say no to those big brown eyes, so Tom was allowed to accompany them.

Sylvia was to fly from Croydon Airfield, which until recently had been used by RAF Transport Command. During the war the need to fly supplies and passengers from America to the UK had made crossing the Atlantic a routine operation, and now commercial companies were beginning to move into trans-Atlantic flights.

They were told to wait in a Quonset hut, from which Sylvia got her first glimpse of the plane she would be taking. It was a DC-4, a four-engined propeller-driven plane, of the same kind that had been used during the war. She felt a rush of excitement and nervousness as she saw the words 'Pan American World Airways' along the side. Here she was, Sylvia Bradley from Woolwich, about to take an aeroplane and go to live in America! Best of all, waiting for her there was the man of her dreams – her beloved Bob.

The Bradleys had to go along a wooden walkway across a muddy field to the runway, where Sylvia was met by a steward to take her onto the plane. Her father handed Sylvia her little suitcase. She had only been able to take 40lbs, so all that was packed in it was a change of woolly underwear, her wedding dress and veil, a robe and a nightie she had made herself and the cake server her friends at work had given her.

Tom said goodbye and wished her luck, still looking as disappointed as he had the day before. Sylvia hugged her father and saw that his eyes were filling with tears. She suddenly felt a flash of guilt that amid all her excitement and happiness she was causing pain to him and her mother. 'We're going to miss you, love, but I hope you're happy,' he said.

Sylvia's mother said her goodbyes next. Mrs Bradley knew she had finally lost the power to watch over her little girl. 'Take care of yourself, and be careful, won't you?' she pleaded. 'If you have any problems, you know you can write to me.'

'Yes, Mum,' Sylvia said, hugging her tightly.

Then, as she turned to go, her mother added, 'You've made your bed, and now you'll have to lie in it.'

16

Gwendolyn

At 6 a.m. on 4 February 1946, the first official war-bride ship, the SS *Argentina*, docked at Pier 54 in New York. Despite the early hour and bitingly cold weather, the war brides were met by a crowd of 200 reporters for print, radio and newsreels, along with the Mayor of New York, William O'Dwyer. In honour of their arrival, the Statue of Liberty was floodlit for the first time since the start of the war. Soon, more than a dozen war-bride boats were crossing the ocean in an almost constant relay.

Press attention was intense on both sides of the Atlantic. Amid the stories of romantic reunions, some darker tales soon began to emerge, especially in the British tabloids. The *Daily Mail* wrote of the 'abandoned' brides who had arrived in New York to find their husbands wanted nothing to do with them, claiming – with little evidence – that hundreds were living in squalor, surviving on Red Cross handouts. There was more than a touch of smugness about such stories, since GI brides had already been stereotyped in the sensationalist press as gold-diggers, femme fatales and even prostitutes. Magazine coverage of GI marriages had predicted 80 per cent would fail, and newspapers had printed letters celebrating the departure of the 'British trash' who had dallied with the Yanks.

Reading the papers in Southampton, Lyn shrugged off the more salacious reports. Despite continued ribbing from her colleagues, she knew Ben was a good man who would never abandon her. In fact, he had recently sent her a photograph of the wedding and engagement rings his mother had tried to send her, which had gone back and forth across the Atlantic. She showed it off at work to prove her GI was as good as his word, but the girls still teased her, joking she would arrive in California to find Ben wearing a zoot suit like a gangster.

The war-bride ships all departed from Southampton, and it was Ben's old company, the 14th Port, who were in charge of the operation. There were now around 70,000 brides waiting for transportation from Britain to America, plus many more from other countries, and Lyn had resigned herself to a long wait. But one day she got a call from Shady Lane, Ben's former CO. 'Pack your bags, sugar,' he told her. 'You've been bumped up the list!'

Lyn rushed to tell her GI-bride friend Jean the good news. 'That's great,' Jean said, but she struggled to hide her envy. They both knew the war-bride transport was predicted to go on for many months, perhaps even years.

Before long, Lyn received a letter telling her to prepare to travel at short notice. There was also a postcard to fill in accepting the offer of transportation, a questionnaire and a railway warrant covering passage to a transit camp near the village of Tidworth, thirty miles north of Southampton. It seemed ridiculous to travel away from the city her boat would leave from, but at least the new camp sounded exciting – recent press coverage had dubbed it a 'country club for GI brides'.

Lyn was instructed to bring her marriage, birth and baptismal certificates, as well as her ration book and clothing coupons, and was warned not to take more than 200lbs of luggage. She tried to keep the excitement from overwhelming her as she packed her bags. She felt sorry to be leaving her parents behind – perhaps never to see them again – but Lyn's desire to be reunited with Ben eclipsed all else.

When the day came for her to depart, Lyn's parents took her to the train station. Mrs Rowe welled up at the thought of her youngest daughter setting off halfway across the world on her own, while Mr Rowe hugged Lyn tighter than he ever had before. It was a bittersweet moment for Lyn, as she climbed into the carriage and waved goodbye to them from the window.

When she arrived at Tidworth camp along with a motley crew of other war brides, Lyn quickly realised it was very far from a 'country club'. The brides slept in huge red-brick dormitory huts, sixteen to a room, in beds sorted alphabetically by surname, some of which were infested with fleas. The huts were freezing cold at night, inadequately heated by little coal fires. At meal times, the brides were ushered into a cavernous mess hall, where German POWs resentfully slopped sauerkraut onto their metal food trays. One US Army representative told a group of brides, 'You may not like the conditions here, but remember, no one asked you to come.'

Lyn's contingent of brides were excited to discover they were to travel on the famous liner the *Queen Mary*. But first they were to undergo several days of 'processing', which involved much queuing, followed by injections, blood tests, X-rays and impertinent questions such as, 'Have you ever been a prostitute?' and 'Have you ever taken drugs?' Then, they were taken for fingerprinting. Lyn couldn't help feeling they were being treated like criminals.

But the worst ordeal was 'The Physical'. Lyn was surprised to be ushered into the garrison theatre, where she was told to strip, put on a robe and join the queue of brides waiting to walk up onto the stage. To her horror, a doctor was seated there with a torch, and as each woman walked up to him she opened her robe and he shone the light between her legs to inspect her.

When Lyn got up on the stage, her legs were shaking.

'Open your robe,' the doctor commanded.

'I – I can't,' she stammered.

'Do you want to go to America?' he demanded.

She nodded weakly.

'Then open your robe.'

Lyn peeled back the fabric and exposed her naked body to the doctor. He shone his flashlight over her, then shouted, 'You're done. Next!'

She gathered up her clothes and dashed to her dormitory, fighting back tears.

Lyn's cohort of brides consoled themselves with the thought that their ordeal was only temporary. But the night before they were due to sail, an American officer announced, 'You've been bumped to the *President Tyler*. You're going to have to stay a couple more days.'

For Lyn, already exhausted and humiliated, it was the last straw. She packed her bag and walked out of the camp.

'If you're not back in two days you'll miss the boat,' a guard shouted after her, but she didn't care.

When she turned up on her parents' doorstep in Southampton, her mother cried, 'Oh my God – you've changed your mind, haven't you?'

'I don't know, Mum,' Lyn replied. 'I just couldn't take any more of that camp.'

Mrs Rowe brought her inside and put the kettle on. Part of her was glad to see her daughter again, but she was anxious about the possible repercussions. 'It's lovely to see you, Gwen,' she said, 'but if you want to be with Ben, you're going to have to go back.'

Lyn nodded slowly. Suddenly she felt terrible for what she had done – putting her mother through false hope, and now yet another difficult parting to come. 'I'm sorry, Mum,' she whispered, now feeling more wretched than ever.

The next morning, she said a second, more tearful goodbye to her parents. 'Promise me you won't come down to the dock tomorrow,' she said. She didn't think she could cope with seeing them wave her off.

'All right, love, if that's what you want,' her father said.

Lyn returned to Tidworth, and the brides were finally transported to Southampton. There, waiting for them, was the SS *President Tyler*, a single-funnelled ship half the length of the *Queen Mary*. 'We have to cross the Atlantic in *that*?' one of the brides exclaimed in disbelief.

Not only was the *Tyler* a smaller vessel, it was considerably slower as well. Their journey time across the Atlantic had been doubled from five days to ten.

Oh well, Lyn told herself, at least she had seen the last of Tidworth, and when they arrived in New York Ben would be there to meet her. He had written to say he was planning to fly from California so they could see the Big Apple together, and then he would take her back with him on the return flight.

Lyn clambered up the gangplank and stood up on deck, looking back at the city she was leaving behind. A crowd of people had gathered to wave off the boat, and she suddenly spotted a couple of faces she recognised. It was her parents, who had broken their promise not to come.

'Happy birthday, Gwen!' her mother shouted, waving frantically. In all the upset, Lyn had completely forgotten the date. It was 19 March, her twentieth birthday.

She tried her best to smile as she waved back at her parents. She didn't want their last image of her to be an unhappy one.

On the boat, the brides were under the care of the Red Cross, which had assigned a handful of its officers to every vessel. As well as running onboard nurseries, the girls provided a regime of entertainment for the passengers, including knitting classes, bingo nights, card tournaments, quizzes, hat-making contests, sing-alongs, classical concerts, ballroom dancing and even writing the ships' magazines, with names such as *Wives Whispers* and *The Porthole Peeper*. Every war-bride boat also had a well-stocked library of books and magazines, and screened a different movie every night.

The Red Cross did its bit to prepare the brides for life in the US with a series of lectures on topics such as 'Behaviour and Conduct in America' and how to pledge allegiance to the flag. The organisation also saw its role as policing the women's morals. The war brides were sharing the *Tyler* with returning servicemen, and had been told that fraternisation with the soldiers was forbidden. The Red Cross took their late-night 'chastity patrol' very seriously, since rumours persisted of girls sneaking off for affairs with male passengers and crew.

For some women, living conditions onboard the transport ships came as a shock. Even the luxury liners were still in their troop-ship arrangements, with many bunk beds or hammocks crammed into each cabin. Lyn didn't so much mind that – it was the washing facilities she struggled with. The girls strip-washed in front of one another, and her awkwardness was taken for snobbery by some of the brides, who started calling out 'La-di-dah' whenever she walked into the room.

At least Lyn found herself unaffected by the queasiness that overwhelmed a large number of the brides, and she soon began looking for things to occupy her time. She was encouraged to enter a beauty pageant, organised and judged by the Red Cross. There were no swimsuits involved, but the girls paraded up and down in front of the serious-looking panel of three Red Cross workers, flashing them their best smiles.

Then they stood waiting as the panel made up their minds. The woman next to Lyn whispered, 'You're going to win this,' and, looking down the row, Lyn thought she was probably right.

She was delighted to see one of the judges heading in her direction with a rosette. The woman pinned it to Lyn's chest, and she smiled proudly. But when she looked down at it, she realised it was blue for second place, not the winner's red she had expected. She looked along the line of women to see who had pipped her to first place, and was annoyed to see a buxom blonde jumping with joy, her red rosette bobbing up and down.

When the ship had been out at sea for about a week, the relatively calm waters they had so far enjoyed began to get choppier. The boat's tipsy movements unsettled the women, and when one bride spotted a dark, inky substance in the water, the others were quick to react.

'It's oil,' said one girl. 'We've sprung a leak!'

'Oh my God,' said another. 'Maybe we've hit an iceberg, like the *Titanic*.'

'But we're too far out now – they'll never be able to rescue us!' the first cried.

By now, other brides had crowded round and their speculations were being passed around as facts. Several girls started to cry and wail.

'What's going on?' asked Lyn.

'Haven't you heard? The ship's sinking!' a girl screamed at her, clearly hysterical.

Two Red Cross girls heard the commotion and realised they needed to get the situation under control.

'Everyone down to the dining room,' one of them called.

The women protested – they weren't going to be shut away to await their deaths.

'We will investigate and bring you information as soon as possible. Now please – go to the dining room at once.'

Reluctantly, the brides allowed themselves to be shepherded into the room, where the Red Cross calmed their nerves with tea and biscuits.

A crew member soon arrived to reassure them. 'We haven't hit anything, and there isn't a serious leak. We lost a bit of oil when the water got rough, but we're not sinking.'

The leak might have been harmless, but the ship was going to have to reduce speed, he told them. Their arrival in America would be delayed even further.

Lyn couldn't believe it. She had just about resigned herself to a ten-day voyage instead of the five the *Queen Mary* would have taken, but now she would be at sea for almost a fortnight.

That evening everyone was quieter than usual. Some were embarrassed at having been so easily whipped up into mass hysteria, while others found it difficult to let go of the fear that had gripped them. All felt it had been a reminder of how vulnerable they were out on the open sea.

On the final night of the voyage, some of the brides staged a variety show, which they called the Tyler Follies. This was a Red Cross innovation that had rapidly spread across the war-bride fleet, assuming different names on different vessels, such as the Gibbon Gaieties or the Argentina Antics. The girls sang, danced and performed short skits – one bride even dressed up as the Statue of Liberty – and the show ended with the final communal sing-song of the voyage before the brides went their separate ways in the morning. Many exchanged addresses and promised to write, fearful at losing their sense of community and starting afresh as individuals in a huge foreign country. But after nearly two weeks at sea, all Lyn wanted was to set foot on dry land and be with Ben again.

Early on the morning of 1 April, the women gathered up on deck to see the iconic landmark that every GI bride had been waiting for: the Statue of Liberty. 'Give me your tired, your poor, your huddled masses yearning to breathe free,' ran the poem around her plinth. But the huddled masses onboard the *Tyler* were not fleeing poverty or tyranny – they were there for love.

Lyn gazed at the statue in wonder. She felt she had never seen anything so magnificent.

As non-quota immigrants, the brides had no need to stop at Ellis Island, so the *Tyler* made her way up the Hudson alongside Manhattan before pulling in to dock at one of the piers, where Lyn could hear a band playing a predictable medley of tunes:

'Sentimental Journey', 'America the Beautiful' and 'Here Comes the Bride'.

Now the slow business of processing the brides could begin. On arrival, responsibility for the young women was handed over to the New York chapter of the Red Cross, which had set up an office nearby. Those brides whose husbands were coming to collect them would be allowed off, while others who required transport to their final destinations on official war-bride trains would stay onboard until the following day.

Lyn was relieved that Ben was to meet her in New York. All that remained was for her name to be called over a loudspeaker, so that he could come and sign for her. She waited as a Red Cross girl called out the brides' names, working her way through the alphabet. One by one their husbands stepped forward to claim them, and the women traipsed down the gangplank.

'Gwendolyn Patrino,' the girl called out.

Lyn waited expectantly, but there was no response from the crowd below.

'*Gwendolyn Patrino*,' the girl repeated.

A murmur went around the women still on deck. They think I'm one of those, Lyn realised – the infamous brides whose husbands never show up, destined to live off handouts.

Lyn wanted to scream that they were wrong, but all she could do was stand there, as the girl moved on to the next name.

After the other brides had gone, the Red Cross told Lyn to wait onboard while they attempted to get hold of Ben. They were used to husbands not showing up, and had dealt with stranger cases than hers. One woman had arrived to find that her husband had divorced her, but she announced that she had an offer of marriage from another former GI and would like to go and marry him instead. The Red Cross had wired its branch in Sacramento, who contacted the man and wired back to confirm that he was willing to accept the girl. Some war brides, though, seemed to be deliberately working the system – one woman's alleged husband turned out never to have heard of her.

Later that day, one of the Red Cross girls told Lyn she had Ben on the line. Lyn rushed with her to the office and clutched the receiver to her ear.

'Lyn, are you there?' he said.

'Ben! Where are you?'

'I'm at home in San Jose. I hate to tell you this, but I won't be able to come and meet you.'

Lyn felt panicked. 'What's happened?'

'Well, my mom says we can't afford the fare.'

'I see,' she said guardedly. 'So what do I do now?'

'The Red Cross are going to put you on a train to California, and I'll meet you in Oakland,' he said. 'It won't be long now. I think the train should take about four or five days.'

Four or five days! How could Ben's mother put her through this, after the journey she'd already endured?

'Will you promise me one thing?' she pleaded.

'Anything.'

'Come to the station in your army uniform, like I remember you.'

She recalled the jibes her colleagues had made about her Italian-American turning up in a zoot suit, and she wanted to know they were wrong.

Lyn spent the night on the ship, and the next morning one of the Red Cross girls told her they had been forced to put her on an army train, since all the special war-bride trains were full.

It was leaving late that evening, and she advised Lyn to take the time to rest. Lyn, however, had no intention of doing that when the whole of New York was waiting outside. She disembarked from the boat and hopped in a yellow cab, asking the driver to take her to Saks on Fifth Avenue. She had seen the famous department store in the movies and couldn't wait to experience it for herself.

'That's forty-five cents,' the cab driver told her when he pulled up outside the store. She opened her purse and looked at the jumble of foreign currency inside – even after two weeks on an American boat she still hadn't got her head around it. She scooped up a handful of coins and held them out to the driver, hoping he was honest.

Lyn stepped out of the cab and looked around her at the huge buildings forging upwards to the sky. Across the road she saw the soaring tower of the Rockefeller Center, while a little further down the street was the magnificent cathedral of Saint Patrick. New York was more vibrant even than London, but as she watched the brightly coloured cars and smartly dressed people whiz by, she couldn't help wondering why everyone seemed to be in such a hurry.

Inside Saks, Lyn made her way to the womenswear department, where she spotted a magnificent fur coat. She tried to take it off the hanger, but found it wouldn't budge.

'Can I help you, ma'am?' came a sharp American voice. A smartly dressed sales assistant was walking over quickly.

'I was just going to try this coat on,' Lyn explained.

'You can't,' she said.

'Why not?'

The woman glared at her. 'It's chained up to stop you from stealing it.'

'I didn't want to steal it!' Lyn protested. 'I just wanted to try it on.'

Her cheeks burning in humiliation, Lyn shoved the coat back onto its hanger and left.

After walking several blocks, she felt desperate to sit down, and stopped at a café on Lexington Avenue.

'Could I get a cup of tea, please?' she asked a waiter.

'Coming right up,' the man replied. Before long a steaming cup was plonked down in front of her.

But to her surprise it just seemed to be hot water, with a strange brown thing floating in it. 'Excuse me,' she said, calling the waiter over, 'I think there's something in my cup.'

'Yeah, that's a tea bag,' he replied.

Lyn had never heard the word before. 'Well, would you take it out and give me a cup of tea?' she asked.

'You're a real smart alec, aren't you?' he said, and walked off angrily.

Confused, Lyn left the café and hailed a cab back to the ship. She'd already had more than her fill of the Big Apple.

As the Red Cross bus pulled up to Grand Central station, it was met by a group of angry-looking women brandishing placards. Lyn peered out of the window and was greeted with the words 'ENGLISH WHORES GO HOME'. Charming, she thought. It seemed the war brides were about as popular among American women as the GIs had been among British men.

The brides disembarked and were taken into the train station, where they were held in a kind of pen, with tags around their necks detailing their final destination. Passers-by stopped to stare, and a few asked them to speak so they could hear their strange accents.

The other brides were soon helped onto official war-bride trains, and Lyn was put on her army train. She found herself sharing a carriage with a group of officers, including a doctor. As the only woman, Lyn felt conspicuous, but the men were kind and the doctor took her under his wing. He told her he was transporting a soldier to a psychiatric hospital in Oakland, to be treated for schizophrenia. 'Cracked up in France,' he explained.

The soldier was held in a small compartment for the entire journey with an armed guard at the door. As Lyn tried to get to sleep that night, she couldn't help shuddering at the thought of him locked up in there.

The next day, they arrived in Chicago, where they had to change trains. Then they were on their way again, heading west across the mighty Mississippi. 'Excuse me,' Lyn asked the porter as he passed through the carriage. 'Would you mind knocking me up in the morning? I don't want to miss anything.'

The man stared at her for a moment, and then a cheeky smile spread across his face. 'Sure thing, ma'am,' he replied.

Throughout the journey Lyn remained glued to the window, watching the giant continent pass by, hypnotised by mile after mile of lonely, empty space and amazed by how big it was. She saw the landscape outside change, from the corn fields of Iowa to the wild barren prairies of Nebraska. Every night she asked the porter to knock her up in the morning, and every time he would say 'Yes, ma'am' with the same cheeky smile.

When the train pulled into Cheyenne, Wyoming, Lyn was astonished to see an American Indian. He was a member of the Arapaho tribe, and had long dark hair and a traditional necklace. Many war brides viewed their first Indian with fear, having grown up on cowboy movies in which they were wild, scalping villains – one bride had crouched on the floor of her carriage in terror, convinced that a man dancing for some tourists was on the warpath. But Lyn had no such worries and, inquisitive as ever, she took her camera and ran straight up to the man. 'Excuse me,' she said. 'Are you an Indian, like in the movies?'

'I am,' the man replied solemnly.

'A real Indian?'

The man nodded.

'Could I take your photograph?'

'No,' he snapped, and walked off.

Lyn returned to the train disappointed. 'That Indian wouldn't let me take his picture!' she complained to the officers in her carriage.

'That's their custom,' one of them replied. 'They don't allow photographs.'

'Oh,' said Lyn. 'I see.' But she couldn't help feeling a little annoyed.

The train passed through the deserts of Utah and Nevada, until finally Lyn was awoken one morning by the usual knock on her door and told they were now in California. 'Thank you so much,' she told the porter. 'I wanted to give you this.' She handed him a crisp dollar bill. 'It's for knocking me up every morning.'

The man smiled more than ever. 'Thank you, ma'am,' he replied. 'Oh, and when you see your husband, I want you to tell him that the porter knocked you up every morning, and you gave him a tip for it.'

'All right,' Lyn replied innocently. 'I will.'

The lush California landscape was a welcome change of scene for Lyn after the stark, alien desert of Nevada, but her mind was not really on the scenery. She had travelled nearly 3,000 miles from coast to coast across America, almost as great a distance as she had crossing the Atlantic, and there was only one thing she wanted to see: Ben.

As the train pulled into Oakland station, she rushed to the door of her carriage, straining to catch a glimpse of her husband on the platform. There he was, clutching a huge bunch of flowers – and he was wearing his old army uniform, just as she had asked.

Lyn threw open the train door and ran into his arms.

'Thank God you're finally here,' he said. Lyn was so overcome with emotion she couldn't reply.

'Here,' he said, handing her the flowers. 'These are to say sorry I wasn't able to meet you in New York. And I've got something else for you.' He took out a small box containing the engagement and wedding rings that had made their way back and forth across the Atlantic so many times. As he slipped them onto her finger, Lyn wished her old colleagues were there to see that, after all, Ben had proved as good as his word.

Suddenly the difficulties and insults of her epic journey melted away, and Lyn felt it had all been worth it.

As Ben began loading her bags into his father's Buick, a thought struck her. 'Oh, there's something I'm meant to tell you,' she said. 'The porter on the train knocked me up every morning, and I gave him a good tip for it.'

Ben's jaw dropped momentarily, but then he laughed as he realised the misunderstanding. 'Lyn, whatever you do, don't tell my parents that!' he said.

17

Rae

While other war brides were waiting patiently for passage to join their husbands, Rae was secretly beginning to dread the day that she received her orders to sail.

She had found waiting for the war to end almost unbearable, and even after victory had been declared in Europe it had been another three months before Raymond returned from France. There hadn't been much time for a proper reunion, however – he had been given two days' leave to visit her before being shipped back to the States.

Rae had been shocked to see the husband she had worried about so frantically for fifteen months sitting on the sofa in her house as if nothing had happened. Suddenly, relief had overwhelmed her – now that Raymond was finally with her again, she could accept that the war was well and truly over. For the second time in recent months, the normally tough Rae had burst into tears.

'Hey, aren't you pleased to see me?' he had joked, as he put his arms around his sobbing wife.

When they first met, she had slammed the door in his face every time he turned up at her billet asking for a date. Yet here she was crying on his shoulder. She felt like she had become a different person.

There had been other changes too. As a welder in the Army, Rae had found an identity and a vocation that suited her, but now she was no longer in uniform. At the end of the war, she and a few other ATS girls had been called into the office at Chilwell and asked if they would like to stay on. Reluctantly, she had turned down the offer – she knew that as a married woman she couldn't commit to several more years in the Army.

With Raymond about to leave for America, Rae had been gripped by a new worry. 'Promise me you won't go back down the mine,' she pleaded. 'It's too dangerous.'

'Okay, baby,' he had replied. 'I'll get a job at the steel mill instead.'

As Rae waved him off again, it had suddenly dawned on her that the next time she saw him they would both be in America. When they had married, it had been in the midst of a war that seemed never-ending. She had accepted Raymond's ring without considering the fact that one day it would mean following him halfway across the world. But now, as she waited for her orders to join him in America, she began to question what she had done. She loved her country passionately – even more so after serving in the forces – and she was also worried about how her mother would cope with her departure. The family had been disrupted so many times already – by death, by the war and by her stepfather's betrayal. The thought of leaving them now was intolerable.

By the time her orders to travel finally came, Rae had found an excuse to stall her departure. She wrote to Raymond telling him that her sister Liz was about to give birth, and she had offered to help out until she had the baby. In the meantime, she had requested a delay from the US Army.

Raymond accepted the disappointing news, and Rae moved in with Liz. She was there when she went into labour, helping the midwife deliver the baby. Raymond sent his congratulations, and asked if Rae would now be ready to leave. But she replied that she couldn't possibly leave Liz now, in the early days of motherhood, when she needed her help the most.

As the weeks slipped by, the normally laid-back Raymond sounded more and more uneasy in his letters. 'When are you coming?' he kept demanding, but all he received were updates on the baby's progress.

Eventually, Rae's mother confronted her, and asked what was going on.

'I don't want to go to America, Mum!' Rae blurted out.

Mrs Burton didn't want her daughter to leave either, but she felt the decision had been made when Rae and Raymond had married. 'Your place is with your husband,' she told her sadly. 'No matter where he is.'

Reluctantly, Rae wrote to tell Raymond that she was ready to leave, and accepted passage with the Army.

Rae's mother and her siblings Vic, Mary and Ron came to see her off at Waterloo, from where she was to take the War Brides Express to Tidworth. The station platform was busy with war brides from all over Britain, and the Women's Voluntary Service bustled about, ticking their names off lists before they were handed over to the care of the Red Cross.

Suddenly, Rae's brother Ron started running back down the platform to the exit. 'Where are you going?' she called.

'I have to meet my mate,' he shouted back, and to Rae's dismay he was gone. Saying goodbye had proved too difficult for him.

A whistle blew and everyone in the crowd started giving each other a last hug, before the women made for the doors. 'Goodbye, love,' said Rae's mother, wiping away her tears with a hanky.

Mary looked utterly desolate as she watched her sister disappear onto the train. This latest loss to the family proved so hard to bear that when Mary returned to her ATS base she spent three days in the camp hospital.

When Rae's contingent of war brides arrived at Tidworth, they handed over their luggage, ration books and identity cards, and endured the endless checking of paperwork and the humiliating medical examinations that were the price of passage to the States.

They were told that their stay at the camp would be for only three days, but three days came and went and still they had not been taken to a ship. Every afternoon they were promised they would be boarding the following day, but the next morning they were always disappointed. Some of the brides became desperate, hearing stories of women who had waited at Tidworth for nearly two months. Unable to bear it any longer, several walked out, declaring, 'If our husbands want us, they can come and get us.'

Finally, after six days, Rae's group of brides were taken to Southampton to board the *Bridgeport*, an old steel-hulled German passenger vessel that the US Army had been using as a hospital ship. When Rae and the other brides went to investigate their quarters, they found that they were in the former psychiatric ward, and their dining area was enclosed within a wire cage – hardly the most welcoming of environments. Before the boat left, five or six brides had a change of heart and demanded to be let off.

As the boat began to pull out of port, Rae and the remaining women rushed up on deck. A ship of wounded British soldiers was coming in, and seeing the war brides, they started yelling, 'You'll be sorry!'

But the brides drowned them out by singing 'There'll Always Be an England' at the tops of their voices, and Rae joined in with gusto, doing her best to blast away the aching sadness she felt as she watched her homeland slide out of view.

Although the *Bridgeport*'s voyage began relatively smoothly, a few days into the journey it hit a storm. The boat lurched violently in the water and waves came crashing over the deck, causing the majority of the brides to suffer terrible sea sickness. One Jewish bride, who had been in a concentration camp, was suffering more than most and as the storm worsened she became increasingly distressed. She had previously spoken in fluent English, but now the language seemed to escape her and she began ranting at the Red Cross girls in German and wailing inconsolably. The girls did their best to calm her down, but it was clear that the fear caused by the storm had triggered memories of her previous trauma and she had to be taken to the sickbay, where she lay delirious for three days.

Even those who had not suffered atrocities in the war could sometimes be driven crazy by the rough seas. During the first ever war-bride voyage on the *Argentina*, a terrible storm had made one bride so hysterical that she tried to throw herself overboard. Her life was saved by another bride, who managed to grab her before she succeeded, and she was taken to the sickbay and sedated.

The closer they got to their final destination, the more troubled Rae felt about having left her home and her family, and the more anxious she became about what was before her. She was not alone. In the last few days of their voyages, many brides began to panic. As well as their other duties, the Red Cross provided a counselling service, and their caseload became heavier as they approached New York. Often these worries simply needed 'talking out', but some cases were more sensitive than others. One Red Cross girl was charged with explaining to a twenty-three-year-old French woman the trouble she and her 'Negro' husband, a bag handler at Grand Central station, could expect to face in America as a mixed-race couple. Many war brides had no idea that mixed marriages were still illegal in some states.

As the *Bridgeport* arrived at the mouth of New York Harbor, the brides rose early to see the Statue of Liberty. For some it was an exciting moment, but the sight filled Rae with dread. She stood up on deck and cried, wishing that she could jump in the water and swim back to England.

In New York Rae was put on an overnight train heading west, which had been commandeered for the brides. Red Cross girls were onboard handing out candy, doughnuts, fried cakes, peanuts and newspapers – in which some brides spotted pictures of themselves that had been taken by the press on their arrival. The Red Cross had become vigilant in guarding against journalists and photographers after hordes of them had jumped a war-bride train in Chicago, which led to the women becoming separated and stranded without their baggage.

The Red Cross girls took good care of the brides, staying up all night and preparing baby formula, comforting those who were 'train sick', talking to the women about their destinations and handing out maps so they could see where they were going. On one train, the women were so grateful to a Red Cross worker that at the end of the trip they made a collection of $23 and suggested that she and the male medic onboard use it to go out for dinner together.

Meanwhile, the Red Cross girls also continued to fulfil their role as counsellors. One tall, blonde bride wept as she told a caseworker how she and her GI both wanted a divorce. She said she intended to leave him and marry a relative in America – who, it soon transpired, was on the train already. The Red Cross called the immigration authorities, who said that if she did not go to her husband she would be deported. When she arrived at her destination, the unwanted spouse, who did not want a divorce after all, was there to meet her. Reluctantly, she went off with him, leaving her boyfriend behind.

As the train pulled into Pittsburgh, Rae saw that the sky was thick with smog and the buildings were blackened and grimy – it was even worse than she was used to in London. The city's steel mills had been booming during the war, and smoke-control laws, passed in 1941, had been put on hold. Not for nothing had the city garnered the nickname 'Hell with the lid off'.

Rae was the only bride who got off at Pittsburgh, where the Red Cross handed her over to a woman from Travelers Aid, who put her on the train to her husband's hometown of Hackett. After about half an hour, the train was passing through woodland, in what seemed like the middle of nowhere, when it came to a stop. Rae peered out of the window. There was no station, just a road running alongside the railway line. She was wondering if they had broken down when a man came running along the tracks calling, 'Rae Wessel?'

Rae grabbed her bag and ran to the door, and the man offered a small stool so she could step down onto the gravel by the side of the tracks. She wondered what kind of a place she had come to, where there weren't even platforms for the trains.

As the train departed, Rae saw a little group of people heading towards her, and at the front of them was Raymond. He was dressed not in his old army uniform but in a white shirt and loose-fitting trousers, which made him look even more laid-back than she remembered.

'Rae!' he called, running up to her, his familiar big grin on his face. She reached up to hug him, but couldn't help feeling a little like she was hugging a stranger. It had been so long since they'd last seen each other.

He took her bag. 'This is my mom and pop,' he said, introducing a short thin man and a little chubby woman, both of them dark haired.

'Hello, Rae!' said Mrs Wessel, giving her a hug.

'Welcome!' said her husband.

'And these are my brothers, Jimmy and Charles,' Raymond continued. Both were shorter than Raymond, like their parents, and all of them greeted her warmly.

'Everyone's going to be calling the police, wanting to know what's wrong with the train,' her father-in-law told her. 'It's the first time in history it's stopped here!'

They walked up to a little road, where Charles's car was parked. Raymond put Rae's bag in the boot and they all squeezed in.

'Charles is the only one around here with a car,' Raymond said apologetically, as they set off.

As they drove along, there was little more than woods and scrubland on either side, punctuated by the occasional house, but after a while they passed a church and a big red-brick school building.

'My other uncle is the janitor there, so we get to use the shower once a week!' said Raymond, pointing to the school.

'Oh,' said Rae. She hoped there would be more washing facilities at their home.

After five minutes or so, a few more houses started to appear, all of them small clapboard constructions with triangular slanted roofs and little porches at the front. They were widely spaced, and Rae could see that behind them there was nothing more than forest.

'Welcome to Hackett,' Mr Wessel said.

Rae blinked. Was this it? This was the 'town' she was to live in?

At every door, women in housecoats, with their hair in curlers, emerged to stare at the new arrival. As the car drew up to the Wessel home, towards the far end of the line of houses and opposite the only shop, one neighbour said, 'I hope she knows what she's letting herself in for.'

Rae did her best to ignore the stares and followed Raymond and his family inside. To the right as she came in was a small living room containing a couch and a rocking chair, and to the left was a little kitchen. Raymond's other brother Bill and his wife Chi-Chi had arrived, and they were also excited to meet her.

While Mrs Wessel busied herself preparing a lunch of meatloaf, they all sat around the kitchen table and began firing questions at Rae: 'How was the trip?' 'Was the voyage very rough?' 'Were there lots of other war brides onboard?' Rae did her best to answer the stream of enquiries, although she was tired from her night on the train and really just wanted to lie down.

'Where's the loo?' she asked, interrupting the conversation.

They looked at her blankly. 'She means the bathroom,' Raymond explained to the others.

Rae wondered why the family had to take showers at the local school if they had their own bathroom.

To her surprise, Raymond pointed out of the window. Around twenty feet away was a small shack. 'In there,' he said.

Rae went to the back door. Between her and the 'bathroom' was a ferocious dog, chained to a fence, which started barking threateningly as soon as it saw her. Rae steeled herself and ran as fast as she could, reaching the door to the little shack just before the dog lunged at her. Inside, she was horrified to see that, far from being a bathroom, or even a proper outdoor toilet, it was just a two-hole outhouse.

The Wessels' neighbours were keen to meet their exotic new arrival, and soon Rae was taken across the road to a slightly larger house belonging to Mrs McClure, who was throwing her a 'Welcome to America' party.

Every woman on the street seemed to have been invited, and they crowded around Rae, firing more questions at her about her trip and about life in England. 'Oh, we suffered during the war too,' one of them said, telling her about the scarcity of petrol. The others chimed in, complaining how they hadn't been able to get this or that. You're lucky, Rae felt like saying – we didn't have anything! But she kept her mouth shut.

Mrs McClure had bought a large case of fruit from Chuck's Corner Store, and the other women had brought cakes, biscuits and sandwiches. Everyone helped themselves, eating and chatting away cheerily.

Rae was grateful for the effort they were making, and did her best to join in, but she couldn't help feeling a little resentful.

They all seemed quite spoilt, complaining about what they lacked even as they stuffed their faces. All she could think about when she saw the piles of food in front of her was her poor mother back home in England, still struggling to survive on her rations.

However friendly they were, these people couldn't understand her, she realised. They had no idea who she was or what she had been through. The welcome party had been thrown in her honour, but Rae might as well have been an uninvited guest. In the midst of all the laughter and merriment, she felt utterly alone.

18

Sylvia

As Sylvia boarded the DC-4 propeller plane that would take her across the Atlantic, her mother's words were still ringing in her ears: 'You've made your bed, and now you'll have to lie in it.'

But she felt more excitement than trepidation. She was about to embark on a new phase of her life, with the man she loved more than anyone else in the world.

The inside of the aeroplane looked to Sylvia very much like the inside of the buses at home, with their straight-backed, leatherette seats. It had about fifty or sixty passengers, and two-thirds of them were women.

Sylvia was pleased to get a seat by a little round window and watched in fascination as the earth beneath her grew further and further away and she was transported into a landscape of endless cloud.

'Going anywhere nice?' the girl next to her asked.

'I'm going to Baltimore to get married,' Sylvia told her. 'My fiancé was stationed in England during the war.'

'Mine too!' the other girl replied. 'We got married in England but he got sent home. We're going to live just outside Baltimore.'

Sylvia began to wonder whether the other women on the plane were also GI brides. Probably like her companion they had been lucky enough to get married before they set off for America.

But Sylvia was shy with people she didn't know, and didn't want to seem to be prying, so she didn't ask too many questions. After a while the other girl took out a book, and Sylvia realised she hadn't thought to bring anything to occupy her on the journey. The estimated flight time was twenty hours, with refuelling stops in Ireland, Newfoundland and Nova Scotia.

The only thing Sylvia had with her was a pen and paper, so she wrote a letter to her mother, telling her all the things she hadn't said at the airfield – how much she was going to miss her, how much she appreciated everything she had done for her over the years, and how she planned to come back and see them often, just as Bob had promised. It was the longest letter she had ever written.

The plane touched down at LaGuardia airport at 6 a.m., and as Sylvia stepped down onto the tarmac she was immediately hit by the heat, which even in the early morning was pushing eighty degrees – twenty degrees higher than in Croydon.

After going through customs, she and the other passengers who were being met were ushered into a little waiting room. She checked her face in her compact mirror and gave her nose a good powdering, then settled down to await Bob. She was so excited at the thought of seeing him again that the hands on the little clock on the wall seemed to be going at half speed. Every time someone arrived to collect their loved ones she looked up hopefully, but each time she saw an unfamiliar face.

After half an hour the room was beginning to thin out. Sylvia was almost bursting with anticipation and began to tap her foot impatiently on the floor. If only Bob would hurry up.

After an hour, she was the last one left in the waiting room, and a janitor poked his head round the door. 'Are you meeting someone?' he asked.

'Yes,' she replied. 'My fiancé's picking me up.'

'Okay then,' said the man, and went back to his rounds.

The second hour that Sylvia waited, she started to become increasingly anxious. Surely Bob couldn't just be running late any more. There must be something else going on.

The janitor came back. 'Are you sure someone's picking you up?' he asked.

'Yes, I'm sure!' retorted Sylvia. But she was beginning to panic. What would she do if Bob didn't show up? The only thing she could think of was somehow getting to the British Embassy and throwing herself on their mercy.

She looked at the clock again. It was just after eight. If he hadn't arrived by nine, she told herself, she would go.

That hour was the longest of them all. As the hand on the clock got closer and closer to nine, Sylvia's hopes diminished further and further and she couldn't help thinking how humiliating it would be to have to return to England and tell everyone that her marriage had never actually taken place.

At three minutes to nine, she got up and walked shakily to the door of the waiting room. She heaved it open and stepped back into the long corridor outside. At the other end of the corridor she could see a man walking towards her. He had glasses and was wearing a double-breasted pin-striped suit with a watch chain and a fedora hat, which made him look alarmingly like a gangster. The man noticed her and started walking towards her more quickly. 'Sylvia!' he called out.

Sylvia stood rooted to the spot. How on earth did this gang-ster know her name? Then, as his face came into focus, she suddenly recognised Bob. She was completely taken aback. He had never worn glasses in the Army, and she had never imag-ined that in his civvies he would dress like this. But it was him all right.

'Bob!' she cried. 'I was just getting ready to go to the Embassy. I thought you'd stood me up!'

Bob laughed and rushed up to her, grabbing her in his arms and spinning her round. 'I've got you at last!' he said. 'I've really got you at last!'

It transpired that Bob had mistakenly gone to Idlewild airport, on the south side of Queens, and spent hours walking all the way to LaGuardia. 'I met some people here who offered to drive us home,' he told Sylvia.

Outside the airport it was even hotter than when she had arrived, and Sylvia immediately took off her fur coat and hat. Bob led her over to a little black Plymouth, and she was surprised to find the GI bride she had met on the plane, with a man who was evidently her husband. 'Hello again!' the other girl said.

Sylvia and Bob got into the back seat, and they set off for Baltimore. Inside the car, Sylvia found the heat was even worse than before. The back windows didn't open, so she tried to fan herself with her hand. 'Too hot for you, babycakes?' Bob asked, laughing.

Sylvia nodded. She was transfixed by how wide the roads were and how many cars there seemed to be on them, not to mention how big the cars were.

Bob chatted and joked away, but Sylvia found it hard to concentrate on what he was saying. She had never been so hot in her whole life, and felt as if she would die. She took off her tweed jacket, undid the bow on her blouse and kicked off her shoes, but even that didn't give her any relief.

She didn't understand it – why was it so hot? She knew Florida and California were meant to be warm, but she hadn't expected the northeast coast to be. She took off her stockings, much to Bob's amusement, and rolled up the sleeves of her blouse.

It was a four-hour drive to Baltimore and every minute of it Sylvia felt like she was in pure hell. Sweat ran down her face, her hair was wet with it, and her face broke out in ugly red bumps from the heat.

At last Bob told her they were nearing his home, in the northeast of the city. They drove through a large, pretty park and came out onto a busy little road called Washington Street with a tramline running through it. The houses were all terraced, brick buildings, each of them with white marble steps up to the front door. Many of the steps had people sitting on them, and all of the people looked with interest as the car pulled up to number 1722.

'They all heard you're coming!' Bob explained. As Sylvia stepped out of the car, giddy with heat and exhaustion and her curly hair now an enormous frizz-ball from the perspiration, she wondered what on earth they must be making of her.

The other couple drove off and Bob's parents emerged from their house. Mr O'Connor was a handsome, fair-haired man with broad shoulders, and was smartly dressed. He looked an unlikely match with Bob's mother, who was short and rather dumpy, with dark hair like her son's, and wearing a loose house-dress. Bob's dad had a big smile on his face, but his mother looked more serious.

Mrs O'Connor tried to disguise her shock at the sight of the bedraggled, half-conscious English girl that her son had brought back from the airport. 'Welcome!' she said, kissing her on a heat-bump-covered cheek. Sylvia winced, but Bob's mother smiled warmly.

His father seemed equally friendly. 'I think you're so brave to leave your home and your family for my son,' he told her.

Sylvia's mother ushered her inside. 'I've filled the tub with cold water for you, if you want to go upstairs and cool off,' she told her. The words were like music to Sylvia's ears, and she followed her to the bathroom. After soaking for half an hour in the blissfully cool water she was a little less red-faced but very sleepy, and Mrs O'Connor showed her to the middle of three bedrooms, which she told her would be hers until after the wedding, while Bob would be sleeping in the back bedroom.

Five hours later, when she awoke, several sleeveless cotton dresses and sets of cotton underwear were lying at the end of her bed. While she had been sleeping, Bob's mother had unpacked her case and, horrified by the sight of her one pair of woollen underwear, had taken the tram down to Monument Street to kit her future daughter-in-law out with more suitable attire. Sylvia still felt woozy from the flight, but she was filled with gratitude at her new family's kindness.

The next day was a Sunday, and Bob proudly showed Sylvia around the local area, all the time holding her hand and stealing kisses whenever he could. It was a pleasant neighbourhood a couple of miles from the city centre, with a seafood shop just across the street and a cinema nearby.

In the early evening they rode the tram into the centre of town and went to the harbour. Sylvia was less than impressed – it looked shabby and unkempt, and there were a few high-rise buildings to be seen around it. Baltimore was nothing like she had imagined.

The government buildings around the post office, where Bob and his dad worked, were more appealing. There was a grand city hall with a dome in the centre and a marble exterior, even if it was rather run down.

The next day, Bob and his father had to get up at 4 a.m. for their postal rounds, but his sister Dorothy, who lived nearby, came round with her three-year-old son. She had a pretty smile and the dark hair and eyes from Mrs O'Connor's side of the family. 'I've come to take you shopping!' she told Sylvia. Bob had left a pile of dollars to fund the trip. 'What have you got for your wedding night?'

Sylvia showed her the nightie she had made herself, and Dorothy shook her head. 'Oh no,' she said. 'We'll have to buy you something else.'

Dorothy left her little boy with her mother and she and Sylvia took the tram into the city, getting off near the downtown shopping area, the other side of Charles Street from the government district. Sylvia was very impressed with the window displays, showing mannequins dressed in the latest fashions, and in all the shops she was overwhelmed by the range of styles and colours on offer. Everything seemed to be made with so much more material, with pleats and folds and layering that would have been hard to come by in post-war Britain.

Dorothy took her to a shoe shop, since she hadn't come with any white shoes for the wedding. Sylvia picked out a pair of white suede heels, with a flower pattern punched into the material at the front. They were exquisitely made.

'Why don't we buy another pair while we're here?' Dorothy asked. 'You can't just have one pair of shoes!'

Sylvia felt giddy buying so many things at once, but encouraged by Bob's sister she asked the salesman if she could look at a pair she'd seen in the window. 'They're the nigger-brown sandals,' she said.

The man stared at her in disbelief.

'Sylvia, we don't use that word over here,' Dorothy whispered.

'Oh,' Sylvia said, confused. Back home in England, 'nigger' was just a shade of brown.

They bought the shoes as quickly as possible and hurried out of the shop.

Next, Dorothy took her into a department store and they headed for the lingerie department, where they bought a beautiful pink lacy nightie for Sylvia's wedding night, along with some satin slips, camiknickers and a dressing gown. Sylvia felt like she'd died and gone to heaven when she held the luxurious items in her hands.

When they took them to the cash desk, the woman overheard Sylvia talking and noticed her accent. 'Where are you from?' she asked.

'England,' Sylvia replied.

'That's so interesting,' the woman said. 'What language do you speak over there?'

This time it was Sylvia's turn to be flabbergasted.

When they got home, Bob and his father had just got up from their daily nap, and Sylvia excitedly showed them and his mother her purchases. Among them was a new powder compact that Dorothy had encouraged her to get, but as she took it out of the cardboard box it had come in, she was disappointed to see that the catch was broken.

'Oh no!' exclaimed Sylvia. 'I've been diddled!'

For the second time that day, her comment was met with shocked looks.

'You can't use that word over here, honey,' Bob whispered.

'Why not?' Sylvia asked.

Bob leaned over and whispered in her ear, and her face turned almost as red as it had been on her arrival.

The wedding was planned for the following Saturday, and the rest of that week was a whirlwind of visits from family members and friends who all wanted to meet Sylvia and discuss the wedding with Bob's mother. Everything, it seemed, had already been planned, from the bridesmaids to the flowers. All Sylvia was required to do was show up. As she sat there hearing the details being discussed, she couldn't help feeling she was going to someone else's wedding. Half the time Sylvia found it difficult to concentrate on what they were saying, since she was still struggling with the heat and humidity.

The morning of the wedding it was hotter than ever. Sylvia felt a rush of excitement remembering it was her big day, followed by a wave of nervousness. Bob's mother was busy downstairs preparing the food for the reception, but Dorothy came round to help her get ready. She knocked on the door and came in with a little bag. 'I brought you a razor,' she told her.

'What for?' Sylvia asked.

'To shave your legs of course!'

'Does everyone do that over here?'

'Oh yes.'

Sylvia took a bath and did as she was told, trying her best to avoid cutting herself. Afterwards she wafted about in her new dressing gown, feeling quite the movie star, while Dorothy helped fix her hair. But as the day got hotter and the hour of the wedding got closer, Sylvia's excitement began to be over-taken by her nerves and she felt suffocated. The thought of getting married in front of hordes of strangers terrified her. The person she really wanted right now was her mother, but she was thousands of miles away.

'Sylvia, are you okay?' Dorothy asked, seeing her sway slightly.

'I think I'm going to faint,' Sylvia replied.

'Lie down on the bed,' Dorothy told her. She went and got Sylvia an iced tea, which revived her a little.

Sylvia began dressing in the gown her mother had made – the only thing in the wedding that was her own. It was a beautiful long-sleeved dress made of heavy slipper satin, the bodice embroidered with imitation pearls and silver bugle beads, with a three-foot train. Sylvia was wearing two petticoats underneath the skirt to help bulk it out, and her mother had made a headpiece out of wax and artificial pearls.

When she had it all on, Sylvia felt hotter than ever, and she was gasping for breath. 'I feel faint again!' she told Dorothy, who rushed downstairs for more iced tea. Mrs O'Connor decided they couldn't risk an unconscious bride, and dispatched a cousin to the corner drug store to purchase some spirits of ammonia, a few drops of which were added to Sylvia's drink. As Dorothy helped her with her make-up, and the bridesmaids arrived to get changed, Sylvia was in a complete fog, and only managed to keep from fainting in their midst by taking regular sips of the liquid.

Bob, meanwhile, was getting ready at his best man Donald's house, but had been told of Sylvia's fainting fits and phoned to see if she was all right. 'How are you feeling?' he asked her.

'Nervous!' she told him. 'How about you?'

'Yeah, me too. Donald had to give me a couple of drinks to straighten me out!'

Mrs O'Connor's youngest brother, Gordon, was to walk Sylvia down the aisle, and since he had a car and the O'Connors did not, he came to pick them up. Outside it was pushing ninety degrees, and Sylvia was so uncomfortably hot as they drove to the Faith Presbyterian Church she thought she would melt inside her heavy dress and two petticoats.

When they arrived, Gordon noticed Sylvia was wobbling as she walked up to the church door. 'Are you okay?' he asked her.

'I feel a bit funny,' Sylvia replied.

Gordon had been forewarned by his sister, and quickly drew out a little bottle from his pocket. 'Here, drink this,' he said. It was more iced tea and spirits of ammonia, and Sylvia gratefully drank a large gulp before she took his arm and they went in.

Thankfully the church was a large, old stone building and it was cooler inside. But when Sylvia saw the sea of unfamiliar faces she felt even more wobbly. All the neighbours had turned up and had kindly filled the bride's side of the church, since Sylvia had nobody there. She clung to Gordon's arm as tightly as she could, scared of looking to the right or left for fear of losing her balance, and somehow made it to the altar without passing out. There was Bob, looking extremely handsome in a rented black tuxedo and shiny shoes. As soon as he saw her, his own nerves were amplified and his leg started shaking uncontrollably.

The Reverend Jackson only added further difficulty by mentioning more than once how sad the bride's family must be not to be part of her special day, and each time he did so Sylvia struggled desperately not to burst into tears. By the end of the service, with Sylvia's faintness and Bob's trembling leg, it was a miracle that neither of them had fallen over.

Around fifty people squeezed into the O'Connors' for the reception. Bob's mother had made an enormous bowl of punch and everyone took a glass and toasted the bride and groom, before helping themselves to food from the buffet in the kitchen. When it was time for the cake to be cut, Bob and Sylvia held the knife together and Sylvia pushed as hard as she could, anticipating hard fruitcake and royal icing. But she hadn't realised that in America, wedding cakes were sponge, with soft icing, and to her horror the knife went through all three tiers at once, wrecking her mother-in-law's creation. Sylvia had hoped to send home a slice to her mother, but looking at the squashy mess she realised she wouldn't be able to.

'Oops!' Sylvia said, and Bob chuckled.

As they ate their cake, all the women inundated Sylvia with questions about England, asking her to repeat everything just so they could hear her 'cute' accent. She did her best to be friendly, even though what she really wanted was to be alone with Bob.

But where was Bob? As she scanned the room, she realised all the men at the party had vanished.

'Where did the blokes go?' she asked Bob's Aunt Catherine, who gestured towards the basement.

'What are they doing down there?' Sylvia asked, confused.

'Oh, they've got one of their card games going,' she replied.

Sylvia had no choice but to deal with the hordes of well-wishers on her own.

She was relieved when, finally, Bob emerged from the basement and his best man Donald said it was time for them to be going. He was to drive the newlyweds to a little bungalow his family owned in the countryside just outside Baltimore.

Sylvia changed into her going-away outfit and they waved goodbye. Somehow, she had survived her American wedding.

It was dark by the time they arrived at the little bungalow, but the moon was out and Sylvia could see a beautiful garden with a wishing well. Once they were finally alone, they breathed a huge sigh of relief. 'At last!' said Bob, kissing her.

They sat out for a while on a bench by the wishing well, looking up at the stars. Opposite them was a field, and Sylvia could see little lights flashing on and off in the distance. 'What's wrong with those lights over there?' she asked her husband.

'Those aren't lights, babycakes,' he said, laughing. 'They're lightning bugs!'

'Lightning bugs?' Sylvia repeated.

'Yeah, don't you have them in England?'

'No,' Sylvia said. 'They're beautiful!'

Bob smiled as an idea came to him. 'Wait here,' he said.

He went into the little bungalow and returned with an empty jam jar, then ran off into the field opposite with it. Sylvia giggled. 'What are you doing?' she called.

'You'll see,' Bob shouted back.

When he returned, Sylvia saw that he had filled the jar with lightning bugs. In the bedroom he put it on top of the chest of drawers, where it glowed all night long.

19

Margaret

With two small children to care for now, life was more constrained than ever for Margaret. Despite Lawrence's promise to find them a proper home, they were still living in the summer house in the middle of nowhere outside Akron, Ohio.

Lawrence was still coming home late, having gone out drinking after work. He collapsed exhausted into bed each night, but slept badly, tossing and turning with nightmares, and in the morning had no appetite for breakfast.

'I promised I wouldn't drink around you and the baby, and I haven't,' he insisted, when she tried to talk to him about it.

'No, you promised you wouldn't drink at all!' she responded, but he didn't seem to listen.

One day, however, she was cleaning the kitchen when she discovered an empty whisky bottle in the bin. Now he couldn't deny any longer that he was breaking his promise.

When he came through the door that evening, she showed him the bottle. 'You *have* been drinking at home,' she told him. 'Lawrence, this has got to stop.'

But he was drunker than she had seen him since they arrived in Ohio, and at this criticism his face contorted into an ugly scowl and his dark eyes flashed with anger. Her heart sank when she saw that he had brought several bottles of Scotch with him. Clearly he no longer thought there was any point in hiding what he was doing, and he was going to keep drinking right in front of her. Margaret was furious.

'I don't want you doing that in the house, with the children here,' she told him.

'You don't like it – don't stick around!' he told her, pouring himself a glassful and knocking it back.

'You know perfectly well I haven't anywhere else to go,' she said, tears pricking her eyes. 'Lawrence, you promised me!'

'I don't owe you anything!' he said, slamming his fist down on the coffee table in front of him. 'I've been working hard all day to feed those babies of yours! A man deserves a bit of relaxation in the evening.'

'I've been with those babies on my own all day!' she retorted. 'When do I ever get to relax? I'm stuck here, hour after hour, with no one to speak to, and when my husband does get home, he's drunk!'

'I told you, if you don't like it, don't stick around, Goddammit!' he shouted. He hurled the glass across the room and it smashed against the wall.

Margaret fled to the bedroom, shaking with fear and anger.

In the early morning, she tiptoed into the kitchen to make some coffee. There, she found her husband passed out on his back in a pool of vomit, an empty bottle of Scotch still clutched in his hand.

'Lawrence!' she cried, rolling him over. She was horrified to think he could have choked to death on his own vomit, just feet away from where she was sleeping.

He winced as if her voice was painful to him. 'Quiet,' he murmured.

She got a wet cloth and cleaned his mouth, then helped him sit up. 'Oh, what have you done to yourself?' Margaret said, unable to stop the tears running down her face. The angry Lawrence was gone and in his place was a man who was as helpless as a baby.

Lawrence slept off the hangover until noon and then headed into the office, telling Margaret he'd smooth things over with his boss. She knew he had the skills to charm his way out of anything, but she couldn't help worrying that even he would get into trouble soon if he made a habit of going into work late and hung over.

The next night was no different, however, nor the night after that – except that Lawrence's tolerance to alcohol seemed to be getting higher and higher, and he was drinking more and more. Margaret was unable to go to sleep herself before he passed out, too scared that he might end up choking on his vomit in the night, so she waited until he fell silent and then snuck in and put a pillow under his head. She would then be up half the night with the newborn, and by morning she was utterly exhausted.

She had other worries too. As his drinking got worse, the housekeeping money Lawrence gave her was dwindling. There was not enough to get a check-up for her or baby Maeve, nor for clothes for the two children. The only time she could speak to him about it was in the morning, before he headed out for work. Often he would promise to bring her back some cash when he returned home, but by then he was usually too drunk to remember. Soon she was finding it hard even to buy enough food from the little farm shop to feed them all, and she had to eke out what she had each day.

She didn't know if Lawrence himself was eating at all, since he now seemed to exist solely on alcohol. He had taken to having a drink first thing in the morning, which he said was necessary to 'calm his nerves', and his hands shook until he had gulped down a glass of Scotch. His face was puffy and he was constantly sweating, and he complained of stomach cramps. He often went into work late, and some days didn't make it in at all.

'If you carry on like this you're going to kill yourself!' Margaret told him, horrified to see him in such a state. But he just didn't seem to care. Even when he wasn't drunk, the old Lawrence had disappeared completely, and an irritable, irrational person had taken his place.

He was coming back later and later, and after a while there were some nights that he didn't return at all. Margaret sat up waiting for him, hour after hour, terrified that he was lying in a gutter somewhere or had crashed his car.

One morning, after he had failed to show up all night, she heard him fumbling with his keys at the door. When she went to open it for him she saw a police car drive off down the dirt path. 'What's happened?' she asked Lawrence anxiously.

'My friends offered to put me up for the night,' he said wryly. Lawrence had been picked up drunk and disorderly and spent the night in a police cell.

Margaret was too ashamed to tell anyone what her life had become, and in her letters to her father she never mentioned her troubles, nor how desperate for money she was. She had even begun to resort to stealing herself – picking her husband's pockets as he lay unconscious – since it was the only way she could get money to feed her children. Still, there hadn't been enough to pay the landlord when he'd turned up at the door, wanting to know why they were behind with the rent. He had arrived clearly angry, but at the sight of the thin, exhausted-looking young English woman with two hungry, crying children, he felt so sorry for them he had gone away again.

Inevitably, Lawrence was sacked from his job at Goodyear. Margaret felt desperate – how would they carry on now, without even the little he had been bringing home?

That weekend, Lawrence's younger sister Judy was getting married, and he had agreed to give her away. The whole family was convening in Atlanta for the wedding, and with no reason to stay in Akron any more, Margaret and her husband packed their bags, took the girls and headed back to Georgia. 'I'll get a job there,' Lawrence told her, confidently.

'All right,' Margaret replied wearily. As they left Ohio, she remembered how hopeful she had felt when they had first arrived, and she couldn't believe what a disaster the whole scheme had been. She didn't care what came next – nothing could be as wretched as living in the middle of nowhere, waiting for Lawrence to come home and drink himself half to death.

The family had booked a suite of rooms in a hotel downtown, and Margaret felt a sense of overwhelming relief at being in a city again, not to mention seeing Lawrence's family. Ellen greeted her like a sister, and Margaret could tell she was shocked to see how thin and tired she looked. 'He's worse again, isn't he?' she asked, and Margaret nodded, too upset to speak. She had coped on her own for so many months, but now that she finally had someone sympathetic to speak to, she couldn't help bursting into tears.

The marriage ceremony took place at the Winship Chapel of the First Presbyterian Church, a beautiful old building with enormous stained-glass windows. Judy, a pretty, red-haired girl, looked stunning in an eggshell-satin wedding dress that had belonged to her great-grandmother, Eliza McCaskill. Around his younger sister, Lawrence seemed like his old self, making her giggle as he walked her down the aisle by whispering, 'Are you sure you want to do this? You just say and we'll turn around and get out of here!'

For her part, Judy clearly adored her older brother. At the wedding reception, she told Margaret how, before the war, she and Lawrence had lived together in Washington, where he was working for the Ministry of Agriculture and she was a secretary for a Georgia senator. 'I remember when I came back crying because I had letters to send out to a whole heap of constituents, and I hadn't got half of them done,' she told her. 'Lawrence said, "Well, that's no problem – we'll write 'em tonight!" and he stayed up all night long helping me finish the job. That's how kind my brother is.'

Her story reminded Margaret of the charming man she had first met in London, and she felt a stab of sadness.

When they got back to the hotel that night after the reception Lawrence was drunk as usual, and quickly fell into a stupor. By the time Margaret woke the next morning he was already on the bottle again.

There was a knock on the door and Margaret opened it to find Ellen and Jack, who had come to say goodbye before they went back to Arlington.

'Wait a minute,' Lawrence called out. 'Can you do something for me? Take the kids until we get settled here. Just until I find a place and get a job.'

Margaret could see from the look on Jack's face that the last thing he wanted was to bail out his brother-in-law again. 'No, Lawrence,' he said, 'we can't do that. We've got four children at home ourselves.'

'Ellen, come on!' Lawrence begged his sister. 'Just till we get settled!'

But Ellen shook her head. This time, she was sticking by her husband.

Lawrence was already halfway drunk, and he was furious at not getting his way. Before any of them could stop him, he grabbed baby Maeve out of her carrycot, ran over to the window, opened it, and dangled the child outside by the back of her collar.

Margaret screamed.

'Lawrence, for God's sake, what are you doing?' cried Ellen.

'No one move, or I'll drop her!' Lawrence shouted. 'Now, promise me you'll take the kids. Promise me! Or I swear I'll let go!'

'I'll take them, I'll take them!' his sister exclaimed.

At that, Lawrence brought the baby back inside and handed her to Ellen.

Shocked by his behaviour, the Cowarts hurried away, taking Maeve and Rosamund with them. Ellen threw Margaret a sympathetic look, and they were gone.

Margaret hurled herself down onto the bed and burst into tears. For the first time since she had married Lawrence, she felt true hatred for him.

Despite his drinking, Lawrence managed to talk his way into a job on an Atlanta newspaper. He had written a few articles for them when he was in the Canadian Army, about being a Georgia boy abroad, and now they agreed to make him a staff writer.

He and Margaret moved to an apartment in Hapeville, south of Atlanta, and she noticed that Lawrence seemed much happier as a journalist than he had been working for Goodyear. She could see that it suited him better than a corporate job – he had more freedom to come and go as he pleased, and he certainly fitted into the heavy-drinking culture.

But she was desperate to get the children back again, and made frequent attempts to persuade him.

'Margaret, can't you see I'm only just getting back on my feet?' he retorted. 'Do you want everything to go downhill like it did before?'

All Margaret could do was keep trying. In the meantime, she got herself a job as a typist, and tried to save as much of her wages as she could. She was determined that when Rosamund and Maeve did come to live with them, they wouldn't go hungry again.

But with no children around, and his wife working, Lawrence simply relinquished all responsibility for the bills. Margaret found herself having to pay for almost everything, which on her small salary was a struggle. She had no choice but to do it or risk them being evicted, but once again she found it was hard to find enough money to buy food.

In Arlington, the Cowarts were struggling to cope with six children to look after. Ellen's patience with her brother was running out, and one day she decided they would have to send the girls back.

Jack Cowart drove Rosamund and Maeve to Atlanta in the pick-up truck. 'Enough is enough,' he told Lawrence, handing the kids over. 'You're taking your children back.'

Margaret was over the moon to have her daughters with her again, but it put Lawrence in a black mood. That night, he railed drunkenly at Margaret, telling her, 'You've ruined my life with your babies!'

Now that she had her children, Margaret could no longer work, and she lived in constant fear that they would be evicted. She begged Lawrence for money whenever she saw him, and once again fell to picking his pockets when he passed out drunk. She was more worried about money than ever, since she had just found out that she was pregnant again.

Meanwhile, she was increasingly concerned about Rosamund, who seemed to be somewhat behind in her development. She hadn't started walking until she was one and a half, and at two and a half she could still only say single words.

Margaret thought back to Rosamund's difficult birth, and how she had started trying to breathe too early. The doctors in England had been unable to say if those first moments being deprived of oxygen would affect her, but now it seemed clear that they had. Margaret was desperate to take her daughter to a doctor, but she knew that would cost money.

She waited for Lawrence to come home that evening, planning what she would say to convince him to pay for the appointment. But when he did, he was drunk as usual.

'She doesn't need to see any doctor,' he slurred. 'We both know why she's like she is, and it's all your fault!'

'What do you mean, it's my fault?' Margaret said. 'She was deprived of oxygen when she was born.'

'You tried to abort her with a coat hanger!' he shouted.

Margaret felt fury rising in her. She had suffered under this man for so long, and to hear him now place their daughter's problems at her door was just too much. 'How dare you!' she screamed. 'How dare you blame me, you worthless drunk. What kind of father are you? You can't even feed your family!'

Lawrence's eyes flashed with anger, and suddenly Margaret felt his fists beating her around the head, pummelling her over and over again until she couldn't see or hear anything any more. She collapsed into a heap on the ground and he stormed out of the house, slamming the door, the sound of his crying children following him down the street.

When Margaret looked in the mirror the next morning, the sight of her bruised face filled her with horror. She had put up with Lawrence's drunkenness and neglect, but he had never been violent before. She was terrified that if he attacked her again he might harm not only her, but the unborn baby.

The next day, a letter arrived addressed to Margaret in Ellen's handwriting. She tore it open and discovered inside a stack of dollars, along with a letter from her sister-in-law, explaining that the money had come for Lawrence from the Canadian Army. 'I'm sending it to you, because I thought you might need it,' Ellen had written.

Margaret knew exactly what to do. She took the money and booked herself and her daughters onto the next boat out of New York.

20

Gwendolyn

Driving through San Jose, along streets lined with palm trees under an azure-blue sky, Lyn felt like she was entering a picture postcard. It couldn't have been more different from the dock town she had grown up in.

Ben chose a route that took them down The Alameda, one of the town's oldest and most exclusive streets.

'Is your parents' house one of these?' asked Lyn excitedly, staring up at the enormous mansions.

'I'm afraid not,' laughed Ben.

Soon they arrived in Little Italy, where Lyn saw delis with awnings in the colours of the Italian flag, old men playing *bocce* and groups of women chattering loudly in Italian.

'This is us,' said Ben, pulling up at a large house. It looked odd to Lyn, and she couldn't work out why. Then she realised – it was made entirely of wood. Where are the bricks? she wondered.

Lyn took out her compact mirror and checked her face. She was never normally one to get spots, but she was run down after the long journey and had an enormous pimple on her cheek. She was painfully embarrassed at the thought of Ben's family seeing it. Hopefully they would realise how tired she was and suggest she go straight to bed.

'My mom's organised a big dinner to welcome you to the family,' Ben told her.

'Oh no – but I just want to lie down!' said Lyn.

'I'm sorry. She kinda insisted.'

Lyn sighed and powdered her nose, as Ben took her things out of the boot. Then she followed him up the steps to the porch, where the door flew open to reveal a crowd of people, all bustling to be the first to meet her. Ben's mother got there first, pulling Lyn to her bosom. A light-skinned Italian, what she lacked in natural beauty Mrs Patrino made up for in her perfectly coiffed hair and smart clothes. Mr Patrino, a handsome man much darker than his wife, took his new daughter-in-law's hand and greeted her in heavily accented English. His eldest son, Leo, had evidently inherited his good looks, while Leo's young wife Thelma seemed like a movie star, with her perfect hour-glass figure.

When Leo went to kiss Lyn on the cheek, she remembered her pimple and instinctively turned away. 'Cold fish,' she heard him mutter to his younger brother Armand.

Before she could respond, Lyn found herself faced with a stream of introductions. It seemed the entire extended family had come round in her honour and she estimated there must be more than twenty people there.

Lyn could see through to an immaculate dining room, which contained the longest table she had ever seen, decorated with beautiful glass candlesticks and expertly laid.

'Why don't you go take a shower before we eat?' Mrs Patrino said. Something in her tone made it sound less like a suggestion and more like an order.

'I don't need to take a shower,' Lyn replied. She had never liked being told what to do.

'Go take a shower,' Mrs Patrino repeated.

Several of the aunties and uncles were listening to the conversation. Lyn felt her cheeks burning. Was Ben's mother suggesting, in front of them all, that she wasn't clean?

'I'm sorry, but I'll take a shower when I want to,' she said. She was exhausted and overwhelmed and sorely wished she could go to bed.

Ben took her by the arm. 'Why don't we sit down?' he suggested, taking her over to the dining table. The other guests followed suit.

'Let's see the rings!' cried her new sister-in-law Thelma, and all the aunties excitedly craned their necks as Lyn held up her hand, now decorated with the diamond engagement ring and gold band Ben had given her at the station, in place of the old pot-metal ring that had been there before.

'You must be so relieved to finally have them,' said Ben's Auntie Catherine.

'Oh, I didn't mind the other one,' Lyn replied. She didn't want to seem like she was criticising Ben's mother for the fact that her parcel hadn't got through.

But she realised from the look on Mrs Patrino's face that her comment had not been taken as intended. Ben's mother didn't say anything, and bustled out to the kitchen.

She returned soon afterwards with the first course: plates of an enormous, spiky, bulb-like vegetable. 'What is it?' Lyn whispered to Ben.

'Artichoke,' he told her.

Lyn watched as the others peeled off a layer at a time and dipped the pieces in oil before sucking on them. Cautiously, she tried peeling off a layer of her artichoke. She sucked on the end of the leaf, but it was hard, and nothing came away.

'You've got it the wrong way round,' said Ben, laughing. He took the piece from her and turned it around.

'Oh, whoops,' said Lyn, trying to cover the mistake, but prompting laughter from around the table.

The next course was equally alien, but Ben informed her it was called ravioli. The little parcels of pasta were covered in a tomato sauce, heavily flavoured with garlic, and to Lyn the taste was overwhelming.

To her surprise, that wasn't even the main course, and now a further dish was presented, this time of meat. Again, tomatoes and garlic featured heavily.

The conversation was mainly about food, as the women discussed the pros and cons of different recipes and, to Lyn's surprise, the men joined in passionately too.

Lyn attempted to contribute. 'We don't eat garlic in England.'

'Oh, don't we?' said Mrs Patrino. Once again, Lyn's comment had not been well received.

Lyn felt more desperate than ever to lie down somewhere comfortable and private, but she knew she had to struggle on until the interminable meal was over.

At last, Mrs Patrino brought out a large apple tart, and Lyn realised the banquet was drawing to a close. She silently thanked God for the sight of something that did not, as far as she could see, contain garlic, oil or tomato. The tart was delicious, and was followed by tiny cups of bitter coffee. Lyn found it undrinkable, but didn't dare ask for tea.

Afterwards, she reached for her cigarettes. A good smoke always followed a meal in her parents' household. But before she had opened the packet, Ben's brother Leo said, 'Put that away.'

Lyn assumed he was going to offer her one of his. 'Can I have a fag off you then?' she asked.

Leo simply stared at her, and Ben nudged her to be quiet. She was too exhausted to work out what she had said wrong this time.

After much hugging and kissing, the Patrinos said goodbye to their guests, and only Ben's parents and his younger brother Armand remained. 'We've put you in our room, so you can get a good sleep,' Mrs Patrino told Lyn. It was the first night Lyn and Ben would be spending together since their honeymoon five months before, and she couldn't wait to be in his arms again. But to her horror, with no spare beds in the house, Mr Patrino had taken the couch in the living room and Mrs Patrino had set up camp in the corridor, right outside their door.

There was little chance of a romantic night with her mother-in-law in such close proximity, and the thought of her out there sent Lyn into hysterics. 'Cut it out!' Ben pleaded, but it was no use – the giggles were unstoppable.

A few hours later, Lyn had finally drifted into a much-needed sleep when she was woken by a shuffling sound. She looked round, bleary-eyed, and saw the outline of a man in just a nightshirt stumbling towards her with arms outstretched. His eyes were open but had a strange, glazed look in them.

Lyn let out a piercing scream that made Ben sit bolt upright. The man, who Lyn now realised was Ben's brother Armand, blinked in confusion.

'What's he doing here?' Lyn cried.

Mrs Patrino came flying into the bedroom, slamming on the light. 'Armand! Back to bed!' she barked, and Ben's brother, now awake and intensely embarrassed to find himself in the wrong bedroom in just his night shirt, scuttled out.

Lyn collapsed into a shaking heap. After her long journey, the endless dinner full of humiliations and now this ordeal, her nerves were frayed. 'Is this how it's going to be living here?' she asked Ben. 'Your mother sleeps outside the door and your brother wanders in with no trousers on?'

Ben tried to soothe her, holding her to him. 'Don't worry,' he said. 'We'll get our own place as soon as I can find a job.'

It was well into the early hours before Lyn fell asleep for a second time.

In the morning, Armand's sleepwalking was not mentioned, but breakfast brought a fresh embarrassment. 'Do you want one egg or two?' Mrs Patrino asked Lyn.

'I couldn't possibly eat two of your eggs,' she replied. She was used to the wartime ration of one a week.

Mrs Patrino stared at her as if she was mad. 'What are you doing with this one?' she asked Ben, gesturing at Lyn, and went off to make the breakfast, shaking her head.

Mrs Patrino gave Lyn one day off to recover from her journey, but after that she began instructing her about her responsibilities as Ben's wife. First, there was the laundry – which, in an Italian household, was solely the responsibility of the women.

Mrs Patrino proudly showed Lyn her brand-new washing machine, knowing she would never have seen one before. 'Aren't you glad you're in America now?' she asked.

Lyn bristled at the comment. It reminded her of people back home who thought GI brides only got married as a ticket to a better life. 'I'm here for Ben,' she retorted.

Mrs Patrino showed her where to put the soap and how to start the machine, and then took her over to the electric mangle. Apparently every sock and pair of underpants of Ben's was to be fed through this contraption so that they came out beautifully pressed.

Next Lyn was taken into the kitchen. Ben's mother was planning a *zuppa di lenticchie* for lunch, and asked her to help by washing the lentils. As Mrs Patrino popped out for a minute, Lyn turned on the tap, picked up a sieve and poured half the lentils into it. They went straight through the holes and down the plughole. She quickly turned off the tap and put the remaining lentils back on the counter.

'Where's the other half of the lentils?' Mrs Patrino asked as she came back in.

'Um, they went down the drain,' Lyn replied.

Mrs Patrino shook her head. It was the last time Lyn was called on to help with the cooking.

That didn't mean she was off the hook, however – she was put on washing-up duty instead. With the extended family visiting frequently, it was quite a job, and Mrs Patrino had a number of strict rules. The glasses were washed first, then the cutlery, then the plates. Then the pots needed to be scrubbed with steel wool, the stove washed down, the sink cleaned and the taps polished to perfection – a total of an hour's work after each meal.

Why do they get to sit there doing nothing? Lyn wondered, as her husband and his father and brother relaxed after each meal. But to Mrs Patrino, a spotless home was a woman's greatest achievement. Everyone said you could eat off the floor at her house, and they were probably right. She could sometimes be found cleaning those floors in the middle of the night to make sure they shone.

Lyn soon failed to live up to Mrs Patrino's exacting standards. Her first load of laundry consisted mainly of Ben's underwear, and she didn't see the point of putting it through the electric mangle. She hung up the clothes and, once they were dry, folded them and brought them to the bedroom. She was just putting them away when Mrs Patrino entered the room.

'What are these?' she asked, lifting up a pair of Ben's smalls.

'Um, a pair of underpants?'

'Iron them, please,' demanded Mrs Patrino. 'Ben isn't used to *this*.' She threw the garment on the bed.

Later, as Lyn passed the kitchen, she overheard voices talking at the table and the words 'My *God*, did you see that laundry?' followed by much laughter. Were Ben's family mocking her behind her back?

Lyn was pleased, however, to find an ally in her sister-in-law Thelma, who was no more a favourite of Mrs Patrino's than she was. In fact, Thelma was something of an outcast in the family, having married Leo only after she got pregnant. Although Leo and Thelma didn't live with his parents, it seemed that they were still required to eat there almost every night of the week, and whenever they did, Thelma was roped into dish-washing duty too. Soon the girls were trading complaints about their mother-in-law.

'Ugh, she's so *boss*y!' moaned Thelma.

'Iron Ben's socks! Press his pants!' mimicked Lyn. 'My son isn't used to *this*.' They both collapsed into giggles, which only intensified when Mrs Patrino marched into the kitchen, looking displeased.

Lyn had begun to notice another problem with her mother-in-law. When Lyn and Ben were around each other they often hugged, held hands or kissed. 'You just can't keep your hands off him, can you?' snapped Mrs Patrino, when she saw the young couple cuddling.

'I think she's jealous over her sons,' Lyn told Thelma.

'It's true,' she agreed. 'Her life revolves around her beloved boys. But you know the difference between her and us?'

'What?' asked Lyn.

'She gets on with apple pie, we get on with a roll in the hay!'

They both burst out laughing again.

After four months back in America, Ben still hadn't managed to find a job. The Army was paying him $20 a month as part of the '52/20 club', which helped servicemen for the first year of civilian life. He and Lyn used the money to go to the movies or eat in burger bars every now and then. But there were no regular dances like in the war.

'Is this all there is?' complained Lyn one day. 'We eat and we wash up and that's it?'

Her natural tendency was to relieve the tedium with humour, but whenever she joked around her lightheartedness was met with contempt from Mrs Patrino. 'She gives me the look,' Lyn told Ben, rolling her eyes heavenwards in a parody of her mother-in-law.

When Mrs Patrino was out of the house one day, Lyn decided she would attempt to cook the dinner as a gesture of goodwill. She found a recipe book and followed it diligently, but the chicken was so rare it was virtually uncooked, and the family almost broke their teeth on her corn on the cob. Mrs Patrino's look of thunder made it clear she thought Lyn had spoiled the meal on purpose.

Lyn ended the day exhausted and in tears. Whatever she did, Ben's mother seemed to despise her, and he did nothing to intervene.

'You have ostrich syndrome,' she told him. 'You just stick your head in the sand!'

'I don't like fighting,' he replied. Growing up, it had always been his role to play peacemaker between his parents and two brothers. But he could see how much the situation was upsetting his wife. He was reluctant to confront his mother directly, but he decided on a subtler way to show his support for Lyn.

On the second Sunday in May, Ben went to the local florist and bought Lyn the biggest bunch of flowers he could afford. When he returned, she was sitting out in the garden, smoking a cigarette and feeling glum. As she saw the flowers, her expression changed. 'Ben!' she exclaimed. 'They're beautiful.'

'I wanted to show you how much I love you,' he told her.

Lyn took the flowers and breathed in their sweet scent. 'I'd better put them in some water,' she said. He followed her into the kitchen, where Mrs Patrino was sitting at the table.

'Look what Ben bought me!' Lyn said.

Mrs Patrino's face darkened. 'You love this, don't you?'

'Yes, I do,' said Lyn, confused. Mrs Patrino stormed out of the room.

It was only later that Lyn discovered the second Sunday in May was when Americans celebrated Mother's Day, and Ben hadn't given Mrs Patrino anything.

'Why did you do it?' Lyn asked Ben. 'It's like you were taunting her.'

'I just wanted to make it clear you came first,' he said hopelessly.

Before long Ben was forced to express his feelings more directly. In her first weeks at the Patrinos', Lyn had taken out her frustrations in a letter to a friend back home. Exasperated with Mrs Patrino's endless cooking and cleaning, she had written a withering description of her slimy pasta and tomato and garlic sauce.

Lyn had never sent the letter and had forgotten all about it, but one day, to her horror, Mrs Patrino found it. 'I've never hit a woman in my life, but I feel like slapping you!' she exploded.

'Why do you have such a problem with me?' Lyn demanded.

'I think you're a lousy wife!' Mrs Patrino cried. 'My son should never have married you. He should have married a nice Italian girl!'

Lyn ran upstairs to the bedroom and began to sob. When Ben found her and heard what Mrs Patrino had said, he knew his days of appeasement were over. He went downstairs and confronted his mother. 'Lyn's what I want,' she heard him tell her angrily. 'She's the wife I've chosen.'

Despite her tears, Lyn felt victorious. At last Ben had shown he was on her side.

But Mrs Patrino wasn't willing to concede defeat just yet. Still confident in the hold she had over her son, she decided to put his loyalty to the test once and for all. A few days later she accosted Lyn and Ben in the kitchen. 'It's her or me,' she told her son. 'Make your choice.'

Lyn was stunned. She couldn't believe the woman was really asking him to choose between his mother and his wife.

Ben was calm, but firm. 'We're leaving,' he said, taking Lyn's hand. They went to the bedroom, threw their clothes into a suitcase and walked out, avoiding his mother's furious glare. They might have no job and no home to go to, but it was better than staying under Mrs Patrino's roof a moment longer.

21

Sylvia

When Sylvia and Bob arrived back in Baltimore from their honeymoon, she found a pile of post already waiting for her. There were telegrams of congratulations from her mum and dad, from her Aunt Lillian and even from her granddad, who had never sent a telegram before in his life. Her friend Peggy from the Piccadilly Hotel had wired her best wishes too. Sylvia realised that, lonely as she had felt on her wedding day, there had been plenty of people back home thinking of her.

To her surprise, among the mail was an envelope with a California postmark that had been addressed to her in Woolwich but had been redirected. Inside was a letter from her first ever GI boyfriend, Andy, in which he asked her to marry him. Sylvia couldn't believe that yet another of the men she had briefly dated during the war had proposed, but, like the others, Andy was to be disappointed. Sylvia wrote back saying that she was flattered, but she was already married.

She could not have been happier with her new husband Bob. He was loving, romantic and considerate, always ready with a compliment or a witty remark. But as time went on, she found living under his parents' roof more and more of a strain. Baltimore in summer was unbearably hot and humid, and to make matters worse Mr O'Connor had some strange views on ventilation. He was so paranoid about burglary that all the windows downstairs were permanently nailed shut, and since the bedroom that Bob and Sylvia slept in was in the middle of the house, it had no windows, only a small access door onto the roof that Bob's father forbade them from opening. His solution to the unbearable humidity was to decree that all bedroom doors be left open throughout the night to allow a through-draught.

But for a newly married couple, this arrangement was far from convenient. Whenever Sylvia and Bob shut their door at night in order to have a bit of nooky, Mr O'Connor would run down the corridor, banging on the door and demanding that they open it again.

'What does he think we're doing in here, playing tiddly-winks?' Sylvia whispered to Bob, as his father hammered on the door.

But Bob felt they had to do as his father wished, and reluctantly he opened the door and they went to sleep instead.

Living with the O'Connors, Sylvia soon discovered that the card game that had taken place during her wedding reception was a regular event. Every Saturday, the huge clan would assemble at one of their houses for an early dinner, before spending the rest of the evening playing poker.

Sylvia and Bob had been back in Baltimore less than a week when she witnessed her first card game. Almost all of Bob's mother's siblings took part. His Uncle Ira was there with his wife Marie, as were Uncle Curtis and his wife Catherine. Mrs O'Connor's third brother, Kenneth, arrived on his own – Bob explained that Uncle Kenneth's wife Katherine wasn't a big fan of poker. His Aunt Erma, meanwhile, had also taken a rain check. 'She likes pinochle better,' Bob explained.

They weren't the only women in the family to give the game a miss. Although Catherine had accompanied Curtis to the dinner, Sylvia soon learned she had no intention of joining in. 'I'll just sit upstairs and do some crocheting,' she said.

Sylvia followed the rest of the family down to the basement. It was the coolest part of the house and its dark environs lent the game a certain atmosphere.

Everyone took their seats around a large table. 'Why don't you sit with me and watch to begin with?' Bob suggested, cracking open a beer. His mother brought Sylvia a glass of iced tea, before taking her seat at one end of the table.

'We play dealer's choice,' Bob explained to Sylvia, 'which means whoever deals sets the rules for the hand.'

His father was already shuffling a deck of cards. 'All right, we'll start with five-card draw,' he said, tossing cards face down in the direction of the players as they each threw a nickel into the pot. They picked up their little piles, fanning them out and inspecting them carefully. Bob explained the basic possible hands to Sylvia, from a simple pair through to a royal flush.

One by one the players threw money into the centre of the table as play went round the group. Some of them swapped cards in their hand for more from the deck.

'I fold,' announced Dorothy after a while, tossing her cards face up onto the table.

Soon she was followed by Kenneth, then Ira and Marie, leaving only Bob, his Uncle Curtis and his parents in the game.

Sylvia looked down at Bob's cards – two aces and three queens. 'We call this a full house,' he whispered to her.

Sylvia nodded, doing her best not to smile. From what little of poker she had seen at the movies, she knew it was important not to give away the strength of your hand.

Play continued, and the pile of coins in the centre of the table continued to mount up. Sylvia watched the other players as they took their turns. Bob's father had a look of profound concentration on his face, as if he might be calculating odds in his head. His wife's steely expression never faltered – she rarely smiled in everyday life, and now Sylvia realised it meant she had the perfect poker face.

Bob's eyes were lit up. He seemed completely gripped by the game.

'I'll raise you a dollar,' Mrs O'Connor said.

'I fold,' Mr O'Connor replied resignedly.

'Too high for me,' Curtis said, tossing down his cards.

'You got me, Mom,' Bob replied, shaking his head.

Bob's mother leaned forward and scooped up the pile of winnings from the centre of the table. 'Wait, don't we have to see what her cards are?' Sylvia asked Bob.

'No, she bid high, and we weren't willing to match it,' he replied.

But curiosity got the better of Bob's sister Dorothy. She flipped Mrs O'Connor's cards up on the table, and a groan went round the group.

Sylvia stared at the cards. They were almost worthless – two threes, a seven, a ten and a jack.

'I don't believe it,' Sylvia cried. 'She took all that money, and with those cards she ought to have lost!'

Bob sighed. 'That's Mom,' he replied. 'She's a pretty good bluffer.'

After a few more hands it was clear that Mr and Mrs O'Connor were the strongest players, he thanks to his good memory and scrutiny of his opponents, and she thanks to her deadpan look. Bob won a few hands, and then lost a few, but his enthusiasm for the game never seemed to dampen.

Only Uncle Ira ever seemed to get really worked up. 'What are you doing, you dummkopf?' he would chastise his wife Marie, while chewing on a cigar he kept permanently unlit in the corner of his mouth. Sylvia was privately rather pleased when Marie confounded his expectations by winning several hands.

'Well, it's time for me to go,' Uncle Kenneth announced after about an hour. 'Katherine will be waiting for me at home.'

Sylvia noticed that the other Catherine had come down from the living room and was hovering in the doorway too. 'Yeah, me too,' Curtis said, catching her eye and obediently heading over to her.

But despite the loss of two players, the game continued apace. 'Do you want to play?' Bob's father asked Sylvia after a while.

'Oh, all right,' she replied. 'I'll give it a go.'

The next poker variant was called five-card draw, jacks to open. 'It's like before, but you need two jacks to open the pot,' Bob explained to her.

Sylvia nodded. It seemed pretty straightforward.

Bob dealt the cards, and she was first up. 'I'm afraid I have to pass,' she said. Play moved round the table, and no one else was able to bid either.

'That's strange,' Bob commented. 'All right, we'll deal again.'

Everyone returned their cards to him and he dealt them new hands. Once again Sylvia told them she would have to pass.

'Are you sure you can't open?' Bob asked her.

'Yeah,' Sylvia replied ruefully, showing him her hand.

'Sylvia, you've got two queens here!' Bob laughed.

'I know,' she replied, confused. 'But you told me I had to have two jacks.'

'I meant two jacks or higher!' he said. The whole family guffawed with laughter.

'She sat there all that time for nothing!' Bob's father said, clearly enjoying the joke.

After Bob had explained the rules again, they began the round for a third time, and this time Sylvia played along correctly. But as much as she tried to enjoy herself, she just couldn't. She didn't like the atmosphere of competitiveness the game created, and the edge of nastiness it brought out in some members of the family. No wonder the other wives had wanted to go home.

As the pile of money in the centre of the table mounted up, she also found herself worrying about the amount she and Bob were already losing, especially since she knew every cent counted if they were ever to move out of his parents' house.

'I think I'll just watch for the rest of the evening,' she told Bob when the hand was over and Mrs O'Connor was once again eagerly sweeping up a pile of winnings.

The play continued for many hours and it was almost midnight before Sylvia and Bob finally climbed the stairs to bed. He seemed to be the last to want the game to end, and had gone away in a great mood, having ended up a dollar and a half richer than he had gone in. But Sylvia had hated the experience. She didn't like the thought of hard-earned money being thrown away like that.

Over the next few months, Sylvia got used to the weekly poker games, which rotated around the various houses in the family. Sometimes she would come along and read a book in the corner, other times she would wait at home for Bob to come back, which was often many hours later than he had promised. If he won, he would take her out for dinner or into town the next day. If he lost, he would say determinedly, 'I'll get them next time.'

The regular poker group was from Bob's mother's side of the family, but his father's sister Myrtle and her husband John were also players. One day, Bob told Sylvia that he had been invited to a special game at their house, and half-heartedly she agreed to come along. He was so excited at the thought of the big game that it seemed unkind not to.

When they got there, the game was already underway and Sylvia was concerned to see a huge pile of cash on the table – not just loose change but a great stack of dollar bills. The guests were mostly neighbours of John and Myrtle's who ran their own businesses in the neighbourhood, and they had more money to gamble than the O'Connors. She estimated there was more than a hundred dollars in the pot.

After a few minutes of intense play, Myrtle scooped the jackpot and Bob was dealt in for the next hand. He played with gusto, but his luck seemed to have deserted him, and as the evening wore on he never won a dime, despite throwing more and more money onto the table. By the time he and Sylvia left he was down by $15. 'I can't believe it,' he said. 'I really thought tonight was my night.'

'Bob,' she replied quietly, 'I don't think I'll be coming with you next time you go to play cards.'

But she could tell he wasn't listening. He was still going over and over the game in his head.

As the weeks wore on, Sylvia found Bob's losses at the poker table increasingly hard to bear, knowing that every dollar he gambled put them further away from ever moving out of his parents' house. He stayed out later and later at the games, sometimes not returning home until four in the morning. There were jubilant celebrations when he brought home the jackpot, but plenty of disappointments too.

'How much did you lose this time?' Sylvia asked him once, when he returned home well after midnight.

'Did I say I lost?' Bob replied defensively.

'You didn't have to. I can see it in your eyes.'

Bob hesitated. 'Not that much,' he said. 'Only about six dollars.'

'Well, that's more time we have to live with your mum and dad then,' Sylvia replied. Bob sloped off to bed without responding.

Sylvia had wanted to go out to work to help her and Bob save up, but soon she had fallen pregnant. His mother, who had just taken a job as a chocolate-dipper, suggested she could take over the housework instead, in return for two dollars a week. It might be a pittance, but it was better than nothing, thought Sylvia.

But meanwhile, Bob was finding new ways to lose money. Since his mum's aunt Marion was the unofficial neighbourhood bookie, his parents had a flutter on the horses every week. His mother began offering to place bets for him as well, which meant he was wasting another six or eight dollars a week.

Sylvia was horrified. 'Please don't ask Bob if he wants to bet,' she begged Mrs O'Connor one day, when the men were out of the house. 'We're trying to save for our own place.'

Her mother-in-law shot her a look of annoyance. 'All right then,' she said.

But the next week Mrs O'Connor took Bob's bets just the same as before, and he continued to lose on the horses.

Meanwhile, Sylvia had started to notice another problem. Ever since she had found out that she was pregnant, Bob's father had been treating her differently. He was surly and sullen around her, making snide and sarcastic remarks at the dinner table, and neither Bob nor his mother dared to challenge him. When Sylvia asked him to pass the salt or pepper, he would stare right through her as if she wasn't there.

One time, Sylvia was singing along to a Vera Lynn song on the wireless when Mr O'Connor came into the room. 'Turn that crap off,' he shouted, twisting the knob to retune the radio to another station. 'We had enough English music during the war.'

Sylvia turned to Bob, expecting him to say something, but he merely gave her a sympathetic look.

She thought back to the day she had arrived in Baltimore, when Mr O'Connor had been so friendly towards her. What had she done to alter his opinion of her? The only change she could think of was her pregnancy. Did he resent someone else being the centre of attention?

One day, they were all leaving the house, when Mr O'Connor, walking in front of Sylvia, purposefully let the door slam right in her face. She turned around to her husband in shock, thinking he would react angrily, but she was disappointed once again. 'I guess we'd better slow down a bit,' he joked awkwardly.

'I wish you'd stand up for me a bit, Bob,' she pleaded tearfully when they were next on their own.

'What can I say?' Bob shrugged. 'We're staying in his house.'

Sylvia could see the true reason for his reluctance to confront his father. Mr O'Connor was a bully, and Bob was scared of him.

Throughout Sylvia's pregnancy, Mrs O'Connor offered her no words of advice. Perhaps she felt it wasn't her place, as Sylvia wasn't her own daughter, but with Mrs Bradley 3,000 miles away in England she could have done with a bit of motherly support. As she had moved into her final month of pregnancy, she had grown huge, and her back ached permanently.

One morning, Sylvia came downstairs at 6 a.m. to find her mother-in-law getting ready to go to work. 'I feel terrible,' Sylvia told her. 'I've been up all night.'

Mrs O'Connor phoned the local doctor, who advised them to take a cab to the hospital.

'We'd better call Bob and get him to come back from work first,' Mrs O'Connor said, giving him a ring at the post office.

Sylvia waited patiently until her husband returned home and then the two of them set off for the hospital. It soon became clear that it was not going to be a simple delivery. The waters were stubbornly refusing to break.

Sylvia was taken onto the maternity ward, leaving Bob in the waiting room. There, she went through a difficult twelve-hour labour, twisting the bed sheets in her hands with every agonising wave of pain. The woman in the next bed was screaming blue murder and cursing the day she ever met her husband, but Sylvia, always shy, felt too embarrassed to shout out.

'You know you can scream if you want to,' one of the doctors told her, but as painful as the experience was, she just couldn't bring herself to make a fuss.

Throughout the ordeal, Sylvia was comforted by the thought that Bob was in the hospital with her, even if he wasn't allowed in the room. But when the baby was finally born and she asked to see her husband, she was surprised to be told that he would have to be summoned from home.

Half an hour later, Bob and his mother arrived, and he rushed over to see his new son, cradling him lovingly and placing a finger in his tiny little palm. 'He's beautiful, Sylvia,' he told her, leaning over and kissing her on the forehead.

But Bob's mother was not so overwhelmed by the spirit of the moment. 'Well, that was great timing,' she told Sylvia. 'You broke up a pretty good card game.'

22

Rae

After a few months, Rae was slowly adjusting to life in Hackett, Pennsylvania. At first she had struggled with how quiet it was out in the sticks, having grown up in noisy London. But after a while she began to appreciate the peacefulness – after six years of war it was something of a relief.

Although Hackett only had one small store, a mile and a half's walk up the road was Finleyville, which had a small cinema and a few more shops. Soon after Rae arrived, she and Raymond had visited a bar and restaurant there called Boyko's, where, to her amusement, everyone already seemed to have heard about the arrival of 'the war bride' and was very excited to meet her. News clearly travelled fast in small-town America.

Raymond's family had continued to be warm and welcoming, and his brothers had moved into their parents' bedroom in order to give him and Rae a room of their own. The neighbours in Hackett still viewed Rae as an object of fascination, and she struggled with their ignorance about the war, but for the most part they treated her with kindness. Rae had already made a few friends in the community, in particular a young woman called Mary Gurem who lived next door.

As he had promised, Raymond had not gone back to the coal mine, and had got a job at the Clairton steel mill instead.

When Rae saw how his father came home black from the mine every day, and how Mrs Wessel had to scrub his back at the kitchen sink, she felt doubly relieved.

But despite it all, Rae was not entirely happy. She felt bored during the long weekdays while Raymond was out at work, and once the ironing was done – her main job in the household – she had nothing to do but sit smoking in the swing chair on the front porch. She found herself longing for the hard-working days of the war years, and imagined herself with her welding torch in her hand, a row of tanks lined up in front of her for mending. She missed the sense of doing something important, and the camaraderie of her friends in the ATS.

But more than anything else she missed her family, and sitting around idly for hour after hour there was plenty of time for homesickness to creep in. She hoped that before long she and Raymond would start a family of their own, and that it would help ease the pain of separation. They were trying for a baby, although so far without success.

Rae was also coping with psychological scars from the war. When Raymond had asked if she would like to come with him to the Fourth of July celebrations in nearby South Park, she had agreed, keen to experience first-hand this famous American tradition. There was music from a small brass band, a hotdog stand and local children waving American flags, and the atmosphere of community and kindness reminded Rae a little of the war years in England.

Then, as night fell, it was time for the highlight of the event: the fireworks display. As a series of rockets shot into the air and exploded, Rae was transported right back to the bombing of London. She felt her stomach tightening and her heart beginning to race. Gripped by fear, she instinctively threw herself down on the grass, her hands covering the back of her head.

Raymond had to prise her off the ground and quickly lead her away. 'It's all right,' he told her. 'You're safe.'

It was the last time Rae went to a fireworks display.

Since Raymond worked at the steel mill, he generally arrived home separately from Mr Wessel, so Rae was surprised one day to see the two men walking back to the house together. She was even more shocked when they got closer and she could see that, like his father, Raymond was blackened from head to toe.

'Hey, honey,' he called, as if nothing was out of the ordinary.

'What's going on, Ray?' she asked him anxiously, as Mr Wessel went through to the kitchen where his wife was waiting to scrub him down.

'I'm working at Mathies Mine now,' Raymond told her. 'I wanted the same money as my dad.'

'You said you wouldn't go back there!' Rae protested. 'You promised me.' He knew how much she hated the thought of him going down the mine, in danger of being buried alive or killed in a dust explosion.

If Raymond was aware of the turmoil his wife was enduring, however, he gave no sign of it. He simply shrugged his shoulders and walked off to join his father.

There was nothing Rae could do. Before long, she was scrubbing the coal dust off his back every day just like her mother-in-law.

A few weeks later, Rae got a new job of her own. She and Raymond were out for the evening at Boyko's bar and restaurant in Finleyville, where she had become a hit with the owner, who liked her English accent.

'How would you like to work here?' Mr Boyko asked her as she was finishing her Pittsburgh salad. 'I'm looking for another waitress, and everyone round here loves to talk to a real English war bride.'

Rae said yes immediately. Any chance to get out of the house and actually do something was hard to pass up, and in a neighbourhood as small as the one they lived in, opportunities for work didn't come along very often. 'You don't mind, do you?' she asked her husband.

'Nah,' he said, putting one of his great big arms around her and giving her a squeeze.

But when the time came for Rae's first shift, Raymond didn't seem his usual laid-back self. 'You sure you want to do this?' he asked her.

'Of course,' Rae replied. 'I'm looking forward to it.'

When she arrived at the bar, Mr Boyko talked her through the different drinks on offer at the bar, and the process for passing orders on to the kitchen. 'Just turn on the English accent,' he told her. 'You'll do fine.'

Rae's previous work as a welder had done little to prepare her for waiting tables, but with her confident, friendly personality she made a good impression on the customers, and before long she had made a decent amount in tips.

After an hour or so, Rae was surprised to see Raymond arrive with his brother Bill and Bill's wife Chi-Chi. Rae felt touched that they had come to support her, but she had little time to talk to them as the restaurant was already heaving.

When the three of them had finished their food, Bill and Chi-Chi rose to leave, but Raymond declared that he would stay for a drink at the bar.

'You know I can't sit and talk with you,' Rae warned him. 'I don't mind if you want to go home.'

'It's all right,' Raymond replied, sipping on a bottle of beer. 'I like to watch you.'

Rae went back to her work and tried not to worry about her husband, but as she dashed from table to table she could feel his gaze upon her, especially when she talked to male customers. He's keeping an eye on me, she realised.

The evening set a pattern for what was to follow. Every night, a few hours into her shift, the door would open and in would walk Raymond, taking up his seat at the bar alone. As Rae went about her work, she would feel his intense stare following her. The bartender, Tubby, began to make jokes about it, which only made her feel worse.

After a couple of weeks Rae could take it no longer. 'I'm really sorry,' she told Mr Boyko, 'but this isn't working out for me. You're going to have to find a new waitress.'

The proprietor was surprised, but he accepted Rae's resignation and she went back to the ironing, feeling bitterly disappointed.

A few days later, Rae and Raymond went out to a small club by the railroad track near his parents' house, which was run by a Slovakian family. They hadn't been there long before a man came up and asked Rae if she was the local English war bride he'd heard so much about.

'That's me,' Rae laughed.

'I was stationed in England,' the man said. 'I sure did have a good time there.'

Rae could sense that Raymond was growing uncomfortable, but the other man seemed to be oblivious. 'So what part of England are you from?' he asked her.

Raymond stood up from the table and looked the man straight in the eye. 'Back off, buddy,' he said. 'She's with me.'

'Raymond!' she said. 'What's wrong with you?'

The other man seemed equally perturbed, and he had no wish to start a fight with someone Raymond's size. 'I didn't mean to make trouble,' he said, backing off and walking away.

Once the other man was gone, Raymond grew calmer, but Rae was shocked. Even at Boyko's she had never seen her husband flare up like this. What was causing these sudden bouts of jealousy in a man who was normally so easy-going that his army nickname had been 'Hap'?

Before long, a thought had occurred to her – and once it had, she found it impossible to shake off. Maybe Raymond was nursing a guilty conscience of his own.

Rae hoped that her own sixth sense when it came to men was not as accurate as her mother's. But it didn't take long for her to discover that her intuition had been correct. Her sister-in-law Chi-Chi confided that while Rae had been on the boat coming over, she and Bill had seen Raymond drunk in the street outside Boyko's with one of his old girlfriends. 'I'm sorry, Rae,' she said. 'It's a disgrace.'

And there was more. When Rae and Raymond went to visit his best man Chet, who lived in the nearby town of Canonsburg, she fell into conversation with Chet's sister. 'There's a girl at my factory who came in one day sobbing like crazy,' she said. 'Raymond had told her his wife was coming over and he couldn't see her any more.'

The more people Rae talked to about Raymond, the more she came to realise that her husband had quite a reputation. 'Oh, he was always a real run-around,' Mary next door told her. Now Rae realised why, when she had first arrived, a neighbour had remarked, 'I hope she knows what she's letting herself in for.'

Faced with all this damning information about her husband, she was caught on the horns of a dilemma. Should she confront him and risk a huge row, or carry on as if she knew nothing? His indiscretions were in the past, and aside from stoking his jealousy when she spoke to other men, there was no reason they should affect things between them now. In any case, she felt sure he had been loyal to her throughout their time together in England, and now that she was living under the same roof as him there was little chance of him straying again. She decided it would be best not to make an issue of it.

In any case, another worry was playing on Rae's mind. After more than six months of trying for a baby, she still wasn't pregnant. She thought back sadly to the miscarriage she had suffered in the Army, and the unborn child she had never known she was carrying. Was it possible that the experience had caused lasting damage? She decided to make an appointment with a doctor.

'There's nothing wrong with you as far as I can see,' he said, after examining her. 'My advice is to try not to worry. Just let nature take its course.'

When Rae got home she found her husband in the midst of a game of cards with some neighbours. She was keen to tell him the good news, so she walked up to him and said quietly, 'The doctor says there's nothing wrong with me.'

Raymond took the comment as an accusation, however. He turned round in his chair and, in front of the assembled card players, announced, 'Well, it can't be my fault you're not pregnant. I've already got a baby in West Virginia!'

A silence fell on the room and the other couples all looked down at their cards. Rae ran upstairs and shut herself in the bedroom.

Up until now, she had avoided telling her family back home about any of the discoveries she had made about Raymond. She knew that they would only confirm her brothers' prejudices about untrustworthy Yanks and that her mum would be beside herself with worry. But she was beginning to feel at breaking point herself now, and if she didn't let them know what she was going through she felt like she was going to burst. She sat down and began writing them a letter.

She told them all about how Raymond had been messing around with his old girlfriend before she arrived, how he had a reputation as a womaniser and how he had fathered a child with a woman in West Virginia. As Rae wrote, her tears dripped down onto the page.

When she had finished the letter, Rae put it in an envelope and went downstairs. There was no sign of Raymond or any of the guests. She knew she wouldn't be able to post the letter until she had a chance to buy a stamp, and in the meantime she didn't want Raymond to find it in their bedroom, so she reached up on tiptoes and placed it on the top of a tall cabinet by the kitchen door. Then she went out for a walk to clear her head.

When she got back to the house a little later, Rae realised the flaw in her plan. The cabinet might be high for her, but at six foot two Raymond could see the top of it easily. She found him sat at the kitchen table with the letter in front of him, scowling as he poured over its contents. He looked up at her with fury in his eyes. 'How could you write this about me?' he demanded.

She held his gaze. 'Because I know it's all true.'

'The hell it is!' Raymond shouted.

Rae took a deep breath. 'I don't want to hear your lies, Raymond,' she told him. 'I'm going up to pack my bags. I'm leaving.'

She climbed the stairs in a daze. Was she really doing this – really walking out on her husband? She went into the bedroom and sat down on the bed to compose herself.

After a while, Rae began looking for the duffle bag she had arrived with, but couldn't find it, so she headed back downstairs. Raymond was nowhere to be seen, but his mother was in the kitchen. 'Have you seen my duffle bag?' she asked.

'Oh, that,' Mrs Wessel replied. 'I threw it out.' Then she added, 'I think there's a note for you in the living room.'

Rae went into the other room and found a folded piece of paper with her name scrawled on it. 'I'm sorry, Rae,' her husband had written. 'Please don't go. I promise things will be different from now on. I've gone fishing with my dad, but I hope you're here when I get back.'

Rae felt torn. She no longer knew what to think. A few minutes before, she had been ready to walk out the door – but now she felt she owed it to Raymond to hear him out. She waited in the living room until he got back, and his parents went for a stroll to give them some privacy.

'Rae, you've got to forgive me,' Raymond said, rushing over and taking her hands in his. To her surprise, he started crying, big tears rolling down his manly face. She had never seen a grown man cry before, and the sight shocked her.

'It was so hard for me when I first came back after the war,' he sobbed. 'The things I saw out there… I can't even tell you, but I saw some terrible things.'

Rae thought back to the Raymond she had first got to know in Mansfield, the cheerful man whose friends had called him Hap. It was true – he didn't seem like the same person now. She remembered the many months she had spent wracked with worry while he was away in France. Perhaps the horrors he had witnessed there were worse than she had ever imagined.

The sight of her big, strong man broken like this was more than Rae could bear. 'All right then,' she said. 'I forgive you, as long as things are different now.'

'They are,' Raymond replied, wiping the tears from his face. 'I love you. I don't want to lose you.'

'I don't either,' Rae replied, and she meant it. She had crossed an ocean for this man, and she was determined to prove that it had been the right decision.

23

Margaret

As Margaret sailed back across the Atlantic on the SS *Argentina*, she was filled with dread. She had escaped a drunk, violent husband in America, but with her father now away with the Army in Israel, the only place she had to go was her abusive mother's house in Ireland. She hadn't been there since the day she escaped with her father during the war, and her mother knew nothing of her real reasons for coming to 'visit', nor that she was pregnant again.

Mrs Boyle was now living outside a little village called Tinahely in County Wicklow, and came with her donkey and trap to meet her daughter's bus at Carnew. To Margaret's surprise, she seemed quite pleased to see her, but it wasn't long before the reason became clear. 'Will your rich American husband be gracing us with his presence?' she asked hopefully.

'I don't think so,' Margaret replied.

Mrs Boyle was renting a little house on a farm called Greenhall, and conditions were even more primitive than they had been before. There was no running water, so it had to be pumped into buckets, which were kept lined up on the table in the scullery.

Margaret's younger sisters Bridget and Susannah instantly fell in love with their little nieces Maeve and Rosamund, but

Mrs Boyle wasn't pleased to hear that another child was on the way. She had intended for Margaret to wait on her hand and foot during her stay, and was furious when she said she needed to rest.

Margaret was not only exhausted, but was suffering from headaches and shortness of breath. She begged her mother to call a doctor, which she eventually did, and was told she had high blood pressure – hardly a surprise given all she had gone through in America. 'Complete bed rest is what you need,' the doctor declared.

But before long, Margaret was feeling even more tense. Lawrence wrote begging for her forgiveness, and announcing that he was coming over to Ireland to win her back.

Margaret was horrified, but her mother was delighted. On the day of his planned arrival, Mrs Boyle set out on the donkey and trap to meet Lawrence's bus. As it pulled into Carnew, no one matching her son-in-law's description alighted, so she marched onboard and shouted, 'Is there a Lawrence Rambo here?'

From the back of the bus she heard a groan, and spotted a dishevelled, dark-haired man who was clearly the worse for wear. She managed to get him into the trap and slowly they made their way back to Greenhall.

Once there, Mrs Boyle stormed up the stairs to the bed-ridden Margaret. 'Your husband is drunk!' she told her.

'I've never known him to drink,' Margaret lied. 'He must be ill.'

The last thing she wanted was for Lawrence to incur her mother's wrath and make the awkward situation even worse.

The next day, when Lawrence had sobered up, he was at her bedside immediately.

'Margaret, I was devastated when you left,' he told her, sobbing. 'You're the only woman I've ever loved and I can't live without you. Please come back to me, I'm begging you.'

'How can I come back to you after what you did to me?' she demanded.

'I'd do anything in the world to take that back,' he said. The tears streamed down his face and there was a look of fear in his eyes that she hadn't seen before. Perhaps her leaving had made him realise for the first time what he stood to lose as a result of his behaviour, she thought.

'Please don't give up on me now, before our child is even born,' he said. 'I'll do anything to make it right between us again – anything. You name it and I'll do it.'

'All I ever wanted', Margaret said, sobbing herself now, 'was for you to stop drinking and hold down a decent job, but you're not capable of it, Lawrence. You're just not capable of it. I tried for so long, but life with you was unbearable.'

'I am capable of it – I'll prove it to you,' he insisted, desperately grasping at her words. 'Give me a little bit of time and I'll make everything right.'

A few days later he left for England, full of promises to make a new life for them there. Margaret doubted very much that he was even capable of getting back to England without falling down drunk somewhere, let alone of finding a job. In the meantime, she struggled through her pregnancy in Ireland, trying to ignore her mother's angry comments about her 'wastrel' husband.

She gave birth to baby Veronica in a little hospital in Baltinglass, where things couldn't have been more different from her traumatic experience in Akron. The hospital wasn't busy and the midwife stayed with her throughout.

But she felt desperate at the thought of returning to Greenhall. How could she cope with a newborn baby, in a house with no running water and a spiteful mother who refused to do anything to help? She remembered how her mother had beaten her as a child, and feared that her own children might suffer the same fate. But she had nowhere else to go.

When she got back to the house, there was a letter waiting from Lawrence. 'I'm working as a journalist for Reuters in London, and I've found us a place to live,' he wrote. 'Things are different now I'm in England. Please give me the chance to meet my new daughter and show you that we can be a family again.'

Enclosed was a boat ticket back to England. At the sight of it, Margaret's heart leaped. She longed to be back there again, and there was no way she would be able to afford to get there on her own.

Living in Ireland with her mother was miserable, and she knew she couldn't stay there indefinitely. Her departure from America really seemed to have shaken Lawrence up – maybe it had provided the impetus he needed to turn his life around. Either way, she had three children by him now, and she felt she had to give him another chance.

Once again, she left Ireland and her angry mother behind.

Lawrence was over the moon to see her and he was as charming and courteous as he had been when they first met. In America, he had been too drunk most of the time to pay much attention to his older two daughters, but Margaret was encouraged to see that he was taking more interest in the children, particularly the baby, Veronica.

As he'd promised, he had found a job and a flat, although when Margaret arrived she quickly discovered that they weren't quite what she had hoped for. The 'flat' was in an empty lawyers' chambers in Temple, and there was no running water to cook with – only a tap in a bathroom across the corridor. Lawrence was working for Reuters, but he was on the night shift, which meant that he slept all day and they barely saw one another.

As long as he was holding down a job and not drinking, however, she was not going to complain. She spent her days taking the children down to Temple Gardens or for walks along the river, and met up with her father's friend, Daphne Steadham, whom she had first stayed with when she moved to London before. She also took a trip to Canterbury to see her grandmother, who was thrilled to meet her great-grandchildren.

Margaret felt a little happier just being in London again, around familiar sights like St Paul's and the River Thames. It seemed as if a lifetime had passed since she was last there, and she thought back to the young, carefree girl she had been when she first arrived in the city. She could have had no idea then that one of her many wartime dalliances would end up taking her on such a rollercoaster. She was only twenty-four, but already she had three children born in three different countries.

Tentatively, Margaret began to hope that she and Lawrence might be able to make a go of it. She wrote to his sister Ellen in Georgia, telling her about their new life in London, and received friendly letters back, along with photographs of her niece and nephews in America. Her sister-in-law told her that no one in the family blamed her for having walked out on

Lawrence, and that they all hoped it had given him the kick he needed to straighten himself out once and for all.

Margaret truly believed it was what Lawrence wanted too, and when he looked into her eyes and told her he loved her, she knew he meant it.

But one day, when she went to kiss him, she smelled alcohol on his breath.

'Lawrence, have you been drinking?' she asked him.

'I just had a little nightcap to relax me before I went to bed,' he told her. 'It's not easy keeping these crazy hours.'

Margaret felt sick to her stomach. Soon she began finding empty bottles around the flat, and Lawrence was waking up in the evenings with shaking hands, clearly craving his first drink of the day.

This time, at least, he didn't try to deny it. 'Margaret, I just don't know what to do any more,' he said hopelessly. 'Every time I try to beat it, it creeps up on me again.'

Margaret looked at his sad, tired face. In his mid-thirties, it was already haggard from years of heavy drinking, and now it was regaining the familiar puffy appearance it had when he drank. It was a pathetic sight to behold, and for the first time, she felt truly sorry for him.

She knew the real Lawrence Rambo was not a bad man – he was charming, intelligent and full of life. But he was a man in the grip of a terrible addiction, one that would follow them wherever they went and whatever their circumstances. She knew that if she stayed with him it would ruin her life as well as his.

'I'm sorry, Lawrence,' she told him, 'but this time it really is the end.'

Lawrence made no attempt to argue with her. He knew as well as she did that their marriage was over.

Margaret had no idea what kind of life she could give her three children as a single mother, but at least she was back in her own country now, with a few people around who cared about her. Somehow, she would have to find a way.

24

Gwendolyn

For a few blissful moments when she first woke, Lyn thought she was back home in her childhood bed in Southampton. But as she blinked, her surroundings came into view: bare wooden walls, a pock-marked floor and a few cheap pieces of holiday furniture.

It was little more than a shack, but ever since the day Ben's mother had forced him to choose between her and Lyn, the cabin in the mountains above San Jose had been their home. It had no hot water and no phone, but until Ben found a job it was all they could afford on his small monthly allowance from the Army.

'Hi, honey,' Ben greeted her, as he emerged from the shower and began towelling himself down. Lyn got up, took their single pan to the sink and filled it with water for his coffee. She set it down on the little two-ring stove and then slumped at the table.

'Don't worry, Lyn,' Ben said. 'Maybe this'll be the day.'

As he dressed, Lyn poured the coffee into a pair of chipped mugs. Coffee-drinking was one American habit she had finally embraced, having given up on what passed for tea in the States.

Ben poked his head optimistically into the food cupboard, but there was nothing that would do for breakfast, so he sipped his drink instead. They sat in silence for a few minutes before he stood up to leave. 'See you tonight,' he said. 'Love you.'

Lyn hugged him. 'I love you too,' she whispered.

She watched from the window as he sped off through the forest towards San Jose in their rented jeep.

Every day, while Ben was out job-hunting, Lyn tried to make herself a useful housewife – but more often than not she ended up feeling like a failure, and he would come home to find her in tears. Her attempts at cooking what little food they had – supplemented by handouts from his Uncle Tony – were mostly disastrous. She struggled to wash their clothes in the cold water, and hung them up on the line outside, trying not to drop them in the pine needles. If Mrs Patrino had seen how crumpled Ben's underpants were now, she would have had a fit. Lyn was beginning to wonder if her mother-in-law had been right to say that she wasn't the wife Ben deserved.

Lyn still knew no one in America outside Ben's family. She had tried to keep up a correspondence with her war-bride friend Jean from Southampton, who was living in Texas, but the letters had petered out. Lyn wrote asking whether she'd said anything to upset her, and eventually Jean wrote back to say that her baby had died and her husband had become an alcoholic. Lyn tried to persuade her to come and visit, but Jean said she couldn't bear her friend to see her the way she was now. Were any GI brides living happily ever after? Lyn wondered.

Around 6 p.m., Lyn decided to get some food ready before Ben got home. She took a handful of beans from the cupboard, dropped them in the little pressure cooker and put it on the hob. Then she went outside to have a cigarette. Gazing out across the mountains she was struck by how beautiful it was here, among the pines and redwoods. When she had first arrived, she had been convinced that beauty and love would be enough to sustain her and Ben. Now she wasn't so sure.

In her reverie, Lyn had lost track of time. She jumped up and headed back into the cabin to check on the dinner. As she entered, she heard a strange popping noise, and saw to her horror that the top of the pressure cooker had burst off and the beans were shooting wildly out of the metal pan like popcorn. Only then did she realise she had forgotten to put any water in. Once again, she felt like an abject failure.

The day might have ended in tears, had it not been for the unexpected arrival of Ben's Auntie Louise. She found Lyn looking dejected, and put her arm around her. 'I once put some apple sauce in the pressure cooker and went to take a bath,' she told her. 'I was still in there when it exploded – there was apple sauce dripping off the ceiling!'

Lyn couldn't help giggling. Seeing Auntie Louise always cheered her up and, even though she was Mrs Patrino's sister, they got on well. Louise's leg was deformed by childhood polio, and Lyn admired the way she never let it stop her doing anything, even going canoeing or horse riding. She seemed to have an unlimited reserve of positivity. I wish I could be more like her, Lyn thought.

'Something arrived for you at my sister's house,' Louise said, handing Lyn an envelope stamped with the Red Cross logo. 'Why don't you read it while I sort out some food.' Louise plonked her bag down and took out some chicken and potatoes.

'Thank you,' Lyn replied gratefully.

The letter was about a new local club called Wise Wives that the Red Cross was starting for GI brides from England, Australia, New Zealand and Canada. Their first meeting was coming up, and they had written to all the local brides whose addresses they had.

Lyn's heart leaped at the thought of finally making some friends in America and spending time with English people.

When Ben arrived later, the three of them settled down to Auntie Louise's delicious dinner, which was some consolation to him after yet another day of fruitless job-hunting. Once Louise left, Ben suggested they go out for a drive in the mountains.

As they drove, Lyn told Ben about the bean explosion, which now seemed quite funny. She had been chattering away for several minutes before she realised that Ben hadn't said a word. 'I'm sorry,' she said. 'I don't know why I prattle on.'

'It's okay,' he said, his voice choked. 'If you didn't, I wouldn't know what to do right now.'

Lyn looked at him and saw there were tears in his eyes. Ben must be almost at breaking point, she realised.

As time went on, life in the shack only seemed to get harder. Soon Ben and Lyn were falling behind on the rent, and the landlord was threatening eviction. Ben had to go cap in hand to Uncle Tony to borrow money.

Meanwhile, Lyn was feeling increasingly exhausted and kept throwing up. She thought she might have stomach flu, and went to see a doctor.

'Well, you don't have stomach flu, Mrs Patrino,' the doctor told her. 'You're pregnant.'

'I can't be!' she exclaimed.

'Why's that?'

'My husband doesn't have a job.'

'Maybe you should have thought of that before,' the man said unsympathetically.

When she saw Ben again, Lyn felt terrible saddling him with more bad news. The two of them could barely cope up in the mountains – how could they take care of a baby?

'We'll work it out,' Ben said. He put his arms around his wife and held her tight.

But not everyone in the family took the news so well. Lyn's sister-in-law Thelma reported that Mrs Patrino had complained, 'Oh great, now we'll never get rid of her.'

Amid the worry about the baby, Lyn almost forgot the Red Cross meeting, but when the appointed day came she was determined to give it a go. Ben dropped her off at the YWCA, and Lyn followed a sign for the Wise Wives club. Inside, a group of wives were listening while an Englishwoman instructed them on the best way to make traditional cucumber sandwiches. 'It's very important the cucumber is paper thin,' the woman was saying as she demonstrated her deft slicing technique. Much discussion followed on how to avoid a soggy sandwich, and soon the women were putting their theories to the test.

Lyn marvelled at the sound of English voices filling the room. As they ate the sandwiches they had made, tea was poured from large teapots – and to her delight it was the proper stuff, not made with a bag.

The women soon found they had more in common than just a fondness for tea. Many of their husbands, like Ben, didn't have jobs, and a lot of them were finding it a challenge fitting into their partner's families.

'My mother-in-law thinks I'm not clean,' admitted one girl, bashfully.

'Mine thinks I should shower every day!' Lyn responded. 'She's fanatical!'

She soon gravitated towards a woman called Leslie, a smartly dressed, fair-haired GI bride from Canada whose rounded tummy announced that, like Lyn, she was pregnant. Lyn admitted that she was worried about having a baby when Ben had no job.

'Maybe I can help you,' Leslie told her. 'My husband's setting up a new business and I know he's looking to take someone on.'

Lyn's eyes lit up. 'That would be wonderful,' she replied.

The job turned out to be the lifeline Ben and Lyn had been waiting for. Leslie's husband Joe had set up a company repairing carburettors, and after a brief interview he agreed to hire Ben on the spot. Ben proved himself a hard worker and was soon indispensable to the business, and before long he and Lyn had saved enough to move out of the cabin.

They started looking for an apartment downtown, and to their delight the first place they saw was perfect. It was on the third floor of a beautiful old house, overlooking the high street. But the landlady had two strict conditions. 'I only rent to people who keep house perfectly, and who don't have children,' she said.

To the woman's astonishment, Lyn began to cry. 'What's wrong, dear?' she asked.

'I'm a rotten housekeeper,' Lyn sobbed.

'Well, don't worry about that,' she replied. 'At least you don't have children!'

'That's just it. I'm pregnant as well!'

Seeing Lyn's tears, the landlady's heart melted. She took pity on Ben and Lyn and decided to rent them the apartment anyway. Before long they were making it their own.

Despite Lyn's former resistance towards housekeeping, she was so grateful to be in a proper apartment rather than a shack that she found it brought out her domestic side, and soon she was happily spending her hours reading recipe books and tuning in to cookery programmes on the radio.

Although relations with Ben's parents remained frosty, he and Lyn continued to see a lot of Auntie Louise, so Lyn thought nothing of it when Ben announced they were going to her house for dinner one evening.

When they pulled into Louise's driveway, however, Lyn spotted her mother-in-law's car. 'She's not coming, is she?' Lyn asked, panicked.

'I don't know,' Ben replied, a little awkwardly.

Lyn noticed the road outside was unusually parked up as well. 'There's Thelma's car, and Auntie Nancy's and Auntie Catherine's. It's looks like they're having a party and didn't bother to tell us!'

Lyn refused to go inside, but Ben tried his best to persuade her. 'Please, Lyn, just do it for me,' he begged.

Eventually she agreed, and they knocked on the door. As soon as it opened, Auntie Louise pulled her into the living room, and dozens of people suddenly emerged shouting, 'Shower!'

Lyn was utterly confused. 'What's going on?' she said.

'Don't you know what a shower is?' asked Auntie Catherine.

'When it rains?' Lyn replied.

'There's she goes again, being a smart alec,' said Mrs Patrino, rolling her eyes.

'It's for you, honey, because you're having a baby,' Auntie Louise explained. 'We thought it would be a nice surprise, to remind you how much we all care about you.'

Lyn barely had a chance to respond before the aunties were gathered round, cooing over her bulge and making proclamations about the sex of the baby. Lyn was inundated with gifts of baby clothes and toys, all of which were held up so the women could coo over them too. It was one of the most bizarre American rituals she had come across, Lyn decided. But they had all been incredibly generous – even Mrs Patrino – and on the drive home she had to admit to Ben that it hadn't gone too badly.

Although seeing Ben's mother at the shower had been a shock, Lyn felt that now she and Ben had their own apartment, she wanted to prove she was not the hopeless wife Mrs Patrino had accused her of being. Ben's parents agreed to come round for dinner, and Lyn pored over her cookery books, perfecting her French onion soup and sirloin steak with mashed potatoes and asparagus. It would be classy but simple – without a single garlic bulb in sight.

When the guests arrived, Lyn played the perfect hostess. As she opened the door to Ben's parents, she could see Mrs Patrino's eyes giving the place the once over. But she had made sure that every surface was dusted and polished until it shined.

They took their seats at the dining table and Lyn announced the menu. She thought she saw Mrs Patrino's eyebrow raise a little at the mention of French onion soup, but she remained silent.

The bowls came out and Ben's parents gingerly slurped their soup. They had reason to be cautious, remembering Lyn's almost-raw chicken and tooth-breaking corn on the cob. But after a few moments, Ben's father emitted a satisfied 'Mmmm'.

Mrs Patrino looked round at him in surprise, and he quickly covered his mouth with his napkin. But she didn't make any complaints.

To their relief, the sirloin steak was well cooked, and Lyn's asparagus was particularly tasty. 'This is good,' Mrs Patrino said quietly.

It was the slightest of compliments, but to Lyn it meant everything. Ben might not have married a 'nice Italian girl', but Lyn had proved that his English bride wasn't completely hopeless after all.

Lyn felt relieved that her relationship with Ben's mother was now cordial, even if they were not the best of friends. But one day, Mrs Patrino called her, sounding agitated. 'Come over, please,' she demanded. 'I need to talk to you.'

Lyn's heart sank. 'What do you think it's about?' she asked Ben.

He shrugged. 'I have no idea.'

Lyn turned up at the Patrino house, and found her mother-in-law waiting for her.

'Sit down,' she told her. 'Now, did you say I was jealous over my sons?'

'What?' Lyn said, taken aback.

'Did you say I was jealous?' Mrs Patrino repeated.

'No!' Lyn said. But then she thought back over the many conversations she'd had with Thelma over the washing up. Had her sister-in-law betrayed her confidence?

'Well, actually, I did say something like that,' Lyn admitted.

'I don't understand you – cutting me behind my back!' Mrs Patrino cried.

'Well,' Lyn said, 'if the person telling you this is who I think it is, she's also telling me what you say about me.'

Suddenly, Mrs Patrino looked less sure of herself.

But Lyn was gaining confidence. 'Didn't you say you'd never get rid of me when you found out I was pregnant?'

Mrs Patrino couldn't deny it, and for a moment she was speechless. Then, she suddenly reached out and hugged Lyn.

Lyn couldn't quite believe it, but she put her arms around her in return.

'Thank you for your honesty,' Mrs Patrino said.

'You're welcome,' Lyn replied, and made a hasty getaway before her mother-in-law could change her mind.

Despite what she had said when Lyn was pregnant, when baby John was born Mrs Patrino and her husband proved to be doting grandparents. For the first year of John's life, Lyn was happy to play mum and housewife in her new apartment, but as time drew on she began to feel restless. Having perfected her cooking, cleaning now became her new obsession, and she spent so many hours washing, scrubbing and polishing that even Mrs Patrino's floors couldn't have competed. Ben finally told her it was driving him crazy, and it was clear that Lyn needed to get out of the house more.

She saw that the University of Santa Clara were hiring and went along for an interview. 'There are two positions vacant,' the interviewer, Mr Stefan, told her. 'One is for a receptionist and the other is for a secretary to the priest here, Father Donnalan. Which would you prefer? I have to warn you, the priest has been known to make people cry.'

But having handled the mother of all mother-in-laws, Lyn knew she could deal with anyone. 'I'll take the secretary job,' she said firmly.

The university gratefully assigned Lyn to the gruff Father Donnalan – who never managed to reduce Lyn to tears.

Lyn realised she was pretty lucky. Things were improving with her husband's family, she and Ben both had decent jobs and they were blessed with a beautiful baby boy. After everything that had gone wrong in her first couple of years in America, life really seemed to be getting back on track.

One night, Lyn and Ben decided to see an English movie in Palo Alto, having left little John with his grandparents. It was nice to spend an evening together just the two of them, but all through the film Lyn was distracted by a pain in her head and neck.

'Do you think it's a migraine?' Ben asked her as they drove back to get John.

'I don't think so,' Lyn replied. 'Maybe I'm coming down with the flu.'

When they got home she went straight to bed, but the next morning she was still in pain and decided to call in sick at work. When Ben phoned at lunchtime to see how she was doing, she told him she hadn't yet got out of bed. 'This doesn't sound right,' he told her. 'I'm going to come home and take you to the doctor.'

Lyn was too exhausted to argue. 'I'll just have a quick bath first,' she said.

She dragged herself out of bed, but walking along the corridor her legs suddenly gave out from under her and she fell to the floor. Something is very wrong, she thought, as she hauled herself up and very slowly made her way to the bathroom.

The heat of the bath felt blissful as Lyn lowered herself into it, even though her head and neck were still hurting. But when she pulled the plug and tried to get out, she found she didn't have the strength to stand. It was like her legs just wouldn't do what she told them.

Lyn managed to heave herself out of the tub by her arms, and lay panting on the bathroom floor in a pool of water. When Ben found her there, he was horrified. 'Oh my God, what's the matter, Lyn?' he said anxiously.

'I just couldn't get up,' Lyn said helplessly. 'My legs really hurt.'

Ben helped her get dressed and carried her out to the car, then drove her straight to the doctor's surgery.

In the waiting room, a nurse took Lyn's temperature. 'Not too high,' she told her with a smile, although beneath it Lyn could tell she was worried. 'But I don't think you should be out here. Let's get you in to see the doctor right away.'

She took hold of one of Lyn's arms and Ben took the other, and between them they helped her into the doctor's room.

'How are you feeling?' the doctor asked, pulling up a chair in front of Lyn and looking into her eyes.

'Terrible,' she told him.

'Well, you don't look sick,' he replied. 'Can you can stand?'

'I'm not sure,' she said. She tried to force herself up from her chair but fell forward into the doctor's arms. 'Good try, Lyn,' he told her. 'You can rest now.'

As he lowered her back into her chair, she caught Ben's eye and saw that he was as terrified as she was.

The doctor applied some pressure to Lyn's neck, pushing her head forward a little, and she gasped in pain.

'Okay, just one more test,' he said, reaching for a small reflex hammer.

He lifted one of Lyn's legs and crossed it over the other. Then he tapped her knee with the hammer. Nothing happened.

He crossed her knees the other way and repeated the test, but again there was no response. 'Good God,' he said. 'I think it's polio. We need to get you into isolation right away.'

Lyn stared at him in disbelief, struggling to take in what he was saying.

Ben was on his feet at once. 'Shall I call an ambulance?' he asked.

'No,' the doctor replied, 'we don't have time. I want you to take her straight to the hospital – she could need an iron lung at any minute.'

25

Sylvia

Although he had been gambling while Sylvia was in labour, Bob proved to be a very proud father. He was over the moon at having a son, and Sylvia hoped it would spur him on to stop gambling and save up the money for a deposit on an apartment so that they could move out of his parents' house.

Meanwhile, now that she had brought a new grandchild into the family, Sylvia felt she had more to contribute to conversations around the dinner table. She had always been quite shy, unable to join in with talk about Leo and Bob's work at the post office, or the goings-on of all Mrs O'Connor's relatives. But now she could chat about baby Barry's latest developments – his first tooth or his attempts to crawl – and she didn't feel like such an outsider.

She was also hoping that the new arrival would soften her father-in-law's heart and stop him ignoring her, making snide remarks and letting doors slam in her face. To begin with, Mr O'Connor seemed to take quite an interest in the baby, and he joined in with all the other family members who came round to dote on him. But it wasn't long before his old jealousy reared its ugly head once more. By the time Barry was old enough for a playpen, Mr O'Connor took to simply ignoring him, just as he had Sylvia, walking straight past as if he wasn't there.

Perhaps he saw the child as an affront to his vanity, thought Sylvia. He was a handsome man, and he didn't even like anyone at the post office to know that his son worked there, fearing it would make him seem old, so she was sure that he wouldn't want anyone to know that he was a grandfather. He had stormed out in a rage one day when Sylvia tried to teach the baby to call him Granddad.

Sylvia was becoming increasingly desperate for her and Bob to move out, but her hopes that little Barry's arrival would curb her husband's gambling seemed to have been misplaced. The card-playing in the basement still continued every weekend, and while she stayed at home with the baby, he would go off for games at his Uncle John's, sometimes not coming home until the early hours. Meanwhile, the family continued to bet on the horses every week, encouraging Bob to do the same, and Sylvia frequently found the money in their little savings tin raided to fund his flutters. When she tried to talk to him about it, he simply grumbled and walked off.

As Barry grew older, Mr O'Connor's behaviour towards him only worsened. At eleven months, Barry started to toddle, and one day, seeing his granddad in the room, began wobbling over towards him, his little chubby hands outstretched. Mr O'Connor stood there until the child had almost reached him and then, at the last moment, stepped aside so that Barry fell over. Sylvia witnessed the incident, but told herself that it must have just been a mistake. Perhaps Mr O'Connor wasn't very good with children.

But a few days later the same thing happened again. This time Barry began to cry, and his grandfather laughed at him.

Sylvia's heart filled with a mother's rage and, uncharacteristically, she confronted her father-in-law. 'You can't let a child fall over like that!' she told him.

But Mr O'Connor ignored her completely, nonchalantly lighting up a cigarette and leaving the room.

The next time Mr O'Connor let Barry fall over, Bob was there to see it too. Mr O'Connor laughed as the child fell and hit his head against a table. Bob rushed over to Barry, rubbing his injured head to soothe his tears, and Sylvia was sure he was about to say something to his father. But he simply picked the boy up and walked out of the room.

Sylvia ran after him. 'You've got to say something to your father,' she begged him. 'He's deliberately hurting his own grandchild!'

Bob sighed. 'I can't do anything,' he said, shrugging. 'We're living in his house.'

Sylvia felt utterly desperate. Living with Bob's father was a nightmare and her husband would do nothing to stand up for her or their son. And with Bob gambling their money away, they were never going to be able to leave. There was only one thing she could do.

The next day, while Bob was at work, Sylvia took their savings tin out of the cupboard and stuffed all the money into her handbag. Then she took Barry and rode the tram downtown to the Cunard office, where she asked for a third-class ticket on the first boat to England. She handed over the money from her handbag and was given a ticket for the *Queen Mary*, departing in three weeks' time.

When she and Barry got home it was gone 4.30 p.m., and Bob was awake after his afternoon nap. 'Hi, babycakes,' he said. 'Where have you been?'

'I went downtown,' Sylvia replied.

'You went where?' Bob said, surprised. 'Downtown?'

'Yes,' Sylvia said. Then she ran upstairs as quickly as she could and put Barry in his crib. He was tired from the outing and fell asleep straight away.

Bob followed her into the bedroom. 'What's the matter with you?' he asked.

'Nothing's the matter with me,' Sylvia said, her heart beating fast. 'I just bought a ticket home.'

'*What?*'

'I'm fed up with the way I'm being treated,' Sylvia blurted out. 'I can't stand your dad's meanness and rudeness, and with you gambling all our money away we're never going to get out of here. I'm going home.'

Sylvia had tears streaming down her face by now, and at the sight of her, Bob began to cry too. 'How long are you going for?' he asked.

She could see he was devastated, but the anger that had driven her to come this far was still burning. 'As long as it takes for you to find us a place of our own,' she told him. 'I'm not coming back unless you do.'

Before long, Mrs O'Connor called them down to dinner. They wiped their tears away and went into the kitchen, Bob looking like a man who'd had the biggest shock of his life. He couldn't believe that his normally docile wife had made such a bold decision.

'What did you do this afternoon, go shopping?' Bob's mother asked Sylvia absentmindedly as they sat down to eat.

'No, Mom,' Bob said quietly. 'She went downtown and bought a boat ticket. She's going back to England.'

Mrs O'Connor looked astonished. Like her son, all she could say was, 'What?'

Sylvia remained calm and collected, but she could feel her cheeks burning red. 'We need our own place,' she said, 'and it doesn't look like we're going to get one at the moment, so I decided I'm going home until Bob can find us somewhere.'

'I thought you were saving up for an apartment,' Mrs O'Connor said, flabbergasted.

'I had to use that money for the ticket,' Sylvia replied. 'Bob's been gambling it away on the horses so I thought I'd better get in there quick while there was still some left.'

Mrs O'Connor couldn't argue with that – after all, Sylvia had pleaded with her to stop asking Bob if he wanted a flutter and she had ignored her.

Sylvia almost felt like smiling. Despite her bright-red cheeks, for the first time since she had arrived at the O'Connors' she felt powerful.

For the next three weeks, Bob stuck to Sylvia like glue, following her around as if he was scared she might do a runner early. He was on his best behaviour, not gambling at all, but it didn't change her mind. She knew that as long as he was surrounded by his family he would go back to it.

Sylvia wrote to her parents, telling them that she was coming home for a visit. She didn't say why – she still hadn't told them how bad things had got, knowing how much her mum would worry. And she had never forgotten what Mrs Bradley had said at the airfield the day she left: 'You've made your bed, and now you'll have to lie in it.'

Since Sylvia had read that the *Queen Mary* had an onboard swimming pool, she went out specially and bought herself a green woollen swimsuit to take with her. But while she was packing the rest of her things for the trip, she made a discovery that filled her with sadness. In a box in the basement of the O'Connors' house, where Bob had spent so many hours playing cards, the wax headpiece she had worn on her wedding day had melted all over the beautiful white dress her mother had made, and it was completely ruined.

When the day finally came for Sylvia to leave, Bob rode the train with her to New York. All the way there he kept playing with little Barry, bouncing him up and down on his knee. 'I'm going to miss you, buddy,' he said sadly. But Sylvia's mind was completely set on the course of action she had begun.

They took a cab to the port and Sylvia's luggage was taken by a steward to be put on the boat. They hung about for an hour or so until the announcement was made for *Queen Mary* passengers to embark.

Bob turned to Sylvia and hugged her tightly. 'I'll find a place for us soon,' he told her. 'It won't be long.'

'Goodbye, Bob,' Sylvia said quietly, hugging him back. All the frustration of the last two years, and her disappointment that he hadn't stood up to his father, had never stopped her loving him.

She walked up the gangplank carrying Barry, and turned to wave at Bob. Barry copied her, and then they were gone.

Now that the war-bride transport operation was over, the *Queen Mary* was once again a luxury liner, and even third-class passengers like Sylvia had a cinema, a wood-panelled lounge and library, a hairdresser's and a large dining room with crisp white tablecloths and mahogany chairs.

The luggage had been delivered to the passengers' rooms, but Sylvia found hers had not arrived. She caught sight of a friendly looking young steward and asked him if he could locate her suitcase. He promised to find it and went off to look.

An hour later, the steward knocked on her door. 'I'm sorry Mrs O'Connor,' he said, 'but there's no sign of your luggage. I don't know what's happened to it – it's definitely not anywhere on the boat.'

Sylvia couldn't believe it – she and Barry had a six-and-a-half-day voyage ahead of them, and all she had were half a dozen nappies and a change of clothes for the two of them. At least she had packed her swimsuit in her hand luggage, she thought. 'Where's the swimming pool?' she asked the steward.

'I'm afraid only first- and second-class passengers can go swimming,' he told her.

He saw Sylvia's disappointed face and felt guilty knowing she had been left without her things. 'Well, I might be able to arrange something,' he said quietly. 'The second-class pool is closed for a couple of hours in the middle of the day – I might be able to sneak you in.'

The next day the steward knocked for her and took her towards the back of the ship where the second-class swimming pool was located. It was a beautiful Art Deco room with columns around the pool, and Sylvia gasped in delight as she saw it. She handed Barry to the steward and went into one of the ladies' dressing boxes to change into her new green swimsuit. Then she dived in, feeling like a movie star.

As her body cut through the water, to her horror Sylvia felt her engagement and wedding rings slip off her finger. She came to the surface as quickly as she could, and swam round in circles trying to see where they had gone. 'I've lost my rings!' she shouted to the steward, who rushed over to the edge of the pool. 'What am I going to do?'

'I'll get someone to help,' he replied. Sylvia hastily got out of the pool, wrapped herself in a towel and took Barry from him.

A few minutes later, the steward came back with one of the life guards, who dived in to search for the rings. Sylvia looked on anxiously as time and again he came back to the surface empty handed. 'There's only one thing for it,' he told the steward. 'We're going to have to drain the pool!'

Sylvia looked on, mortified, as the *Queen Mary*'s swimming pool was drained just for her – a third-class passenger who wasn't even meant to be there in the first place. To make matters worse, her woollen swimming suit had stretched a good five inches in the water, leaving her looking very far from the movie star she had felt like when she arrived.

Sylvia's rings were eventually returned to her, but the poor steward got in trouble for sneaking her in and she never saw him again.

When Sylvia arrived in Southampton, her mother, father and two little sisters – now eleven and thirteen – were waiting for her. She could see that her normally strong mother was struggling not to cry, but as Sylvia approached tears began rolling down her cheeks.

'You've made it, love!' Mrs Bradley cried, throwing her arms around her daughter.

Seeing her mum's tears, Sylvia realised just how much her family had missed her. When she had left England, all her thoughts had been about her future with Bob and she hadn't really thought about the impact her departure would have on the lives of those around her. But her sister Audrey told her that, when she left, their mother had cried every night for three months.

Mr Bradley's face lit up as soon as he saw Barry – his first grandchild – and he covered him in kisses. Meanwhile, Sylvia's sisters were delighted to have a little nephew to pet.

Back in Woolwich, all the neighbours came round, eager for news about America. 'What's it like?' 'Is it as big as they say?' 'Does everyone have a car?'

'Well, not everyone has a car,' Sylvia had to admit. 'But it is very big.'

Sylvia hadn't wanted to burden her mother with how bad things had got at the O'Connors', but once everyone else had gone home, she told her a little of how her father-in-law had treated her. Mrs Bradley was outraged. 'Bloody old sod,' she fumed. 'I'd like to punch him on the nose!' Nor was she happy to hear that Mrs O'Connor had her daughter doing all the housework for a mere two dollars a week. 'She must have thought you were her skivvy,' she said.

Over the next few days, Sylvia saw how different Barry's relationship with his English grandfather was to that with Mr O'Connor. He was the apple of Mr Bradley's eye, who clearly loved having a little boy in the family. Barry, meanwhile, could call him Granddad without incurring his wrath.

After three weeks, Sylvia's luggage finally arrived with an apology note from Cunard. It turned out that her suitcase had gone on the *Queen Elizabeth* by mistake. 'Typical!' she said.

A letter also arrived from Bob. 'I miss you and Barry so much,' he wrote. 'I've gotten used to having you around, and now I'm all on my own at home. Please come back soon.'

But Sylvia knew she had to be strong. 'If you find somewhere for us to live, I'll come back,' she wrote to him.

As the weeks went by and she waited to hear whether Bob would be true to his word, Sylvia settled more and more into her old life. She felt an enormous sense of relief to be surrounded by familiar things and familiar people once again. She met up with her former workmate Peggy for lunch in London, taking the train up to Charing Cross, just like she had done so many times when going to work at the Piccadilly Hotel. She remembered how exciting it had felt the first time she made the journey, when she had gone to work 'Up West', and smiled to think how much further west she had ended up travelling just a few years later. After eating at Lyons Corner House, they took Barry to feed the pigeons in Trafalgar Square. It was strange to see central London now empty of Americans – as if the 'friendly invasion' had been just a dream.

After a few months, Bob had still not written to say he had got them an apartment, and Sylvia realised people were beginning to wonder whether she was really planning to return to America. A friend had even offered her a job in the offices of the Woolwich Co-op. It was hard for Sylvia to know what to say to such offers when she herself didn't know how long she was going to be in England.

When a letter finally came announcing that Bob had found them somewhere to live, Sylvia felt torn. She still loved Bob, and she was glad that he had at last done what she wanted, but she had been so unhappy in America that part of her recoiled at the idea of returning.

Sylvia was a girl of strong principles, however. She had

sworn in her marriage vows that she would stand by Bob for the rest of her life, and she had promised him she would come back to America once he found them a place to live. She didn't feel she could break either of her pledges.

The next day, Sylvia went up to the Cunard shipping office in London to book her return journey. But it seemed that every man and his dog suddenly wanted to travel, and she was told there was no availability. A small part of her felt relieved that she had been given an extension to her trip. 'I'm sorry, but I can't get passage at the moment,' she wrote to Bob. 'I'll try again soon.'

Back in Baltimore, her husband was getting more and more nervous. He feared that if Sylvia stayed too long, she might change her mind.

A few weeks later, Sylvia tried again to buy a ticket at the Cunard office, but again she was turned away.

Bob was now frantic. It was nearly seven months since he had waved his wife and son goodbye in New York. In desperation, he contacted a local politician in Baltimore, mentioning that he was an ex-serviceman and begging for help in returning his wife to him. A month later, he wrote to say that he had managed to get Sylvia passage on an American ship, the SS *Washington*.

When she gave her parents the news, Sylvia could see the pain in their eyes. Once again, they dutifully went to see their daughter off as she left them for America, not knowing how many years they would be parted. 'Promise you'll write this time if things get really bad,' Mrs Bradley said.

Sylvia could see how difficult it was for her dad in particular to be parted from the grandchild he had grown to love so much. Poor Barry called out 'Granddad! Granddad!' as they set sail on the ship, looking around desperately for the man who had become like a second father to him.

The SS *Washington* was nothing like the luxurious *Queen Mary*, and when they hit stormy weather in the Irish Sea, it rocked ferociously. Sylvia was very seasick, but she had to keep going to meal sittings in order to feed Barry, no matter how queasy she felt.

Despite her sickness, Sylvia began to feel more and more hopeful the closer they got to New York. At last, she and Bob would be away from his hateful father, and free from the influence of his gambling relatives. They could finally make the proper start they should have done before.

When the ship arrived and Sylvia finally saw Bob, she felt a rush of love for him. He threw his arms around her and Barry, and they were a family once again.

'I've got something to tell you,' he said. 'The apartment we've got isn't going to be ready for a few days…'

'Okay,' Sylvia said cautiously.

'But my best man Don's moved into a new place and he says we can stay there while he's on holiday.'

They took the train back to Baltimore, and then rode out of town several miles on the bus to an area of new-build starter homes called the Elmwood Development, which had recently been constructed on former farmland.

'This is Don's place,' Bob said, taking out a key to one of the houses and ushering her inside. 'What do you think?'

Sylvia took a look around. Everything was brand, spanking new – a white L-shaped kitchen with a wall of cabinets, a washing machine and a small refrigerator, a sitting room furnished in American colonial-style furniture and a good-sized master bedroom.

'Did you see the back room?' Bob asked. He led her into a smaller room that had a child's bed in it.

'I didn't know Don and his wife had a child,' Sylvia said, confused.

'They don't. It's for Barry,' Bob said, grinning impishly from ear to ear. 'This is our house. I got a GI loan and bought it for us!'

'Bob!' Sylvia cried, throwing her arms around him.

She was overjoyed. The painful eight months of separation had all been worth it. Now she had a beautiful, fully furnished house to call her own. And best of all, it was a good six miles from Bob's parents.

26

Rae

Since she had confronted Raymond about his past infidelities, Rae had done her best to put her feelings of hurt and betrayal behind her. She had thrown the letter she had written to her family onto the fire, watching the corners of the paper curl in the flames as she tried to exorcise from her mind the awful things she had heard about her husband.

In a way, it surprised Rae how quickly things had gone back to normal, at least on the surface. Raymond would go off to work every morning, she would stay at home as before and do the ironing, and when he got home she would scrub the coal off his back like a dutiful wife. But there was a crack in the relationship that no one else could see – Rae and Raymond were no longer sleeping together.

At the weekends, Raymond was also spending less and less time with her. When he wasn't out hunting or fishing with the other men in the family, he and a friend would often drive to Steubenville, a town just over the state border in Ohio. Raymond explained that his friend was buying costume jewellery for a business he was setting up, and that he enjoyed tagging along for the ride. Rae was a little disappointed that despite repeated trips Raymond never bought any jewellery for her, but she didn't push the issue. She already felt like there was a growing distance between them and she had no intention of provoking another argument.

But one day, when she was round at her next-door neighbour Mary's house, Rae let slip how frustrated she was about her husband's repeated trips out of state.

'Did you say he goes to Steubenville?' Mary asked quietly.

'Yes,' Rae replied. 'Why?'

'Oh, nothing,' said Mary. 'Don't worry about it.'

'What's so special about Steubenville?' Rae asked her.

'Well…' Mary hesitated. 'It's got a bit of a reputation.'

'A reputation?'

'For disorderly houses,' Mary admitted awkwardly. She looked embarrassed, and rushed off to the kitchen to make coffee.

As Rae sat alone in Mary's living room, she felt a feeling of dread creep through her. It had taken such strength of will to overcome her hurt at Raymond's past infidelities. Was it possible he had gone back to cheating on her again – and worse, with prostitutes?

Rae drank her coffee in near silence, before heading back to the Wessel house. Alone in the bedroom, she struggled to decide on the best course of action. Part of her wanted to confront Raymond, but she knew if her suspicions were incorrect it would only push them further apart. There was no actual evidence that Raymond had done anything wrong – just because there were brothels in Steubenville, it didn't mean that was why he was going there. Perhaps she had grown mistrustful after all the problems they had encountered in the past, and her free time was leading to too much thinking and paranoid notions. It was better, she decided, to give him the benefit of the doubt and assume his weekends away were as innocent as he claimed.

Despite Rae's best efforts, however, the distance between her and Raymond continued to grow.

One day, Rae was walking to Finleyville when she passed a group of local boys larking about in the street. She had seen the kids before, usually playing Cowboys and Indians, oblivious to any adults who were present. This time, though, as soon as she approached, the boys ducked down behind a wall, and once she had passed she heard a peal of laughter go round the group.

Rae turned to see what the fuss was about. 'It was right here,' she heard one boy tell the others. 'He was so tall, and she was so short, he was almost on his knees!'

They all sniggered.

Rae walked up to them. 'Who are you kids talking about?'

The boy who had spoken looked down at the floor. One of his friends took a step forward and spoke to Rae. 'Your husband,' he told her, smirking.

Rae felt her blood chill. 'Was my husband here with a woman?' she asked the second boy, in as calm and measured a voice as she could muster.

'Yeah,' he replied boldly. 'He was having her right up against this wall.'

The other boys burst out laughing again.

Rae had heard enough. She turned and marched away as fast as she could. She could still hear their voices behind her, but the noise barely registered. She was already so overwhelmed with humiliation that no amount of jeering could make her feel worse.

Rae cursed herself for ever having fallen for Raymond. Why hadn't she held her ground as he had chipped away at her resistance, asking her out again and again? Why hadn't she listened to her sister Mary when she had said she didn't like him, and to her brothers, who had warned her not to date Yanks?

Now that she had discovered Raymond's true colours, Rae realised that she had been made a fool of from the moment she had arrived in Hackett. The happy-go-lucky, easy-going man she had married, the brave soldier whose safety she had worried about so much when he was off in France, had been nothing more than an illusion. Everyone else in the town had seen her husband for what he really was – even the local kids knew him better than she did.

She couldn't bear to go back to the Wessels' house after what she had heard, but who could she turn to? As she came into Finleyville, she spotted a local policeman riding on his horse. In desperation, she ran up to him. 'Can you help me?' she asked breathlessly. 'I need to get away from my husband. He's a womaniser and I can't live with him any more.' Rae could hardly believe the words were coming out of her mouth.

The policeman laughed. He probably knew exactly who her husband was, Rae realised.

'You'll need to see the squire,' he told her. 'Follow me.'

Rae walked alongside the policeman and his horse until they arrived at the address of the Justice of the Peace in Finleyville. 'Go talk to him,' the man told her. 'I'll be outside.'

Rae explained her situation to the JP, and he took a careful note of all the details. It was an uncomfortable interview for her, but after a year of putting up with her husband's outrageous behaviour she was determined to see it through.

When he had gathered all he needed, the JP scribbled something on a piece of paper and summoned the policeman inside.

'Go and pick up Mr Wessel,' he told him, handing over the paper. 'This is a warrant for his arrest.'

Rae couldn't believe what she was hearing. She had just got her own husband arrested! She waited nervously for Raymond's arrival.

An hour later, the policeman came back with Raymond in tow. As he was brought into the room, he avoided Rae's gaze.

'I'm ordering you to pay your wife $46.50 every two weeks,' the JP told him.

'Yes, sir,' Raymond said. Despite the circumstances, he almost seemed his usual laid-back self, as if what was happening didn't bother him at all. He left without giving Rae a second glance.

The JP turned to her. 'Do you have an attorney?'

She shook her head.

'You can pick up the cheques from Louis Oppenheim. He's a lawyer with an office in Monongahela. I'll write down the address. Now, do you have anywhere to stay tonight?'

'Yes,' she said. She knew her friend Mary next door wouldn't turn her away, although it was hardly ideal being so close to Raymond.

Rae went back to Hackett and knocked on Mary's door. She explained the sorry situation, and was immediately welcomed inside.

The following morning, Rae needed her clothes, so she steeled herself and went to the Wessel house. The door was open and she walked in, finding Raymond and his mother in the kitchen. He had come back from a night shift at the mine, and she was scrubbing the coal off his back, just as Rae herself had done a hundred times.

Mrs Wessel turned as Rae came in, a pained look on her face, but her son stood stock still, staring out of the window as if no one was there.

Rae looked into her mother-in-law's eyes, remembering how kindly she had welcomed her to Hackett a year before. In the time that Rae had spent in the Wessel household, she had come to feel like a member of the family. Yet all along they must have known what their son was up to, just like everyone else.

'You knew what was going on,' she said to Mrs Wessel. 'Why didn't you tell me?'

'He's my son,' Mrs Wessel replied simply.

But for Rae that wasn't good enough. 'I'm my mother's daughter,' she told her, 'and I came here all by myself.'

Mrs Wessel returned to washing her son's back, and Rae left them to it.

Since her mother-in-law had thrown out the duffel bag she had arrived with, she was forced to stuff her clothes into a couple of laundry bags, but right now she really didn't care. She just wanted to be out of the house as quickly as possible.

Living next door to her estranged husband was an uncomfortable experience for Rae. Often she would see Raymond sitting out on the porch, but he always acted as if she was a perfect stranger. Hanging her washing out in the back yard, she would catch sight of Mrs Wessel doing the same, and remember with sadness how well they had got on. As the trains trundled past at the bottom of the garden, Rae thought back to her own arrival in Hackett a year before, and realised how little she had known of what she was coming to. She longed to shout for one of the trains to stop so she could hop onboard and go back to New York.

In the rare interactions they had with each other, Raymond treated Rae with cold hostility. One day she lost her purse at a restaurant in Finleyville. There wasn't much money in it, but it contained some irreplaceable photos from England. When she made inquiries, she was told it had been returned to the Wessel residence, but when she asked Raymond, he claimed he didn't have it. 'Come on, Ray, I know you do,' she protested, but he just flashed her his laid-back grin and turned away.

Every two weeks, Rae travelled by tram to Monongahela, a small town about seven miles away, where her lawyer, Mr Oppenheim, had his office above a furniture store he also owned. A Jewish man in his early forties, his legs had been crippled by childhood polio and he walked with two sticks, but he struck Rae as an unusually upbeat man.

To begin with, Raymond kept up his maintenance payments to Rae, but one day, when she went to collect her money, there was only $29 waiting for her. The next time, there was nothing. 'Don't worry, I'll get the money off him,' Mr Oppenheim told her.

But Rae didn't like the idea of hassling Raymond for the money. She had heard of other women who took such payouts from their estranged husbands, and how the men thought they were paying for conjugal rights. 'I'll just have to find myself a job,' she told him.

'I might be able to help you with that,' he replied. 'Our housekeeper quit just last week, and my wife needs some help with the kids.'

'I'm not sure,' Rae replied. Working as a nanny was not a role she had ever seen herself in – and her previous experience as a welder hardly qualified her for it.

'I tell you what,' he said, 'we have a summer house at Deep Creek Lake in Maryland, and we're driving down there tonight for the weekend. Why don't you come along and see how you like the job?'

The offer was hard to refuse. A weekend by a lake, far away from the stares and whispers of folk in Hackett – and best of all, far from Raymond. 'All right then,' Rae replied, smiling. Mr Oppenheim told her to pack a bag and meet him outside the office later.

That evening, Rae returned just as a large red station wagon was pulling up. In the driving seat was an elegant blonde woman, and on the seat next to her was a carrycot with a baby in it, while two little boys squabbled in the back seat. Rae looked at them all nervously.

The woman got out and offered Rae her hand. 'Hello, I'm Minna,' she said warmly. 'I understand you're going to work for us.'

'Well, I didn't really say that,' Rae replied awkwardly. 'I don't know very much about housekeeping.'

Their attention was diverted by Mr Oppenheim coming out of the furniture store, walking along slowly with the help of his sticks. 'You know how to set a table, don't you?' he asked.

'Yes,' Rae replied.

He smiled. 'Well, that's the kind of thing we need.'

Rae stashed her bag in the boot of the car and got into the back seat with the boys.

'This is Jay – he's twelve,' Minna told her, gesturing to the older boy, who had jet-black hair like his father's. 'And this is

Donny, who's ten.' She gestured to the other child, whose hair was as blond as her own.

'Hi,' the two boys replied in unison.

Mr Oppenheim got in the driver's seat and reached forward for a lever that operated the accelerator on the car. It was an hour and a half's drive to Deep Creek Lake, but they stopped along the way for ice cream. It was then that Rae got a look at the baby, who had been asleep in his carrycot. 'This is Billy,' Minna said. 'He's five months old.' The most beautiful big brown eyes Rae had ever seen blinked up at her, and she fell instantly in love.

It was late by the time they arrived at the summer house, and Rae was relieved to be shown to a pleasant little room where she was to sleep.

The next morning she was able to have a proper look around. The building was a spacious converted farm house, set a little way up from the shimmering waters of the lake, surrounded by forest. Down below, Rae could see a number of boats moored, and holidaymakers splashing about in the water. The sky was a brilliant blue, not the smoggy grey she had grown used to around Pittsburgh.

Rae spent most of the weekend playing with the two older boys, but the highlight of the trip for her was helping Minna look after baby Billy. He was so adorable and good natured that it hardly felt like work at all.

The Oppenheims didn't treat her like the hired help, but as one of the family. She was told to call Mr Oppenheim 'Pap', like the rest of them, and they ate all their meals together.

By the time the weekend was over, Rae was in no doubt about her decision. 'I'd like to take the job,' she told Pap and Minna, who were thrilled.

On Monday morning they drove back early to Monongahela, and Pap got out at his office. Then Minna drove Rae back to Hackett, where she collected her things from Mary's house. When they went outside to load her bags into the station wagon, Raymond had come out of the Wessel house and was sitting on the porch. As she got into the car, he watched her go and didn't say a word.

Life with the Oppenheims was better than Rae had ever imagined. Because they didn't put on any airs, she hadn't realised quite how wealthy they were – until she saw the size of their townhouse in Monongahela. It was a huge mansion set a few streets back from the town's main road, with an enormous living room, dining room, library and kitchen. Rae had a whole suite of rooms to herself on the third floor – a bedroom, sitting room and bathroom.

Monongahela itself was a small but charming little town on the bank of a river, and felt worlds away from Hackett and Finleyville. There were shops, bars and restaurants, and even a little green with a bandstand. Rae soon found herself making new friends there, among them two young women called Rose and Myrtle who she often went out dancing with on Saturday nights.

Rae's work routine suited her well. Every day, Minna would walk down to the furniture store after lunch, leaving Rae to look after little Billy. She loved having the baby to herself for a few hours to feed, wash and cuddle. It was almost like having a child of her own.

Rae and Minna divided up the household chores between them. Minna would cook the meals, while Rae would set the table and wash the dishes. Minna would wash the clothes and Rae would iron them. Sharing the work made her feel more like a sister than a servant, and the Oppenheims were generous with her time off as well, allowing her to spend her evenings and weekends as she liked.

But Rae's life wasn't all plain sailing. Once her ex-husband had worked out where she was staying, he began phoning the Oppenheims' house with increasing regularity. Rae would always hang up as soon as she realised who it was, but the nuisance calls kept coming.

Then one night, when Pap and Minna were out for the evening and the kids had all been put to bed, Rae heard a knock at the front door. She opened it to find Raymond standing on the doorstep with tears streaming down his face. 'Please, Rae,' he wept, 'you've got to take me back.'

Rae didn't know what to do. She had never wanted to see Raymond again, but she couldn't quite bring herself to slam the door on a man who was crying. 'Come inside and we'll talk,' she told him instead.

Raymond followed her into the Oppenheims' spacious living room, and they sat opposite each other on a pair of plush armchairs. He was in such a state of abject misery that he seemed not to notice the opulent surroundings.

'Please, Rae,' he begged in between sobs. 'Don't give up on me.'

Rae heard a noise on the stairs and saw Donny poking his head between the banisters to see what was going on. 'Are you all right, Rae?' he asked her anxiously.

'I'm fine,' she told him. 'You go back to sleep.' The boy disappeared back to his room.

Rae turned to look at her husband again, bawling his eyes

out like a child and talking about how remorseful he was. If it had been anyone else in the world, Rae would have felt sorry for them, but right now she felt absolutely nothing. Her anger for Raymond had gone, but so had her pity. The realisation felt like a weight off her shoulders.

'I'm not taking you back, Raymond,' she said calmly. 'I think you ought to go now.'

Reluctantly, Raymond allowed himself to be led to the front door, and he walked out into the street without turning back. Rae closed the door and breathed a sigh of relief.

When Pap and Minna got home, Rae told them what had happened. 'You should have called me,' Pap said. 'I would have come straight home and dealt with him.'

'It's all right,' Rae replied. 'I felt safe here.'

Rae slept soundly that night, convinced that she had seen the last of her cheating husband. But early the next morning the phone rang. 'Rae, it's me,' Raymond told her. 'I'm giving you one last chance. I'm at the Greyhound station in Pittsburgh, and if you don't take me back, I'll be on the first bus to California.'

'You go right ahead,' Rae replied. 'Be my guest.'

Raymond's voice turned cold. 'Fine,' he said, 'but I want you to know something. If we're not together, you've got no right to stay in America. I'm going to have you deported.'

He hung up.

Rae was incensed. After everything she had put up with from Raymond, now he was trying to throw her out of the country. As she put down the phone, she realised her hands were trembling with rage.

27

Margaret

Margaret kissed Rosamund, Maeve and little Veronica goodbye and walked away from the Orchard Nursery. Sunday afternoon was always the hardest part of the week, leaving them in Canterbury and going back to London alone. But she had no choice – she had to work to support them, and at least they were around the corner from their great-grandmother, who visited them every day.

During the week, she travelled from her small rented room in North London to the office where she worked on Oxford Street, not far from where she had once been a secretary at the ETOUSA headquarters. Seeing her go past in her smart skirt suit, no one would imagine that the pretty young woman had already lived a whole other life in another country.

Margaret had a job as a copywriter at Lintas, the advertising arm of Unilever. She had got the position thanks to the man she was currently dating, Clifford Twelftree. He worked at the Australian High Commission, and was a kind, older man with glasses, who was separated from his wife back home.

Margaret's life had been at crisis point when she met Clifford. Having left Lawrence, she had turned up with her three daughters at the house of her father's friends the Steadhams in Holland Park, begging them to take her in. But now, thanks to her new boyfriend, she was standing on her own two feet again, even if she had to endure the pain of separation from her children.

Margaret could tell that Clifford was falling in love with her, and he had talked of divorcing his wife in Australia so that they could marry. She knew if she said yes she would be able to have her daughters back, and there would be no need to struggle any more. She wasn't in love with him, but he was reliable and she liked him. It was a relief to be with someone normal and stable after her tempestuous life with Lawrence, and she knew that not many men would be willing to take on a woman with three children.

She would be sorry to give up her job when they married, however. For the first time in her life she felt she had found an occupation that she enjoyed and that used her intelligence. She was one of a group of five female copywriters at Lintas, working on campaigns for Unilever's many products, from Pears soap to Birds Eye frozen peas.

One day, the copywriters were taken on a tour of the old Pears factory in Isleworth, West London, to get an insight into the product. They were taken into office after office, and introduced to various managers who all talked at length about soap. Margaret was beginning to lose interest, but as they walked into one office, a young man caught her attention. He was in his late twenties and good-looking, with dark hair and grey eyes. As he looked at her, Margaret felt as if an electrical charge passed between them. Then their little group was led out of the room and off to yet another part of the building.

When she got back to Oxford Street, she found the only thing she could remember about the trip was the face of the young man who had made such a strong impression on her.

There was no point thinking about him, however – that evening she was due to see Clifford for a date at Queens Ice Skating Club near Notting Hill.

As Margaret glided confidently onto the ice, Clifford struggled to keep up with her and she realised she had lost him in the crowd.

Then she felt a tap on her shoulder. 'Hello, again,' said an unfamiliar voice. She turned to see the young man from Isleworth. Margaret felt a rush of excitement at the sight of him, a sensation she had not experienced for a very long time.

The young man began to skate alongside her, and as they went around the rink, they laughed about the dreary tour Margaret had endured at Pears. 'I bet you never knew that anyone could get so excited about soap,' he said.

'No, I didn't,' she replied. 'But now my job is to get everyone in Britain just as excited as they are!'

Margaret learned that the young man was a management trainee at Unilever, and that his name was Patrick Denby. They hadn't been talking long before she spotted Clifford slowly skating along and felt a pang of guilt. 'I'm terribly sorry, but I've got to go,' she told Patrick. 'It was nice meeting you properly.'

The young man watched as she skated off and took Clifford's arm.

The next day at work, Margaret was at her desk staring blankly at pictures of Pears soap when her phone rang. 'Hello Margaret, it's Patrick Denby here. I just wanted to make sure you got home all right last night.'

Margaret couldn't help giving a little laugh. Patrick knew perfectly well that she had been out with another man, and that it wasn't *his* job to make sure she got home safely.

'Yes, I did, thank you,' she replied.

They began to chat, but before long Margaret spotted her manager looking over at her, so she told Patrick she had to go.

'Well, I hope to see you on the ice sometime,' he said.

As a management trainee, however, Patrick often had to visit the Oxford Street office, and the following week, Margaret looked up to find him standing at her desk. 'I'm afraid I can't take you ice-skating during the working day, but how about lunch?' he asked her.

It was an open-plan office, and she could see the other copy-writing girls watching them, smiling. 'Yes, that would be nice,' she said quickly, following him out.

They went to a little café on Oxford Street, and as they sat down opposite each other, Margaret once again felt an overwhelming attraction to Patrick.

Over lunch, he told her how he had been recruited from Oxford University during the war to work as an interpreter of intercepted German and Italian communications. He had been second onboard the Italian flagship *Caio Duilio* when Italy's Navy surrendered, translating the terms of disarmament to Admiral Da Zara.

'We didn't have much warning that the Italian fleet was coming across, and we went out to meet them in a little tug boat,' he laughed. 'We felt pretty insignificant sailing under the battleship's big guns!'

The more Patrick spoke, the more Margaret's attraction to him grew. He was clever and interesting, with a cheeky sense of humour. He had a quiet confidence, and unlike Lawrence he wasn't showy.

But as she cut her food, Margaret was painfully aware of the wedding ring in full view on her finger. She and Lawrence were still legally married, even though he was back in Georgia and hadn't made any attempt to contact her again.

She didn't want to put Patrick off by mentioning her marriage, but nor did she want him to think she was still with her husband and was considering having an affair. She decided it was best to be honest, and explained that they were separated. Even if Patrick hadn't noticed her ring at the ice rink, he must have seen it by now, she reasoned, so there was no point in hiding the truth.

Patrick seemed to take the information in his stride, but when Margaret went back to work she couldn't help feeling despondent. As soon as he found out that she was not only separated but had three children, she felt sure that he would run a mile. Clifford was her only hope of a future now. She would have to put Patrick out of her mind.

A few days later, however, Patrick asked her out to lunch again, and Margaret felt unable to resist. This time they stayed out far longer than their one-hour lunch break, and she could tell he found it as hard to tear himself away as she did. By the end of the date they were holding hands, and Margaret felt like a schoolgirl again, more excited just to feel her hand in his than she had felt in her whole relationship with Clifford. She knew that she was falling in love with him.

Margaret realised it was no longer fair to carry on seeing her Australian boyfriend, and that evening she told Clifford it was over. She knew she was giving up a man who could offer her the security she and her children so desperately needed, but her feelings for him paled in comparison with those she had for Patrick.

It had been only two weeks since that first moment when they had met each other's gaze in Isleworth, but she thought about Patrick constantly. One day, she was daydreaming about him as she got onto the Tube at Oxford Circus when suddenly he happened to jump into the same carriage. Margaret immediately felt self-conscious, and he looked equally flustered.

They both said hello at the same time, and laughed at their clumsiness. Then his expression became very serious. 'Margaret,' he said, 'I've been thinking about you all the time since we last saw each other. I've never met a woman as beautiful or as lovely as you are.' He grabbed her hand. 'Will you marry me?'

'Oh!' Margaret exclaimed. The other commuters did their best to keep their noses in their newspapers.

'Say you will,' Patrick urged.

Margaret felt like screaming 'Yes!' with all her heart, but she knew that what she was about to say would ruin any hope of them having a future together.

'Patrick, I need to tell you something,' she said quietly. 'I'm not just married – I've already got three children.'

'That doesn't change how I feel about you,' he insisted. 'If I have to adopt them, I will. Just say that you'll be my wife.'

She had only known him for a fortnight, but Margaret had no hesitation in telling him: 'I will.'

Margaret was anxious to get a divorce, but she had no idea how Lawrence would react. She wrote to her sister-in-law Ellen, who told her he was now in Panama City, Florida, working as a journalist. 'Don't worry,' Ellen wrote. 'I have a friend in Blakely who's a lawyer. I'll see to it that Lawrence divorces you.'

Meanwhile, Margaret introduced Patrick to her three daughters, Rosamund, Maeve and Veronica. It was important to her that they liked him, so she began bringing him with her on her weekly trips to the nursery in Canterbury. Although the girls were wary at first, they slowly began to trust him. Around them Patrick's playful side came out more than ever, and Margaret could see they loved having him around.

But Patrick's own family were less easy to please. His parents had been horrified to find out that their only son was planning on marrying a divorcee and adopting her three children. His father, a Yorkshire solicitor, wrote him a long letter setting out the financial burden he would be taking on, having added up exactly how much it would cost to educate the three girls over the next two decades.

Patrick was furious. 'I'm a grown man,' he exclaimed. 'I've been independent of them for years. How dare they tell me what to do with my life?'

'I can see it from their point of view,' sighed Margaret. 'I hardly look like a good prospect!'

'Well, they're wrong,' he told her. 'And we'll prove it to them.'

When Patrick's parents got a wedding invitation in the post, they agreed to attend, but informed him they would be changing their wills to ensure that any children he adopted would not inherit their money.

But there was nothing they could do to ruin his and Margaret's big day. The wedding took place at St John's in Kensington, and this time Margaret's father was there to walk her down the aisle. As Patrick turned to see his bride, dressed in a smart dark-red suit and holding a bunch of tulips, they both felt the same charge pass between them as they had on that first day at Pears when they had fallen in love at first sight.

Once they were married, they moved to Putney, and Margaret was at last able to bring her three children back to live with her. Finally, they had the proper family life that they had been lacking for so long.

When they had settled in, Margaret asked the girls, 'What would you like to call Patrick? You could carry on calling him by his name, or you could call him Daddy if you like.'

'We would like to think about it first,' said Maeve, the most precocious of the three. The little girls huddled together in the corner, holding a whispered conference. Then they pushed Veronica, the youngest, forward to announce their decision.

'We have decided to call him Daddy,' she said.

When Patrick came home from work that evening, he was delighted to be greeted by his new name.

Margaret thought their happiness was complete, but one day her husband came into the kitchen with some news. 'How would you like to live in Geneva?' he asked her.

He showed her a letter from a friend he had been billeted with during the war, who was now working for the International Labour Organization, a part of the UN promoting workers' rights. He had offered Patrick a job that was not only more interesting than his current role at Unilever, but that paid more money too.

Margaret knew it would also be a chance to start afresh, in a place where no one would know that their family was any different to anyone else's. 'Yes, please!' she said.

A few weeks later, the whole family were boarding a flight to Switzerland. Once again, Margaret was leaving England for a new life in a foreign land – but she had no fears for the future. This time, she knew she had married the right man.

28

Gwendolyn

The pain was almost unbearable, a searing, ripping sensation that passed repeatedly through Lyn's legs and lower back, leaving them feeling like dead weights after every ferocious pulse. Unfortunately painkillers were forbidden on the isolation ward, where suspected polio cases were kept so as not to risk further contagion. A hit of morphine could depress a patient's breathing, putting them at risk of suffocation.

A young doctor arrived on the ward, decked out in a white surgical gown and face mask. 'I've come to do your spinal tap,' he informed her.

The words sent a shudder of fear through Lyn, and she wished that Ben could be there with her, instead of waiting outside in the corridor. As the doctor rolled her onto her side and wiped her back with iodine, she said, 'I'm a bit scared. Do you think I could hold your hand?'

'No, I'm afraid I need them both,' the doctor replied, readying a needle.

A nurse standing by his side stepped forward. 'You can hold mine instead if you like,' she offered.

'No offence, but it isn't quite the same,' Lyn said, with a weak laugh.

Suddenly, she felt a cold, sharp pain, as the doctor slid the needle in between her vertebrae. 'This one's just the local anaesthetic,' he told her.

The second, bigger needle was much worse, and Lyn felt like a stake was being driven into her spine. 'Just keep breathing,' the doctor told her. 'Not too deep, but constant.' She tried to focus on her shallow breaths and ignore the horrific digging and scraping going on inside her back as the doctor tried to extract the spinal fluid. The procedure only lasted about ten minutes, but to Lyn it felt like hours.

The next time she saw the young doctor, he confirmed the diagnosis of polio. 'I'm afraid it's as we thought,' he told her. 'Now we just have to wait and see how severe your case is.'

Even the word polio was enough to strike fear into anyone living in America at a time when there was at least one major outbreak every summer, sometimes claiming thousands of lives. And assuming she survived the illness, Lyn wondered what kind of life she would have. She might spend the rest of her days confined to a wheelchair, or hobbling along with misshapen limbs – or worse, stuck in an iron lung forever. It was hard to believe that just a few days before she had been perfectly healthy, yet now she had no idea if she would ever walk again.

The doctor went out into the corridor to inform Ben of her diagnosis. Ben put on a brave face, but at his parents' house afterwards he cried like a baby. What had his poor Lyn done to deserve this?

At the hospital, there was little the doctors and nurses could do beyond making Lyn as comfortable as possible as her fever increased and the pain grew even worse. She spent much of the next few days unconscious, as bit by bit the disease crept up her body, burning out her neurons as it went.

In her wakeful periods, Lyn lay staring up at the ceiling in terror, wondering if she would ever leave the bed she was in. As she felt the burning sensation shoot up her legs and into her back, she was haunted by an ominous shadow cast upon the wall of the ward. It was the outline of the iron lung, a terrifying metal coffin, which could well become her only means of breathing if the polio got as far as her chest.

In isolation, the only real distraction from the pain – and the delirious fever that accompanied it – came with the arrival twice a day of the hot-pack machine, an aluminium spin-washer that contained steaming woollen bandages, which a nurse would drape over Lyn's legs. Many patients found the wool treatment unbearable – they hated the scalding heat of the packs and the clammy coldness that followed – but for Lyn the distraction they provided was blissful.

At first, Ben was not allowed to visit Lyn in isolation. He stood anxiously outside the room day after day, looking in through a tiny little window. On one visit he brought young John with him to show the boy that his mother was all right. John was too little to see into the ward, so someone found a stepladder for him to stand on, and he clambered up it and nervously peered through the window. 'Look, there's Mommy,' Ben told him, pointing towards Lyn, who turned her head towards the window and smiled.

But John was traumatised by the sight of his mother laid out on a hospital bed, surrounded by mysterious machines and strange figures dressed head to toe in white with only their eyes showing. 'I want to go home,' he wailed, so Ben picked him up and hurried him away.

Lyn's doctor came to see her afterwards. 'I think it's best the boy doesn't visit you here,' he told her.

'If you say so, doctor,' she replied, doing her best to hide how heartbroken she felt.

After a while, the doctors and nurses agreed to let Ben onto the ward with her. After all, if Lyn had been contagious he would probably have caught the disease already – and in a country where polio outbreaks were frequent, the chances were that Ben had developed an immunity in childhood without ever showing any symptoms. Nonetheless, he was forced to wear the regulation white gown and mask on his daily visits.

As Lyn's fever and the worst of the pain subsided, to be replaced by a dull, insistent ache, the damage done by the polio began to become clear. 'Well, it could be a lot worse,' the doctor told her. 'The paralysis hasn't reached your lungs, and your arms are strong. We're going to transfer you to a convalescent ward, and there we can work on improving your condition with physiotherapy.'

'Will I be able to walk again?' Lyn asked him. It was the question that had been plaguing her ever since she had arrived at the hospital and she was terrified of what he might say.

'I can't tell you that right now, I'm afraid,' the doctor replied. Then, seeing the devastated look on Lyn's face, he tried to offer her a little more hope. 'I've seen plenty of people in your condition get back on their feet and walk again eventually,' he told her, 'whether that's with braces or throwing one foot out ahead of the other.'

Despite the doctor's good intentions, every word he had said made Lyn feel worse. She didn't want to be a cripple, hobbling along with mismatched legs. She just wanted to go back to how she was before.

The year's polio epidemic had been the worst ever in California, and over 3,000 people had died. In many respects, Lyn was lucky – but right now she certainly didn't feel it.

When Lyn had first arrived in hospital, she had imagined she might be there for a few days or weeks, but on the convalescent ward she began to realise she was in for the long haul. She soon settled into a routine. First there were more hot-wool treatments, which her physiotherapist explained would stop her muscles from contracting. 'It's to prevent the limbs from deforming,' he told her, 'as one muscle tries to take over from another that's been damaged. If this muscle pulls too tight, the other one will end up like the strings on a tennis racket.'

After each application of the boiling-hot bandages, Lyn's limbs would be forcibly stretched by a nurse, a process that was agonising to begin with. Then they began asking her to do some of the stretching herself, which Lyn found exhausting and demoralising. Making tiny improvements day by day, it was hard to imagine that she would ever have the strength to walk again, and Lyn spent many tormented hours wondering how far her recovery would take her.

At least on the convalescent ward Ben was allowed to visit without having to wear a mask. But it was a source of constant sorrow to Lyn that he couldn't bring John with him. She missed her son more every day, and felt desperate to get out of the hospital and back home to him.

As well as Ben, Lyn had regular visits from Auntie Louise, who as a polio survivor herself knew more than anyone else in the family what she was going through. 'You'll be all right in the end,' she told Lyn. 'I know it's hard work, but bit by bit you can make a big difference.'

It was good to have Auntie Louise's support, but Lyn still found the progress unbearably slow, and the motivational posters plastered all over the ward by the physiotherapists – Aesop's tortoise beating the hare in the race, along with insightful quotations about the rewards of hard work – did little to help boost her spirits.

At least with some help from the nurses Lyn was able to sit up in bed, which meant that she could read and write to keep her mind occupied. There was a task she had been putting off for some time that she knew she had to face – writing to let her parents know what had happened. After much delay and procrastination, Lyn finally put pen to paper. She told her mum and dad not to worry, that she was being well looked after, and that with enough physio she hoped one day to walk again. She waited anxiously to see how they would respond.

The letter she got back from Southampton made her feel worse than ever. Mrs Rowe was devastated to hear what her daughter had been through, so many miles away from home. 'You broke my heart, Gwen,' she wrote.

Lyn felt awful – all through her time in the cabin in the mountains, and through her struggles with Ben's mother, she had never told her parents how hard she was finding life in America. Now that she had finally risked it, all she felt was guilt.

But the worst part of the letter was an off-hand remark. 'I'm sure you'll be up and walking again soon,' Lyn's mother told her, 'but I hope you don't have to wear those ugly iron braces.' Lyn wept as she read those words – right now, she would have given anything to be walking with the ugliest braces in the world. For months she had been unable to move from her bed.

While Lyn's mother was 6,000 miles away, wishing she could afford to fly over and see her beloved daughter, Mrs Patrino, who lived hardly any distance away, never came to visit her. But back at home, she was making her own adjustments to the new situation.

One day, Ben came in to see Lyn with an anxious, hangdog look on his face. 'Hi, honey,' he said. 'How are you feeling?'

'Terrible,' Lyn replied honestly. 'How are things in the real world?'

'Well,' Ben replied cautiously, 'actually, I have something to tell you. John and I have moved back to my parents' house for a while. We've given up the rent on the apartment.'

Lyn was used to feeling numb in her lower body, but now her whole spirit felt paralysed. Ben's mother had got him back, and the home that she loved so much was gone.

Perhaps sensing that her spirits were low, her physiotherapist decided Lyn needed a motivational boost. 'There's someone I want you to meet,' he told her, as he wheeled her in a chair through to another part of the ward. There, to Lyn's horror, a woman lay encased in an iron lung. 'She's been here eight years,' the physiotherapist told Lyn. 'So you see, you could be a lot worse off.'

The poor woman told Lyn about the battle she was fighting with the city to be allowed home with a nurse and a special bed. 'I'm not sure how much longer I can bear it in here,' she said. And hers wasn't even the worst polio story in the hospital – one man on the ward had been in an iron lung for almost a decade. 'I keep asking the nurses to help me end it all, but they won't,' he told Lyn pathetically.

Despite the physiotherapist's intentions, the sight of these people living through her own worst nightmare only made Lyn feel even worse. Her doctor was furious when he found out about the excursion. 'What were you thinking?' he asked the physiotherapist.

His own belief was that the carrot was more effective than the stick. 'I'm going to make you an offer,' he told Lyn one day. 'If you can get to the point where you can sit up in bed without assistance, I'll let you get out of here for Thanksgiving. We can get a nurse to look after you at home.'

'Thank you!' she replied. 'I'll try my best.'

The doctor's offer had the desired effect. With a clear goal ahead of her, Lyn pushed herself like never before, strengthening her muscles day by day with excruciating and exhausting exercises. Sometimes it was a case of reawakening muscles that the polio had all but destroyed, and sometimes it meant learning to use new muscles to take over their functions. She had just one thought in mind: getting home in time for Thanksgiving dinner with her husband and son, even if it was at Mrs Patrino's.

On his daily visits, Ben offered plenty of encouragement. 'John is really looking forward to seeing you after all this time,' he told her.

Bit by bit, Lyn continued to make progress, until one day, when the doctor arrived on his rounds, she was able to prove how far she had come. With tremendous effort, she raised herself up from her back and heaved her way to a seated position.

'Well done, Lyn, you did it!' the doctor beamed, as she sat there breathing heavily. She had never in her life imagined that she would feel so proud of such a seemingly minor accomplishment.

When Ben arrived, she shared the good news with him. 'That's wonderful, honey!' he said. 'But I'm afraid I have something to tell you.'

'What is it?' Lyn asked.

'I've been talking to Mom,' Ben continued. 'Of course, she's as pleased about you getting better as the rest of us, but...' He broke off for a moment and sat looking at the floor. 'She doesn't think you should come back and stay in the house. She says Pop will find the wheelchair upsetting.'

Lyn was staggered. 'You know that means I'll be stuck in here for months?' she said desperately.

Ben was clearly upset by the situation himself. 'I tried talking to her,' he said, 'but she wouldn't budge. I don't know what else to do, honey.'

When Ben had gone, Lyn wept. She was powerless to fight his mother now. She couldn't even get out of bed.

The next day, Ben's Auntie Louise came to visit Lyn in the hospital. 'I heard about what my sister said,' she told her, 'and I want you to know that I'm here for you.'

'Thank you,' Lyn replied. Louise had always been good to her, even before she had been ill.

'I didn't get much help myself when I had polio,' Louise told Lyn, 'and I want things to be different for you. If they're willing to discharge you, you can come and stay with me and Sid.'

Lyn felt overwhelmed by Louise's kindness. 'That's so sweet of you, but I couldn't do that to you,' she replied. 'I'm going to need a hospital bed and a nurse and all kinds of things.'

But Louise wouldn't take no for an answer. 'You're moving in with me, kid,' she said.

As Auntie Louise wheeled her out of the hospital, Lyn was transfixed by her surroundings. The trees, which had been fresh with blossom when she had arrived in July, were now bare, and the crisp smell of autumn filled the air. After four months in an air-conditioned ward full of clinical smells, it felt like breathing in life itself again.

Louise helped Lyn into her car and put the wheelchair in the boot. 'We'll be having some visitors tonight,' she told her, as they drove to her house. Lyn felt overwhelmed by all the cars whizzing by, and the noises of the city as they drove through it. 'Okay,' she murmured.

Thankfully it was no great gathering of the Patrino clan, just Ben and John, who were already there to greet Lyn when she arrived. 'Oh, honey, it's so good to see you,' Ben told her, rushing over to help her out of the car and into the wheelchair. He pushed her up to where little John was standing with Uncle Sid in the front drive, nervously hanging back. 'Aren't you excited to see your mommy?' he asked the boy.

John nodded obediently, but there was something a little hesitant about him as he approached the wheelchair and awkwardly hugged Lyn's legs.

He's scared of me, she realised with a jolt of sadness.

'Don't worry,' Ben whispered. 'He'll soon get used to the chair.' He wheeled Lyn up the drive and into the house, where her private nurse was waiting.

That night, Lyn's family ate their first meal together in what seemed like a lifetime. But when the time came for Ben and John to leave, Lyn felt so sad she could barely say goodbye. 'Don't worry, honey,' Ben told her. 'As soon as you can wheel the chair yourself, we'll find a ground-floor apartment and we can all be together again.'

Now Lyn had another goal ahead of her, and once again she approached the challenge with relish. Day by day, working hard on her physical therapy with the help of her nurse, she continued to improve, until she was able to get from the bed into the chair with only minimal assistance.

Living with Auntie Louise and Uncle Sid, Lyn was able to see Ben and John every day now, but every time they left to go home to Mrs Patrino she felt another pang of frustrated jealousy. To make matters worse, John remained very nervous around the wheelchair, something Lyn found extremely upsetting.

'I can't bear it,' she told her doctor when he came to visit for a check-up. 'My own son is scared of me now.'

'Lyn, that's perfectly normal,' he replied. 'It's not you, it's just the chair.'

'You don't understand,' Lyn protested. 'Do you realise how much it hurts me?'

'Come on Lyn, he's a child,' the doctor insisted.

It was true, she realised. What could she expect of John, after being without his mother for so long, and at such a young age? Suddenly, her sadness was replaced by a feeling of guilt.

Living at Auntie Louise's, there were no set visiting hours, and Lyn found more people coming to see her. Mrs Patrino continued to stay away, but Ben's sister-in-law Thelma began to turn up regularly, and Lyn even had a couple of visitors from the University of Santa Clara. Among them was Mr Stefan, the manager who had hired her. He had already written to Lyn in hospital offering his best wishes for her recovery, and letting her know that they had found someone to cover for her while she was off sick. 'So, how's the new girl working out?' Lyn asked him when he came to see her a few months later.

'Oh, she's great,' he replied without thinking. 'We've just signed her on for a year.'

Lyn was devastated. 'Does that mean I'm not coming back?'

'Lyn, be realistic,' Mr Stefan replied.

They were the most crushing words that anyone could have said to her. Lyn was terrified that she might never get out of the wheelchair – her physiotherapist was constantly encouraging her to keep going, but knowing that others had already decided her efforts were pointless, she struggled to find the will to continue.

Nevertheless, bit by bit Lyn continued to improve, until she had mastered the use of the chair by herself, and could even manage to get into and out of it from her bed. If she ever fell over she would be stuck on the floor until someone came to rescue her, but aside from that she was pretty much mobile.

It had been almost a year since Lyn first moved in with Auntie Louise, and when her physiotherapist told her, 'I think it's time you and your husband started looking for a place of your own,' she was over the moon. She might still be confined to a wheel-chair – with no guarantee from her doctor that this would ever change – but soon her little family would be together at last.

Before long, Ben found them a nice ground-floor apartment in a quiet part of town. Finally, Lyn and Ben felt like a real couple again, and despite the wheelchair they were able to lead a relatively normal life.

The next challenge for Lyn was to learn to walk using leg braces. The heavy steel encumbrances were intended to keep her legs straight, and had a catch that allowed them to bend at the knee so that she could sit down in them, and then lock when she stood up again. The mechanism took a lot of getting used to, and at first Lyn found it would often lock or unlock unexpectedly.

Clomping around in the braces was exhausting, and nothing like the easy movement she had been used to before the polio, but for Lyn the newfound freedom was exhilarating. She no longer had to look up at other people the whole time. Best of all, she no longer felt trapped – her greatest fear, that she would never leave the wheelchair, was behind her.

Once again, however, Lyn found that her disability was distressing to her son John, who disliked the braces even more than he had the wheelchair. Lyn explained patiently that they were to help her walk. 'I'll get rid of them as soon as I can,' she promised him.

With the help of the braces, Lyn was able to regain her independence. She was gradually getting used to the awkward contraptions as the muscles in her legs began to grow stronger, and she even began to go out on her own. One day, she decided to go into San Francisco, to visit Macy's in Union Square. It was a beautiful day, and as Lyn walked slowly up to the store's grand marbled frontage, she felt a sense of pride and accomplishment. It wasn't so long ago that she had been confined to a bed in the county hospital, staring up at the ceiling for hours on end, afraid that she would never walk again.

Inside the store, Lyn passed through the jewellery and

cosmetics departments and took the elevator up to womens-wear. She picked out a beautiful cashmere cardigan in bright pink, just the sort of thing the old Lyn would have bought.

'That's a pretty colour,' the girl at the cash desk told her. 'It'll look nice with your complexion'.

It felt good to be noticed for something other than her braces, Lyn realised. She thought of Auntie Louise, always so impeccably turned out despite her own limp, and decided that she would always follow her example. She spent a good while wandering around every inch of the department, although her legs were already getting tired, and picked up several more garments before she decided to head home.

Since the elevator was at the far end of the department, Lyn decided to take the escalator down to the ground floor instead. She gripped the rail carefully with her right hand as she stepped onto the moving staircase. Then she heard a sudden click. The noise sent a jolt of panic through her as she realised her braces had locked. Lyn tried to jiggle her leg to release the catch but it was no use – the knee stubbornly refused to bend. She didn't dare take her right hand off the rail in case she fell over, so she tried to use her left to disengage the catch, but as much as she fiddled the damn thing refused to budge.

The staircase was moving quickly and Lyn could see the ground getting closer. In a few seconds she would be there. She could see herself now, being thrown onto the ground, or caught up in the machinery of the escalator. Her heart raced as she continued to fumble wildly with the catch.

At the last moment, as the escalator reached ground level, Lyn heard a second click and felt the catch release, allowing her leg to bend slightly. She pushed herself forward with all her strength and then took a moment to regain her balance, her heart still racing. All the confidence she had felt before seemed to have drained out of her, and she felt powerless and scared again.

'Hey, lady, what's the matter?' a security guard demanded, rushing over.

'My brace locked,' Lyn replied breathlessly.

'Your what?'

She gestured to the catch. 'The brace locked on my leg.'

'Well, stay off the escalator then,' the man replied brusquely, before turning and walking away.

Lyn staggered to a nearby bench and lowered herself onto it, taking care to ensure the catch on her brace was properly released this time. She was still panting and she felt almost dizzy with the stress of the ordeal. It was yet another reminder of how far she still had to go on the road to recovery.

Lyn had always done her best to stay strong in the face of adversity, but right now, knocked by yet another setback, a new feeling suddenly overwhelmed her. For the first time since she had come to America, she felt an intense pang of homesickness. All she wanted was to go home and see her mum.

29

Sylvia

Sylvia woke suddenly in the dead of night. Lying next to her, Bob was yelling incoherently, sweat dripping from his brow. 'Get down!' he screamed, convulsing frantically and tangling himself up in the bed sheets.

'Bob, it's all right,' Sylvia whispered soothingly. She cautiously reached a hand out to stroke his brow.

He started awake and stared at her with a horror-struck look on his face.

'It's all right,' she repeated. 'You're safe here.'

He nodded, and drew a deep breath. 'I thought I was back in France,' he said.

She stroked his forehead again. 'I know,' she said softly. 'You can go back to sleep now.'

Bob had never spoken to Sylvia about his experiences in Europe during the war. When she had first met him at the Red Cross club in London, he had already returned from the front lines for the last time. She knew that he had been at the Battle of the Bulge, and in a prelude to the Battle of Remagen, which was when he had been wounded in the shoulder and received the Purple Heart, but those were all the details he was willing to give. Years of carrying heavy mailbags were beginning to take their toll on his bad shoulder, but despite the pain and the occasional nightmares, the cause of his injury was still clearly off-limits.

Aside from Bob's occasional nightmares, though, Sylvia's life was a happy one. She was living in a dream home, with a husband who loved her and a child they both adored – and the distance between them and Bob's gambling-obsessed family was proving to be a godsend.

Sylvia could not have been more pleased with their new house. Their neighbours were mostly young couples like themselves who had also bought starter homes, so it was the perfect place to raise a family. Looking back on it, Sylvia couldn't quite believe that she had been brave enough to sail back to England, leaving Bob with the ultimatum to find them a house or never see her again. But clearly her own gamble had paid off.

Sylvia had already begun putting her stamp on the place, repainting the bathroom, changing the curtains and adding splashes of colour to the neutral living room with some bright cushions. Meanwhile, she had brought a number of trinkets back from her visit to England, and these were soon dotted around the mantelpiece and window sills. Every so often a parcel would arrive containing another ornament, posted to her by her mother.

With Bob out at work during the day, Sylvia devoted much of her time to housework. She was also working her way through an English cookbook her mother had given her, trying to perfect her culinary skills. Before long, she was serving roast dinner every Sunday, and at Bob's request she soon mastered some American dishes as well. When he arrived back from his mail route in the afternoon, Sylvia would have a jug of iced tea waiting for him. It was an idyllic life for the whole family.

Then one day, Bob returned home with some unexpected news. 'I've just been talking to my dad at work,' he told Sylvia, 'and apparently they're thinking of moving. A coloured family just moved in two blocks away and Dad says the neighbourhood's going to the dogs.'

'Right.' Sylvia had better things to do than get involved in an argument about Bob's father's racist views.

'They're thinking of buying somewhere up this way,' he told her.

Sylvia was silent for a moment as the news sunk in. She couldn't believe it. It had taken her two years of badgering, and an eight-month trip to England, to get Bob away from his family and their gambling. Now the in-laws had decided to follow them.

Once Bob's family moved in nearby, the gambling resumed with a vengeance. There were late-night poker sessions every weekend, and more flutters on the horses than ever before. At least Bob was only betting within limits, thought Sylvia – and there was no more secret raiding of their savings tin. He paid her regular housekeeping money, and it was enough for a family of three to live on fairly comfortably.

But with Bob spending more and more time with his family, Sylvia started to feel lonely. Fortunately, she soon found an opportunity to socialise, thanks to an organisation called the Transatlantic Brides and Parents Association. The TBPA had originally been set up in England by the father of a GI bride who wanted to negotiate group charter rates with airlines so that he and others like him could come and visit their daughters in America. It had rapidly expanded into a social network for GI brides living in the United States.

Sylvia's local TBPA group called themselves The Bluebell Branch, while others were known by such names as The Tea Bags and The Crumpet Club. It comprised two women called Vera, two Phyllises, and Rose, Florence and Ethne. The women soon bonded over their shared frustrations at everyday life in America: being misunderstood by the locals, how much they missed fish and chips and Yorkshire pudding, and, most important of all, the trouble they had getting hold of a decent cup of tea. The meetings would always end with a sing-along: 'We'll Meet Again', 'The White Cliffs of Dover' and 'There'll Always Be an England'.

Before long, Sylvia felt she had known the other girls her entire life. She no longer felt alone in America – being part of a GI-bride sisterhood, she felt like she had family to support her.

The more she got to know the other women, the more Sylvia realised that she wasn't the only one with problems stemming from her marriage. One of the Veras had already divorced her husband by the time she joined the club, while Ethne's husband was a very domineering man. As a captain in the Army he had been used to ordering people about, and he did the same with his wife as well. 'She practically has to ask him if she can blink her eyes,' one of the other brides commented.

Well aware that Ethne's marriage could not be a happy one, the girls did their best to intervene. 'Why don't you leave him?' they asked her. 'You don't have to put up with the way he treats you.'

But Ethne looked them straight in the eyes and replied very calmly, 'We got through the war. We're British, we can stand anything.'

Before long, her words – often repeated – had become the unofficial motto of the group. Whenever one of the girls shared a story of misfortune, the other women would chorus, 'We're British, we can stand anything.'

Those simple words brought great solace and support to a group of women building lives far from family and home.

The Bluebells weren't the only Brits in Baltimore with whom Sylvia had grown friendly. Through another organisation, the Daughters of the British Empire, she had encountered an older couple called Bill and Dot Langston. Bill was a painter and decorator from the East End of London – 'He's a proper cockney,' Sylvia had told Bob excitedly – and his house on Harvard Road boasted a magnificent English-style garden.

When Bob wasn't out playing cards with his family, he and Sylvia would often visit the Langstons, whose door was always open to them. They cooked traditional English food, including sausage rolls and Banbury tarts, and after dinner there would always be some old East End games, such as pass the orange. Bob did his best to join in, but the games didn't mean anything to him – they evoked no nostalgic memories as they did for Sylvia. In any case, she thought ruefully, the only games he truly loved were those you could bet on.

The years rolled on, and Bob and Sylvia's little family grew larger. First, she gave birth to a daughter, Victoria, and then two more sons, Brad and Rodger. As the number of mouths to feed increased, Sylvia began to struggle on the housekeeping money she got from Bob.

'Are you sure you can't give me a little more?' she asked him.

'I'm sorry, honey,' he replied. 'Mail carriers just don't get paid that well.'

Sylvia accepted Bob's answer and determined to tighten her belt another notch or two. He had never told her how much he earned, and she hadn't pressed him.

Then one day, Bob came home and announced that he was being transferred to a different district.

'Does that mean more money?' Sylvia asked hopefully.

'No,' he replied. 'Just a new patch.'

The new patch meant new colleagues, in particular a man called Bernie, who stood next to Bob filing the mail at the sorting office, and with whom he struck up a firm friendship. Bernie soon invited Bob out to play golf with him.

'You could come along too,' Bob suggested to Sylvia, but she decided to give it a miss.

When Bob came home to announce that he had won some money on the golf game, Sylvia was a little surprised. Was it normal to bet on golf? she wondered. But with four kids to feed, she wasn't about to look a gift horse in the mouth.

Unfortunately, the odd flutter on a round of the green was the least of Bernie's betting activities. Soon Bob was playing cards with him every lunchtime, and losing badly.

When Bob announced that he and Bernie were taking a vacation in Las Vegas, Sylvia tried to reason with him. 'You know, love, Bernie only has a wife to take care of,' she told him, 'but you've got four children as well. We can't afford to bet the kind of money he can.'

'Don't worry, honey,' Bob told her with a kiss. 'I know what I'm doing.'

Bob set off for Las Vegas convinced that he could beat the casino, but when he returned home a few days later he was several hundred dollars worse off.

'I just don't know what to do with him,' Sylvia told her friends at the Bluebell Branch. 'He's always so convinced that he's going to win.' She thought back to the plane ticket Bob had sent her to fly over to America, which he had paid for with his winnings from a craps game. That time luck had been on his side, but he didn't seem to realise how rare that was.

'You'll be all right, Sylvia,' the other girls told her. 'Just remember, we're British, we can stand anything.'

As time went on, though, Bob's gambling became more and more of a problem. Under Bernie's influence it was turning into more than just an occasional habit – it was compulsive. 'Sometimes I think he'd bet on a drop of water coming down the window,' Sylvia joked to her friend Dot Langston.

As Bob's gambling increased, Sylvia noticed it was affecting his personality too. On the rare occasions that he won he was on top of the world, as charming and full of life as when she had first met him, but when he lost he was sullen and low-spirited.

One day, when Bob came home from work in a particularly miserable sulk, Sylvia said, 'Don't you see what this gambling is doing to you, Bob? It's poisoning your happiness.'

But Bob just went upstairs, giving no acknowledgement that she had spoken.

Sylvia felt on the verge of tears. She wanted so badly to get through to him, but it was as if a glass wall had gone up between them. The only person Bob let into his life now was Bernie.

Sylvia decided that a change of scene might be good for Bob, so she persuaded him to take the family away for the weekend, renting a little apartment on the coast. But while Sylvia played in the surf with their four children, Bob refused to budge from his armchair. He was too absorbed in the latest horse-racing almanac, comparing facts and figures in an attempt to devise a fool-proof system to beat the odds.

'Bob, you're missing out on your children,' Sylvia told him. 'Please won't you come down and play with them?'

'This is my vacation,' Bob replied. 'I'll spend it how I choose.'

When Sylvia's parents flew to Baltimore to visit her and the grandchildren for the first time, they were shocked at the change in Bob's personality. Where once he had seemed charming, he now merely moped around in a perpetual sulk. Worse, he seemed resentful of the attention Sylvia paid to her parents, even though it had been years since she had seen them.

'Are you sure this is the same chap we met in London?' Mrs Bradley asked when Bob left the room. 'How long has he been like this?'

'Oh, I don't know, Mum,' Sylvia replied. 'It feels like forever.'

'Well, for goodness' sake girl, why didn't you come home?' her mother asked her.

Sylvia choked back tears. 'You told me I'd made my bed and I had to lie in it.'

'Oh, love,' Mrs Bradley sighed, 'I never meant that.'

When the time came for her to depart for London with her husband, she did so with a heavy heart. If she could have bundled Sylvia and the kids back onto the plane with her, she would have.

Sylvia's parents weren't the only ones worried about her. The Bluebell girls asked her why she didn't just leave Bob, since he was making her so unhappy.

'I couldn't afford it,' Sylvia replied. 'We barely manage as it is. I can't raise four children on my own.'

Despite what her mum had told her, she didn't see returning to England as a viable option either. Her parents were near retirement age and she didn't want to be a burden on them.

'I'll be all right,' she told the girls. 'After all, I lived through the Blitz. We're British, we can stand anything.'

But each time she repeated the motto it sounded more hollow.

Sylvia knew that Bob must be gambling a sizeable proportion of his earnings, and she begged him to give her more to help bring up their children. 'There are four of them now, Bob,' she pleaded. 'I can't manage on the same amount of money as before.'

But Bob was resolute, and refused to offer up another dime. Sylvia started looking for jobs that she could do in the evening, when Bob was at home and could look after the kids. Soon she was working part time as a waitress, and putting in shifts at a local bowling alley.

Back at home, Sylvia found ways to make what little money she had stretch further than ever before, applying the old wartime ethos of make-do-and-mend. She began cutting the children's hair herself, rather than taking them to a hairdresser, and even started making their clothes.

One night, when Bob's parents had come round for dinner, his father mentioned a big raise all the postal workers had received. Sylvia was dumbfounded – Bob hadn't mentioned anything of the kind. Once they were alone, she asked him how much his salary had gone up by.

'Oh, not that much,' Bob replied evasively. 'It'll be a few more dollars a month.'

'Well, can I have this month's now?' Sylvia asked.

'I already spent it,' he muttered.

'You mean you gambled it?'

Bob didn't reply.

'You weren't going to tell me, were you? You were going to let me carry on struggling month after month while you blow the extra money on your gambling.'

Silently, Bob sloped off out of the room.

Sylvia was livid. She knew that Bob had a problem with gambling, but she had always assumed he was honest.

The next month, Bob gave Sylvia a little more housekeeping money, which helped ease things slightly, but feeding the family of six remained quite an art. And something had changed within Sylvia too. Her trust in Bob had been broken. Who knew whether this was the first raise that he had received without telling her. She might be killing herself, working evening jobs and making the kids' clothes, all for nothing.

One day, Bob arrived home from work with a rare smile plastered across his face. 'So, you won some money today then?' Sylvia asked him.

'I sure did,' Bob replied excitedly. 'In fact, I won a whole bunch of it. Enough to pay for a vacation abroad.'

Despite herself, Sylvia's heart leaped. Maybe he would take her back to England, like he had promised all those years ago.

'I've already booked the tickets,' Bob continued. 'Bernie and I are going golfing in Scotland. There's a course there he says is the best in the world.'

Scotland! Sylvia couldn't believe it. Bob wouldn't take her back home to see her parents, but he would fly the same distance to play golf!

Not long after Bob returned from the trip, Sylvia made a discovery that shook her to the core. She received a letter from the bank about some loans they claimed she had taken out recently.

'Do you know anything about this?' Sylvia asked Bob, showing him the letter.

He shrugged. 'Yeah, I took out some money, but I'll pay it back soon enough.'

'You took out loans in my name?' Sylvia cried. 'How could you do something like that?'

'I just needed a bit of dough to tide me over. I'm going to win big, Sylvia, I know it. I've got a system now.'

Sylvia felt like she had reached breaking point. 'Well, a fat lot of good your bloody system has ever done us!' she shouted angrily. She stopped for a moment, surprised at herself.

'I know what I'm doing!' Bob bellowed. 'You're my wife, it's your job to stand by me.' He stormed out of the room and headed upstairs to bed.

Sylvia had never imagined that she would be the sort of woman to end up screaming and shouting at her husband, but once the pressure valve had been opened, she and Bob seemed to be fighting almost every day. Where once she had been wary of broaching difficult topics and he had skulked off at the first sign of conflict, now they were having blazing rows. One time, Bob grew so irate that he raised his hand to hit her.

'The minute you do that, you'll be sorry,' she told him. 'You see all them?' She gestured at the collection of English knick-knacks dotted all over the room. 'You lay so much as a finger on me and you'll find every one of them flying at your damn head, and you can bet I ain't going to miss!'

Bob backed down and crept out of the room.

Sylvia flopped down on the sofa and burst into tears. She had put up with so much, but she felt she couldn't take it any more. His gambling was ruining their lives.

In desperation, Sylvia looked up the number for Gamblers Anonymous and called them. 'My husband's gambling is tearing us apart,' she told them.

The woman on the end of the line was sympathetic, but told her there was nothing they could do. 'Your husband has to admit he has a problem,' she told Sylvia. 'He has to ask for help, not you.'

Sylvia felt as if the last breath of hope had been sucked out of her. She had tried everything she could think of to get her husband to change, and it had come to nothing. She felt hollowed out, helpless and desperate. If only she had stayed in England when she first walked out on the O'Connors all those years ago. She had come to the United States for the love of a man, but the man she had fallen in love with was long gone – his very soul had been taken over by the addiction.

A single straw had been enough to break the proverbial camel's back, and for Sylvia all it took was a few stray hairs. She had been giving her son Rodger a haircut one evening, and was just getting him settled in bed, when she heard a commotion in the bathroom. Her daughter Victoria had got out of the bath and begun to dry herself on the nearest available towel – which just happened to be the one that Sylvia had put around Rodger's neck.

'Urrghh!' Victoria cried. 'This towel's got hair on it!'

Bob's response was to side with his daughter. 'It's disgusting,' he shouted. 'What kind of a woman would do something like that?'

Sylvia felt like something within her had shattered. She walked straight down into the living room, picked up the phone and dialled the number of a cab firm. Then she went out onto the street and waited for the car to arrive. She felt like she was in a daze – just as she had all those years before in London, when the V-2 rocket had hit her train on the way to work. Right now, her brain was only focused on one thing – getting away as quickly as possible.

Bob heard the click of the front door and came down to investigate. 'What are you doing?' he called.

'I'm getting out of here,' Sylvia replied. 'I can't stand it any more.'

The car pulled up and Sylvia got inside. She gave the driver the address of her English friends Bill and Dot Langston. They had always said she could call on them any time, day or night.

As she sped off in the cab, Sylvia felt a kind of calm settle over her, but it didn't last long. By the time she arrived at the Langstons she was shaking all over, and she fainted as soon as they got her into the house.

Bill called a doctor to come and examine her, and was told that Sylvia was having a breakdown brought on by extreme stress. 'She just needs time to rest and recover,' he told the Langstons.

When Sylvia came round, she was frantic with worry. 'I walked out on my children,' she told Bill and Dot desperately. 'I never thought in a million years I would do that.'

'It's all right, love, Bob'll look after them,' Dot told her soothingly. But Sylvia was not to be reassured. Eventually, in a state of extreme anxiety, she picked up the phone herself and dialled Mr and Mrs O'Connor's number, begging Bob's mother to go round and check that the kids were all right.

But her mother-in-law said coldly, 'They're your children, not mine.'

'Try not to worry, love,' Dot Langston told her. 'The kids'll be fine.'

The older couple were like surrogate parents to Sylvia, and as she recuperated in their house they took good care of her, offering plenty of tea and biscuits and listening as she talked about how bad things had got with Bob. The warm, cosy environment and the Langstons' cockney accents made Sylvia almost feel she was back in Woolwich.

After several days at the Langstons', Sylvia was beginning to feel calmer, but she continued to worry constantly about the children. 'I think I need to go back there,' she told Bill and Dot.

'All right then,' Bill replied. He picked up the phone and dialled Bob's number. 'Get over here right now and pick up your wife,' he told him gruffly. 'She wants to come home.'

But Bob was in no mood to be dictated to. 'She left on her own, why can't she come back on her own?' he demanded.

'Don't be so bloody daft,' Bill shouted angrily. 'You come and get her right now or I'll bring her round myself, and you'd better be there.'

Suitably chastened, Bob came and picked Sylvia up. When she returned to their house, the four kids were standing waiting for her at the front door. The younger ones were bawling their eyes out as they saw the car draw up, and Sylvia rushed out and hugged them, wiping away their tears with a handkerchief. She felt terrible at having walked out on them and was almost beside herself with guilt.

At Bill and Dot's suggestion, Sylvia booked herself and Bob in for a course of sessions with a marriage guidance counsellor called Dr King. The idea was that in the first session they would take turns seeing the counsellor individually, so they could each explain their view of the situation, and then in succeeding sessions he would see both of them together and try to work towards a solution.

In the course of the first private session, Sylvia talked Dr King through the ups and downs of her relationship with Bob: how they had met and fallen in love at the Red Cross club in London, how he had bought her a ticket to fly over to America with his winnings from a craps game – 'That should have been the first warning sign,' she told him, 'but I didn't know it at the time' – and how she had encountered his difficult family, with their constant poker games and betting on horses. 'It was an alien world to me,' she said.

She explained how Bob's gambling had become worse and worse as the addiction had taken hold, and the effect that it had had on their relationship. 'He used to be so loving and affectionate,' she said, 'and then something seemed to dry up inside of him. He became moody and difficult, and it just seemed like he didn't love me any more.'

The doctor listened patiently as Sylvia told her story and explained how she had suffered a breakdown. Then it was time for her to go, and Bob took his turn in the consultation room.

The next week, Sylvia was getting ready to return for their first session together when Bob announced he wouldn't be coming. She was furious. 'Well, I'm going on my own then,' she told him, and she marched out the door.

'Where's your husband?' Dr King asked when Sylvia walked into his office on her own.

'He decided not to come,' she explained.

'To be honest, I'm not surprised,' Dr King said. 'I shouldn't really tell you this, but in his private session last week, Bob told me he doesn't think he should have to see a psychologist, since he's not the one who had a breakdown. Whenever I asked a question about your marriage, all he did was talk about money.'

'That's Bob,' Sylvia replied. 'All he ever thinks about these days is how to come up with a system to beat the odds, and how once he works it out we'll be rich beyond our wildest dreams.' She sighed. 'So, what am I supposed to do now?'

'Well, it seems to me you have two options,' Dr King replied. 'Either you have to leave Bob…'

'I just can't do that,' Sylvia interrupted. 'I couldn't afford to bring up the kids on my own, and I couldn't live with being a burden on my parents.'

'In that case,' the counsellor continued, 'you have to accept that Bob isn't going to change, and you can't make him. The only thing you can change is yourself.'

'What does that mean?' Sylvia asked.

'It means you have to learn to stand up to him,' he told her. 'You can't bottle everything up inside until it explodes again. You've seen where that got you before – you ended up having a breakdown.'

Sylvia carried on seeing Dr King on her own, and over the course of their sessions he taught her how to assert herself with Bob. She learned to state calmly but firmly what she needed, rather than suffering in silence. If Bob tried to ignore her requests for things like money for the kids' clothes, she would keep repeating them, refusing to let him shut her out. It didn't always get the desired result, but at least she felt that she was being heard.

To begin with, Bob didn't like it that his previously shy wife was becoming more confident, and it made him angry. One day he told her that if she didn't stop it, she could get out. 'No, you get out if you want to,' Sylvia replied coolly. 'I'm not leaving again.'

She had learned to control her own anger, which meant that their conversations didn't spiral so often into rows. Dr King had taught her that when she found herself feeling over-whelmed she could express her frustrations in writing, pouring out her troubles in a diary, rather than lashing out. As a result, she no longer felt that she had resentment building up that risked making her ill again.

At the same time, Sylvia had acknowledged that she would never be able to change Bob. As Gamblers Anonymous had told her before, his addiction was his problem, and he was the only one who could tackle it. Sylvia knew that he was unlikely ever to do that, but finally giving up her battle to stop him gambling brought her a certain amount of relief. She learned she could choose to compromise without having to feel like a victim – deciding to stay with Bob despite not agreeing with what he did.

Sylvia had long since given up the romantic notions she had held when she first married her GI boyfriend and came to

America. It was far from the Hollywood ending that she had dreamed of, but she had come to realise that, rather than looking to him to make her happy, she would have to find happiness elsewhere. She put her energy into her relationships with her children instead, and into her friendships with the Bluebell girls, who had become like a second family to her.

She set her own boundaries now, carving out a life for herself that was increasingly separate from Bob's. They moved into different parts of the house – he upstairs and she downstairs – and saw less and less of each other. She also kept her finances separate, making sure that her money was out of his reach. She had accepted the fact that she would always have to keep working, so that she could cover the inevitable shortfalls in the money she got from him, but it also enabled her to start putting aside a small amount each month in a savings account of her own.

After many years of hard work, Sylvia had put by enough to fulfil her long-held ambition to return to England for a holiday. Bob might have failed in his promise to take her home, but together the Bluebell girls managed to get a cheap flight by chartering a plane.

Finally, Sylvia was able to show her children the place that, in her heart, she still called home. Bob might not be by her side, but she had got there thanks to her own strength of will and determination – and she knew that was enough to carry her through.

30

Rae

'I hereby declare, on oath, that I absolutely and entirely renounce and abjure all allegiance and fidelity to any foreign prince, potentate, state or sovereignty, and particularly to Great Britain, of which I have heretofore been a subject.'

At the Washington County courthouse, near Pittsburgh, Rae stood and recited the words as instructed. The most patriotic of British subjects, she had never imagined herself taking out American citizenship, but Raymond's threats to deport her had only made her determined to stay in the United States. She might have been desperate to jump off the boat and swim home when she first arrived, but she wasn't going to let her cheating husband force her out now when she had done nothing wrong.

When she had told her mother that she and Raymond had separated, Rae had expected her to beg her to return to England. But to her surprise, Mrs Burton was so outraged to hear how he had treated her daughter that she told her: 'Stay and fight him.'

Luckily, Rae had a formidable lawyer on her team, in the shape of her employer Pap Oppenheim. Every time Raymond had approached an attorney about his scheme to boot Rae out of the country, Pap had intervened and dissuaded them from taking on the case. Word had spread quickly, and Raymond had been forced to abandon his campaign.

Over the past few years, Rae hadn't heard from Raymond at all, and her life with the Oppenheims had proved a full one. There was never a dull moment with Donny, Jay and Billy around. The older two were always up to some prank or other – peeing in the builders' coffee when they were working on the house, or sneaking unexpected things into the wastepaper basket before Rae emptied it into the fireplace at night, causing sparks to fly out and burn holes in the carpet. Their reputation as little rascals preceded them, and other women often asked Rae how she coped. But she always replied, 'I wouldn't change them for the world.' Pap Oppenheim, meanwhile, often told Rae that she was like the daughter he and Minna never had.

Rae really had the ideal set-up, living in the lap of luxury with the kindest employers imaginable. But after three years, she was beginning to wonder if it was all a little too easy. As much as she liked the Oppenheims, she couldn't help thinking that perhaps she was putting her own life on hold by staying with them.

Another matter was beginning to weigh on Rae's mind. She had fallen in love with baby Billy as soon as she had seen his big brown eyes, and over the years she had spent more time with him than his own mother had, looking after him while Minna worked at the furniture store. Rae had begun to notice that when Minna left the house, Billy would say, 'Bye bye, Mommy,' quite contentedly, whereas when she left, the boy would scream blue murder. She knew that he was getting too attached.

Rae loved Billy like her own flesh and blood, and saying goodbye to him, and to the Oppenheims, who had been so kind to her in her hour of need, was heartbreaking. But she knew she had to find her own way in life and prove that she could stand on her own two feet again.

She decided to make a fresh start in McKeesport, a bustling steel town a little further up the Monongahela River that was known affectionately as 'Tube City', since the famous National Tube Works was based there. She already had a friend in the town, Marlene, who had offered to put her up.

On her first day in McKeesport, Rae set off to look for a job, working her way along the main shopping street, Fifth Avenue, and calling in at every building to ask if they were hiring. She tried everything from the National Bank and Murphy's Five & Dime to Immel's Clothing and the Minerva bakery, but at all of them she met with the same answer: 'There's no work here.'

After walking for hours, Rae was exhausted and beginning to despair when she reached a large shoe shop called Forsythe's. Inside, it was thronging with customers, but she eventually managed to catch the attention of the manager.

'Do you have any jobs going?' Rae asked, bracing herself for yet another rejection.

'Are you good at learning stock codes?' he asked her.

Rae thought back to her first job in the Ordnance Corps, learning the code numbers for parts and equipment. It had been boring work, but she had quickly mastered it. 'Yes, I am,' she told him confidently.

'Well, if you can learn these overnight, then I'll hire you.' He handed her a card on which each type of shoe was listed next to a series of numbers and letters, before rushing off to see to the next customer.

That evening, Rae sat for hours poring over the list of codes. In the morning, she returned and asked for the manager.

'Nurse's Oxford, white?' he demanded.

'J-8650,' replied Rae.

'Arrabuk suede high-heel, black?'

'C-39793.'

'Pennywise sandal, beige?'

'V-74656.'

'You're hired,' he told her. 'Now go help that customer over there.'

Rae found she didn't at all mind selling shoes. She enjoyed being around people, and the store was always busy. It was a welcome distraction from thoughts of the three little boys she had left behind, whom she missed terribly. She had decided that she needed to be independent, and this was a step in the right direction.

There was one more hurdle Rae had to jump, however. She told her friend Marlene that she appreciated her generosity, but she had decided to move out. She wanted to live on her own.

Rae scoured the rentals section of the local newspaper and found an apartment above a shop on Walnut Street, in downtown McKeesport.

Marlene helped her move in and then left her to unpack. When the door closed, Rae breathed a contented sigh as she looked around at her apartment, the first she had rented with her own money. Finally, her wellbeing didn't have to depend on anyone else – especially not a man. When her landlady asked her if she was likely to bring any boyfriends back, Rae replied, in no uncertain terms, 'I don't plan on having any boyfriends.'

Not long after Rae had moved in she exercised her most fundamental right as an American citizen and voted in a presidential election. When she had first become a citizen, Pap Oppenheim had encouraged her to register Republican, and out of loyalty to him she had agreed. But now Rae wanted to make her own decisions. She read up on the two candidates, Dwight D. Eisenhower and Adlai Stevenson, and despite all that the former Allied Supreme Commander had done during the war, she decided she was going to vote Democrat.

Rae's life fell into a familiar routine, working at Forsythe's and eating her lunch in the canteen at the nearby Murphy's Five & Dime – where she befriended a couple of girls who worked there called Ruth and Jenny. The three of them would go to a local bar and restaurant called Gill's in the evenings and chat over soda pops and fish sandwiches, watching the comings and goings at the bar.

One day they were laughing over their sodas as usual when a well-built, dark young man in his late twenties came over to their table. Ruth and Jenny knew him already, and introduced him to Rae as Joe, and they began chatting away with him. Rae had absolutely no interest in getting to know a member of the opposite sex, and had been quite happy just talking to the girls, but Joe made an effort to involve her in the conversation. 'How did you come to live in America?' he asked, having noticed her accent.

'How do you think?' snapped Rae. 'I was married!' That seemed to shut him up.

When they left Gill's, Ruth told Joe that she and Rae were walking home in the same direction, and he insisted on accompanying them. Rae's place was first so they dropped her off, and then Joe and Ruth carried on to her house. He must be after her, Rae reasoned.

From then on Joe started coming into Gill's more and more often, and he would always join the three girls in their booth. Now that she was convinced there was something going on between him and Ruth, Rae didn't mind chatting to him as a friend. He told her he came from a large Slovak family and worked at National Tube, just like his father. He was considered the best tube-cutter in the mill, he said proudly, because he could cut almost 1,000 tubes a day.

One evening, Ruth was busy, so Rae and Jenny went to Gill's without her. Joe turned up as usual, and at the end of the evening he insisted on walking Rae home even though Ruth wasn't there. It was a short walk to her apartment and as they arrived, to Rae's surprise, he asked, 'Would you like to go out some time?'

'I'm not going out with you,' Rae retorted. 'What about Ruth?'

'What *about* Ruth?' Joe replied.

'Well, isn't there something going on between the two of you?'

'No. We've never even been on a date together!'

Confused, Rae said a brusque goodbye and went up to her flat.

Inside, she thought back over all the times she and Ruth had chatted with Joe at Gill's. Could he have been coming to see her, not Ruth?

After her disastrous marriage to Raymond, Rae had done her best to avoid men. But Joe had slipped in under the net, and she had grown to like him as a friend.

The next time he saw her, Joe asked her out again. Rae had no intention of allowing another man close enough to hurt her, but she didn't see any harm in dating him – she would just be sure to keep him at arm's length.

Being with Joe felt easy and natural, but Rae was careful not to give him the false impression that she was after anything serious. 'If he tries to tell me he loves me, I'll drop him,' she told Jenny and Ruth.

One Saturday night, Rae and Joe caught a movie together and then went out on the town. By the time he walked her back to her front door it was two in the morning. 'Can I see you again tomorrow night?' he asked. 'How about I call for you at eight?'

'Okay,' Rae shrugged. 'See you then.'

On Sunday evening, she was ready and waiting for Joe at eight o'clock, but there was no knock on the door. Rae started pacing around the apartment, hating the feeling of waiting helplessly for a man. She kept looking out of the window, but there was no sign of him. Quarter-past and half-past went by, and still he wasn't there.

He must have stood me up, Rae thought angrily. She should have known better than to trust another man, especially a Yank. What had she been thinking, going out with him?

There was one last possibility – perhaps Joe had gone to Gill's by mistake, thinking they were supposed to be meeting there. She grabbed her coat and ran out into the street. She had just got to the bank on the corner when she spotted Joe walking along on the other side of the street. 'Oi!' she called. 'Where do you think you're going?'

He turned around with a surprised look on his face. 'Oh, hi, Rae,' he said.

'You were supposed to be at my apartment at eight o'clock!' Rae shouted, struggling to control her anger. She had a lump in her throat, and she didn't want to give away how hurt she felt.

'No, that's Monday night,' Joe replied blankly.

'You said last night you'd see me tomorrow,' Rae insisted. 'We went out on Saturday, so tomorrow means Sunday.'

'No,' he replied calmly. 'I took you home at two this morning, so tomorrow night is Monday.'

Rae couldn't believe he had come up with such a ridiculous story to cover for having stood her up. 'Oh, get lost!' she shouted. She turned on her heel and ran back along Walnut Street and into her apartment, slamming the door behind her.

That night, Rae barely slept, furious with herself for letting a man make her feel vulnerable again. All day on Monday in the shoe shop she wasn't her normal chatty self. She just wanted to get home and hide away.

That evening, Rae was curled up under the covers when there was a knock on the door. Reluctantly she went downstairs and answered it.

Joe was standing on the doorstep.

'What are you doing here?' Rae demanded.

'It's eight o'clock,' he replied. 'We've got a date.'

'That was yesterday,' she said. 'You didn't turn up!'

'No, you crazy limey,' he replied. 'I told you, the date was for tonight.'

Rae was thrown. Maybe it hadn't just been an excuse, she realised.

'So are you coming, or do I have to go on my own?' Joe asked her.

Rae hesitated. She wanted more than anything to believe him, to know that she could trust him.

There was only one way to find out. 'All right,' she told him. 'You've got one last chance.' She ran and got her things, and they set off together.

'Rae, are you sure you're an American citizen?' Joe asked her, as they walked up the street.

'Yeah, why?' she asked.

'Because you sure as hell acted like John Bull last night!'

Joe never pressed Rae to define their relationship, but after more than a year of dating it was obvious to everyone that they were going steady – not least to his parents. 'When are you going to marry this girl?' his mother asked. 'After one year, a man should know his intentions,' his father added.

One night, Rae was cooking Joe roast beef and Yorkshire pudding for dinner when he told her, 'You'd make somebody a great wife, you know.'

'Yeah, anybody but you!' came the prickly reply.

That silenced Joe for a few more months, until parental pressure began to build up again. 'Either marry her or drop her!' demanded his father.

The next time Rae saw Joe, he told her, 'My parents want to know when we're getting married.'

'Tell them I don't want to get married again!' she retorted.

Joe passed on this information to his parents, but they didn't believe him. 'Of course she does!' his mother said, exasperated. For years she had been turning down approaches from the parents of Slovak girls in their neighbourhood who wanted to arrange a marriage with her son. She had been determined that

Joe would marry for love, but here he was at the age of twenty-eight, with no sign of a wedding on the horizon.

The next time they were together, Joe told Rae, 'My parents have been asking about us getting married again.'

'Did you tell them I don't want to?'

'Yes, but they don't believe me!'

Rae couldn't help laughing at that.

'Rae, why *won't* you marry me?' Joe asked her. It was the first time he had tackled the issue head on, and Rae suddenly found herself put on the spot.

'Marry you? I don't even know if you love me!' she blurted out. She was taken aback by her own words.

'Of course I do!' he replied. 'Otherwise I wouldn't be asking you. But I heard you tell your friends that if I said I loved you, you'd drop me.'

Rae thought back to the comment she had made to Jenny and Ruth. Poor Joe had overheard and taken it to heart, and for nearly two years he had been unable to tell her how he felt.

Only now that he had done so did she realise she felt the same way. 'Yes, I'll marry you, Joe,' she told him. To her surprise, there wasn't a trace of doubt in her mind.

That night, Joe was finally able to give his parents the news they had long been waiting for.

'You see?' his mother said, triumphantly. 'She did want to marry you all along!'

In order to marry Joe, Rae would first have to get a divorce from Raymond. She employed a lawyer, who contacted Raymond's father in Hackett to get his address. The lawyer discovered that Raymond was living in California with his former girlfriend from West Virginia – only now she was his wife. He had married bigamously, just as Rae's own stepfather had done all those years ago.

The last thing Rae wanted was to dredge up the painful memories of Raymond's adultery, so she sued him for 'indignities to the person' rather than going into specifics. He signed the divorce papers willingly, and the error of judgement she had made as a naive nineteen-year-old was finally erased from her life.

Rae was going into this marriage as a very different woman. She may have opened her heart again, but she was determined to maintain her independence. She let Joe pay for the engagement ring she had picked out at a jewellery store on Fifth Avenue, but she bought their matching platinum wedding bands herself.

Since Rae's first wedding had taken place in a Methodist church, the Slovak National Catholic Church didn't recognise it, and to her new mother-in-law's delight she and Joe were allowed to get married at the altar. This time, no one gave the bride away – she and Joe walked down the aisle together.

The reception was held at a local club, where they had planned a simple gathering. But Rae hadn't counted on Joe's mother and aunties, who had gone down to the club earlier and been busy cooking chicken noodle soup, stuffed cabbage, pyrih pies, haluski dumplings, turkey schnitzel and delicious layered torts filled with apricots and pineapple. It was a beautiful spread, a million miles away from Rae's fish-and-chip wedding in Mansfield.

The room was packed with people, and although her own family couldn't be with her, Rae's friends from McKeesport,

Monongahela and Hackett had all come to celebrate. The Slovaks knew how to throw a good party, and it was well into the early hours by the time people started to head home.

On their wedding night, Rae and Joe went back together to her apartment. She had decided it was where they would live now that they were husband and wife. It was still her place, but she didn't mind sharing it with Joe.

He might be a Yank, but he was a good one.

31

Gwendolyn

Since the incident on the escalator in San Francisco, Lyn's pangs of homesickness had grown into a burning need to return to England. Although she and Ben could scarcely afford the plane ticket, he agreed to borrow some money for her and John to go, aware of how important it was to her. Soon they were booked on a Trans World flight from San Francisco to London.

Ben dropped them off at the airport and kissed them both goodbye. 'Are you sure you'll be all right?' he asked, looking anxiously at the braces on Lyn's legs.

'I'll manage,' she said, but inside she was terrified. She had never been in an aeroplane before, and she couldn't help thinking about the hundreds of miles of ocean that they would be flying over. The old Lyn would have seen it as a big adventure, but she was more anxious now.

The flight was long, with stopovers in Newfoundland and Ireland, but when she finally stepped onto English soil again, Lyn felt overwhelmed with relief. 'We're home!' she told little John, who looked at her confused. This wasn't home to him – just a place he didn't recognise.

Mr and Mrs Rowe were waiting at Arrivals. As soon as they saw her, Lyn's mother cried, 'There's my Gwen!'

People stared at the overwrought woman with tears running down her face, but she didn't care. She rushed over and threw her arms around her daughter.

Lyn had remembered her family as being reserved, but after so many years apart their natural restraint went out of the window.

'Now, don't you use that "Lyn" word in front of me!' joked her mother, wiping away her tears. Lyn was worried about how she would respond to the sight of her in leg braces, after the comment in her letter about how ugly they were, but to her relief she didn't mention them.

'John, say hi to Grandma and Grandpa Rowe,' Lyn told him.

'Hi,' said John shyly. His grandfather put him on his shoulders, and the family headed back to Southampton.

Over the months that she had been planning the trip, Lyn had imagined the house in Padwell Road time and time again – her childhood bedroom with its fireplace, lit every night, the grand front room that no one was ever allowed to use, and the big kitchen table that they all sat around, chatting.

'Here we are, Gwen – home again!' said her mother, as she ushered Lyn through the door. But Lyn was speechless. The house seemed to have shrunk significantly. The hallway was narrow and the little staircase pokey and strange, and now that she was allowed to sit in it, the front room looked cramped and sparsely furnished.

That night, Lyn slept in her childhood bedroom, but instead of feeling she was truly home, she felt like Goldilocks in someone else's bed.

The next day, Mr Rowe took John so Lyn could have a wander around Southampton. The city had healed from the wounds of the Blitz, but so many new buildings had sprung up that the character of the town was very different. Lyn found it difficult to remember her way around now that so many old landmarks had gone, but she found her way to the Polygon Hotel, where Ben had been billeted in the war.

On a wall of the hotel a plaque had been erected to commemorate the Americans' arrival in Britain. The sight of it brought tears to Lyn's eyes. She thought of Eugene sitting in his jeep outside her front door, and the other brave young men she had chatted to on D-Day before they went off to risk their lives on the far shore. The GIs had passed into history, she realised. Did anyone really remember them now, when the only sign that they had ever been here was a plaque on a wall?

Standing outside the Polygon brought memories flooding back – of Ben and Lyn's early courtship, of the elegant dances in the ballroom, when Lyn had felt so beautiful twirling around the room. She wouldn't be able to dance like that now, she thought, looking down at the braces on her legs.

For months Lyn had felt desperate to return home to England, but now she realised that the thing she had been looking for no longer existed. It was her younger self – that confident, carefree girl who hadn't had any knocks in life, who could stand on her own two feet without braces to support her.

On her way back to her parents' house, Lyn sat on the bench where Ben had proposed all those years ago. She remembered the absolute trust she had felt in him then, a trust which had never faltered. As much as she loved seeing her parents, Lyn realised that Ben and John were her family now, and her home was in California with them. Whatever life in America had to throw at her, she would have to face it.

When the day came to leave, saying goodbye to her parents was even harder than when she had gone the first time. On the plane home, Lyn cried non-stop.

Back in the States, it wasn't long before Lyn was finally able to get rid of the clunky braces and walk unaided once again. Her family and friends congratulated her on her achievement: she had finally beaten polio, and could return to a completely normal life.

One afternoon, Lyn was driving home from a friend's house, with her son John asleep on the back seat. It was a peaceful early summer's day with little traffic on the road, and she drove slowly, taking in the sight of flowers in bloom and the perfect blue of the California sky.

Suddenly, she was gripped by the overwhelming conviction that she was about to die. The thought hit her like a punch in the gut and she struggled to breathe, her fingers tightening around the steering wheel.

Terrified, Lyn checked the rear-view mirror to see if John had noticed. But the boy was still sleeping soundly, unaware of the crisis his mother was enduring. Outside the car, the lazy midday traffic cruised by and the birds were singing. But inside Lyn felt pure fear flooding every inch of her body. All she knew was that she had to get home, to the one place she felt safe. She put her foot down on the accelerator and sped back to the apartment.

Once she was inside with the door shut, Lyn's breathing gradually returned to normal and the feeling of blind terror started to dissipate. She told John to play with his toys, and went to lie down.

She wondered what on earth had just happened. Where had that certainty of impending death come from? And why now, when she was finally over the polio?

That evening, Lyn did her best to forget about the horrible episode. It made no sense to her, so there was no point in dwelling on it. Perhaps she had just spent too much time in the sun.

But a few days later, Lyn was out shopping in the supermarket when once again she was suddenly gripped by fear. She leaned her hand against a wall to steady herself, her breathing becoming tighter and her heart racing. As women pushed their shopping trolleys past her, oblivious to her suffering, Lyn tried her best to regain control of herself. Once again, there was one thought paramount in her mind: she had to get home. She couldn't cope out here on her own for one moment longer.

Back at the house, the feeling quickly subsided. But this time Lyn knew that it would come back again.

Over the following weeks and months Lyn began to dread leaving the house. She never knew when the panic attacks would strike, and there was no way of protecting herself from them. Even the most familiar places provided no guarantee of safety.

Inevitably, she began to find excuses to stay at home. When she and Ben were invited out by friends and family, she would plead a sore throat or headache. Ben did his best to support her, and if there were tasks to be done outside the house, he offered to take them off her plate. Having stood by unable to help as she went through polio, he was anxious to protect her now. 'You don't have to do anything you don't want to,' he told her, and as time went on, Lyn became increasingly withdrawn.

To begin with Lyn's excuses seemed plausible, but it didn't take long for the Patrinos to suspect something was wrong.

Soon Ben's mother was demanding to know why Lyn was no longer attending family dinners, and Ben was having to brush off her questions.

One day, Ben's older brother Leo called and asked to speak to Lyn. She took the phone cautiously, afraid of receiving an earful for deserting the family. Leo had never shown her much kindness.

'Lyn, I need to talk to you,' he said.

'Yes?' she replied, bracing herself.

'Are you feeling afraid right now?'

Lyn was taken aback. 'No.'

'I think you are, and I want to tell you something. I've been there – I know exactly what it's like.'

Leo told her that the reason he had never been drafted during the war was that he had suffered from panic attacks. 'It was a kind of nervous breakdown,' he explained.

Lyn was shocked that he would admit such a thing to her, and for a moment she didn't know what to say. 'How did you get over it?' she asked eventually.

'I went to a shrink,' Leo told her, 'and he helped me out of it. I think maybe you should do the same. I promise I won't tell the family.'

'Thanks,' Lyn replied. Part of her felt relieved that there was someone who understood what she was going through, but another part felt exposed, knowing he had seen through her excuses.

Back in England, the idea of seeing a psychotherapist would have been unthinkable, but here it was different. And Lyn knew Leo was right – she couldn't go on the way she was. She needed help.

The following week, she found herself sitting on a psycho-therapist's couch. 'I can't understand why all of a sudden this has happened,' she told him. 'I used to be so independent and strong.'

She thought back to the old Lyn, who was never afraid to go anywhere or do anything. The Lyn who had crossed the Atlantic to start a life in a new country.

'You've become like a house that's all shut up,' the psychia-trist explained. 'The door's been locked and the shutters have been closed.'

'Why did the house close?' asked Lyn.

'That's what we're going to find out.'

Lyn's visits to the psychotherapist soon became the focal point of her week, while the rest of the time she hardly left the house. Her life was becoming more and more constrained.

In the meantime, her mother-in-law was becoming increas-ingly suspicious. One day, when Ben was out, she turned up at the door, and Lyn had no choice but to let her in.

'Why don't you come round for dinner any more?' she demanded. 'Why do we never see you?'

Lyn felt weary of excuses and decided to come clean with Mrs Patrino, even though she didn't expect her to understand. 'I didn't want to tell you this,' she sighed, 'but I'm seeing a therapist. I've been having panic attacks.'

The look of exasperated annoyance fell from Mrs Patrino's face, and to Lyn's surprise it was replaced by one of concern. She reached out and took her daughter-in-law's hand. 'Let me help you,' she said.

Lyn was caught off-guard. She had expected Mrs Patrino to tell her to stop being lazy and get on with things, but she took the issue very seriously. She had been through it all before with her own son. 'I know this is real,' she said. 'It is not weak. It is not phoney. Don't let anybody tell you that.'

Lyn didn't know what to say, but it meant a lot to her to know that she had her mother-in-law's support.

A few days later, Mrs Patrino returned. She had seen from her last visit that Lyn was struggling to keep on top of the housework.

'Do you want me to do a few things for you?' she asked gently. 'I can change the sheets if you like.'

In the past, Lyn would have responded with indignation to any comment her mother-in-law made about her housekeeping, but there was something very different in the way that she broached the subject now. There was no tone of authority, no implied criticism. And instead of insisting, she had actually asked for permission.

'Yes,' Lyn replied. 'That would be helpful.'

Soon there were fresh sheets on the bed and new towels laid out in the bathroom. The laundry basket had been emptied, the mess had been tidied away and the cabinet tops had been cleaned. 'Thank you,' Lyn said to Mrs Patrino, who gave her a smile and left.

Mrs Patrino began to visit Lyn every few days. Sometimes she swept the floors or dusted the shelves, other times she looked after John so that Lyn could rest, or got the dinner ready before Ben came home. Lyn thought back to how wretched she had felt when she had been stuck in the hospital with polio and Ben and John had gone back to live with his parents. Then she had been desperate for the three of them to be in their own home again, independent once more from Ben's family. But now, for the first time in her life, she was beginning to appreciate having an extra person she could lean on. This must be the flip side of the overbearing Italian family, Lyn thought.

When Mother's Day came round, Mrs Patrino made a comment that touched Lyn's heart. 'It's the worst day of the year for me,' she admitted. 'Leo calls up and has some kind of excuse for not coming round, and Armand shows up asking for a piece of cake. Ben's not too bad. But they see it as an obligation.'

Lyn looked at her own son and imagined how hurt she would be if he felt that way about her when he grew up. She couldn't help remembering her first Mother's Day in America, when Ben had brought her flowers but not given Mrs Patrino anything. The more she thought back to her actions in those early days, the more she realised that Ben's mother had not been entirely to blame for souring things between them. Perhaps Lyn had been more homesick than she had liked to admit, and it had made her overly defensive. 'Maybe I had a chip on my shoulder,' she told Mrs Patrino.

'Maybe we didn't take into account that you were only twenty, and you'd just been through a war,' Mrs Patrino replied.

But while Lyn was finding Ben's family surprisingly supportive, she was beginning to grow frustrated with the professional help she was receiving. The therapist had laid down strict rules about what could and couldn't be discussed in their sessions, and Lyn found them ridiculous. Whenever she tried to talk about her wartime experiences, leaving for America or suffering from polio, he would tell her, 'You're looking in the wrong place.'

It seemed that all he wanted to talk about was Lyn's relation-ship with her parents. She searched her heart, but she could find nothing to complain about regarding Mr and Mrs Rowe, who had always been loving and supportive.

Meanwhile, if she ever tried to ask the therapist a question, the answer would invariably be: 'What do *you* think?'

After each session, Lyn came away feeling worse, yet the next week she would feel the need to return even more strongly. Meanwhile, her life was still as narrow and closed as it had been before.

One day, Lyn was sitting in the psychotherapist's room when a thought came to her. 'I can't leave the house because I'm too afraid, and yet every Friday I drive out and spend an hour with you,' she told him. 'Don't you think there's something strange about that?'

'That's for *you* to figure out,' he responded.

Lyn felt rage bubbling up within her. 'Why do you do that?' she demanded.

'Do what?' he asked calmly.

'*That*,' said Lyn. 'You just sit there, while I get nowhere. I've been coming to you for ages, and I'm getting worse and worse, but you don't say or do anything! I'm so angry with you!'

Had it been his intention to provoke her? she wondered. Perhaps in the end it didn't really matter. Something inside her had snapped, and as she drove home that day, she knew she would never go back. There was only one person who could help Lyn Patrino – and that was herself.

The following Friday, when Lyn didn't go to therapy, she felt a sense of freedom. She realised she had become dependent on the sessions and had convinced herself she couldn't stop going. Now that she had proved herself wrong, she began to look at what other assumptions she had made about her life.

Gradually, she started doing things that she had given up.

Mrs Patrino tactfully retreated as Lyn took over responsibilities for her own household again. Ben was as protective as ever, but now Lyn could see that in his desire to shield her he had aided her withdrawal from the world. She had to stop hiding behind him.

The first time Lyn ventured out on her own again, she closed her eyes and thought back to her younger self, getting on the *President Tyler*. She drew on the spirit of that carefree young girl, even though she now regarded her as naive, and even a little childish. The older Lyn was learning to get in touch with that sense of independence again.

After a few months, Lyn was feeling stronger, but there was one last challenge she felt she had to face. 'I want to go back out to work,' she told Ben.

'Well,' he said, 'it's all right with me – provided that, if I get worried about you, I can tell you to quit.' His protective instinct was still strong, and he didn't want to see his wife taking on too much.

Lyn was determined, however. When a friend told her about a temporary secretarial job coming up at the San Jose Police Department, she jumped at the chance.

Being busy again took Lyn out of herself, and her old love of being around people returned. She became a popular presence at the department, and once the temporary contract was up they asked her to become permanent.

One night after work, Lyn and Ben drove up to Monterey for a picnic. After a short walk along the pier they sat and watched the sea lions playing in the water, honking at each other and rolling on their fat bellies.

Lyn had brought fresh bread from the bakery, and they ate it with Italian cheese, salami and crunchy pickles. Then they shared a thermos of hot coffee and some homemade cookies.

As they walked on the rocks afterwards, feeling the mist against their faces, they watched the seagulls flying overhead and the waves crashing against the shore. 'This is the life,' said Lyn, smiling.

Her time in America hadn't been easy, but with her husband at her side she felt truly happy.

Epilogue

Lyn and Ben remained happily married for many decades, and in 1985 they celebrated their fortieth wedding anniversary. Despite all that had happened to her in America, Lyn felt lucky. Unlike other GI brides she knew, her marriage had worked out for the best.

In fact, despite gloomy predictions during the war years, the divorce rate among GI brides and their husbands was lower than the national average, and over the years many visited England to renew their vows in the churches where they had married decades earlier.

When the Vietnam War came, Lyn's son John was drafted into the Army, and put on a GI uniform just as his father had done. Lyn's heart ached at the thought of her boy fighting in a war thousands of miles away, and she wrote to her parents back in Southampton saying that now she understood what she had put them through by moving halfway across the world.

Lyn finally felt part of her family in America. Despite a difficult start, she had grown to love her Italian in-laws, and over the decades Mrs Patrino became like a second mother to her. Minutes before she died, she drew Lyn close and whispered, 'I'm so sorry about how things started out between us.'

'There's nothing to apologise for,' Lyn replied. 'I know I wasn't an angel myself.'

Mrs Patrino left Lyn her treasured glass candlesticks, which Lyn made sure to take good care of. But she took something else from her mother-in-law as well – a lesson that has stayed with her ever since. When her granddaughter Jenny got married a few years ago, Lyn had one piece of advice for her: 'Just remember, you don't marry a man, you marry a whole family, and you've got to bend over backwards to make it work.'

In 1989, Ben died of a brain tumour, following a long and difficult illness. Although it was a distressing time for Lyn, she took great comfort from the care that she was able to give her husband. Nursing him through his final weeks, Lyn felt she was finally paying him back for all he had done for her throughout their marriage. Ben had stood by her through thick and thin, supporting her with gentle love and kindness however bad things got. Now, at last, she felt able to look after him in return.

A few years after Ben's death, Lyn was on a bus one day when she heard a woman of about her own age speaking with an English accent in the row behind her. 'Are you a GI bride by any chance?' Lyn asked her.

Lyn's hunch turned out to be correct. The other woman was a war bride by the name of Jean Borst who came originally from Welwyn Garden City. Jean was a member of an organisation called the World War II War Brides Association, which she told Lyn met up for a grand reunion one weekend a year, each time in a different American city. Jean also ran a local chapter in San Jose. 'Maybe you'd like to join us?' she suggested.

Lyn leaped at the chance to meet some fellow GI brides. At her first big gathering in San Diego, she was surprised to discover that the group encompassed not just British women, but Italians and Germans as well. At first, she felt an instinctive hostility towards them, but she soon found herself thawing out, sharing a bottle of wine at the bar with a German bride who had also been widowed. 'Isn't it funny,' Lyn said, 'that I can be friends with you, after what your people did to my city?' The German woman turned to her and said, 'You don't know what your people did to mine!' After that, they decided to keep off the topic of the war, but they have remained the best of friends ever since.

Every month, Lyn continues to attend Jean Borst's regular lunches at the Hickory Pit diner in San Jose, where a large group of local brides gathers to reminisce and share their memories of the war years. And these days she doesn't go there on her own. Seven years ago, Lyn met a former GI called Richard, who was getting over the sudden loss of his wife. The chemistry between them was instant.

Richard and Lyn live in separate houses, a few blocks away from each other, but they meet up every day, and enjoy holidaying together in Reno and Las Vegas. But despite their close relationship, Lyn will always keep a special place in her heart for her beloved Ben. On his gravestone, in a beautiful plot in California, her own name is carved alongside his, along with the title of 'their' song: 'Till the End of Time'.

* * *

Sylvia and Bob remained married and living in the same house, but they continued to have largely separate lives. He retired early from the post office, convinced that he could make his fortune on the horses – but as ever, his 'system' came to nothing.

In his final years, Bob had a leg amputated as a result of diabetes and was confined to a wheelchair. Although he and Sylvia spent little time together, they continued to attend family events as a couple. A few weeks before he died in 2001, they were at Bob's nephew's wedding together when, halfway through the ceremony, he asked Sylvia if she could pass him a pencil.

'What for?' she asked.

'I want to write down the hymn numbers.'

'Why, Bob?' Sylvia asked. It wasn't like him to take such an interest in religion.

'I'm going to play them on the lottery,' he replied. 'I think maybe they've been chosen for a reason.'

Sylvia sighed and handed over a pencil from her handbag. Even at the end of his life, when all his hopes had come to nothing, still Bob could think of nothing but gambling.

Although Bob had not turned out to be the husband Sylvia had hoped for, he had given her four wonderful children, and she also had the love and support of her English friends at the Bluebell Branch. She continued to work hard and save, and as a result she was able to go home and visit her family in Woolwich every few years.

Sylvia's last trip home was in 2007, and she doesn't think she will make the trip again. Not long after she returned to Baltimore she was diagnosed with cancer, and although she made a good recovery, the experience has made her fearful of travelling too far away from home. But she still enjoys all things English and made sure to watch Prince William and Kate Middleton's wedding in 2011 and the Queen's Diamond Jubilee in 2012, dressing in red, white and blue for the occasion.

Although Sylvia may never take another trip back to Woolwich, she knows she will be going home eventually. When she dies, she wants her ashes to be taken back to London to join those of her parents.

If Sylvia had her time again, she would live her life differently and never agree to become a GI bride. But she consoles herself with the thought that many women had worse experiences than her own. Her marriage may have become one of compromise, but her good humour saw her through the difficult times and she never lost her love of singing. Now, at the age of eighty-five, she is a member of the choir at the local seniors' centre, which tours around nearby nursing homes, cheering up the residents with old wartime songs.

* * *

When Rae married Joe Zurovcik, she did her best to forget her first husband. But one day, as she walked out of the Five & Dime in McKeesport, she ran into her former sister-in-law, Chi-Chi, who was out shopping with her little daughter.

Chi-Chi greeted Rae warmly before turning to the child. 'You don't know this lady,' she told her, 'but she was married to Uncle Ray before he died.'

'Raymond died?' Rae asked her in shock.

'Oh, yeah,' Chi-Chi said. 'He got black lung disease from working in the coal mine. By the time he passed, he only weighed ninety-eight pounds.'

Rae thought back to the big, strong man she had known. 'What a horrible way to go,' she replied, shaking her head sadly. She had always warned him not to go down the coal mine, and it seemed that she had been right. Despite the misery that Raymond had caused her, Rae felt pity for him now.

Once she was happily remarried, Rae began craving a baby again, but despite their best efforts, after several years she and Joe had not managed to conceive. Rae thought back to the unborn child she and Raymond had lost all those years ago. Had that been her only chance to be a mum?

Neither her doctor nor her priest could suggest anything that might help, and she had all but given up hope. Then finally, at the age of thirty-eight, she discovered she was pregnant. Rae gave birth to little Lynda, and another baby, Sue, followed two years later. Her third child died soon after birth of German measles, but despite the distressing experience, Rae was determined to try again. At forty-two, she gave birth to a baby boy, Michael. 'Okay, now I quit,' she told Joe.

Although Rae has spent more than half her life as an American citizen, she has never lost sight of her English heritage and in her garden she flies both the Stars and Stripes and the Union Jack. She spends much of her time visiting local schools to tell children about her memories of the war, and even puts on her old ATS uniform. In July 2005, she was honoured to be asked to come to London for the Queen's unveiling of the National Monument to the Women of World War II in Whitehall, an event attended by Dame Vera Lynn.

On 7 July, two days before the ceremony, she was standing near Edgware Road Underground Station when a bomb was detonated on a train there, one of four in the city that between them claimed 52 lives. But despite the post-traumatic stress she has lived with all her life as a result of the war, Rae felt more angry than afraid. She couldn't believe that young men who had grown up in Britain could commit such acts of violence against their own country.

Like many of her compatriots in America, Rae enjoys reminiscing about the war with fellow GI brides whenever possible. She is a member of the War Brides Association, through which she and Lyn became friends several years ago. At one point she was the WBA's secretary, although now she limits herself to organising the annual sing-along. Despite having now been diagnosed with emphysema, every year without fail Rae can be found in a hotel conference room somewhere in America, belting out a two-hour set of old wartime tunes including 'Roll Me Over', 'It's Been a Long, Long Time' and 'Bless 'Em All'.

* * *

Margaret and Patrick made the most of their glamorous life in Geneva, where he worked his way up to Assistant Director-General, Treasurer and Financial Comptroller of the ILO, the highest non-elected position in the organisation. He was even honoured by the Queen with a CMG. Margaret felt great pride in her husband's achievements, and threw herself into the role of the perfect wife and hostess, organising sumptuous dinner parties and mixing with the great and the good.

She never lied about who the father of her children was, but when people assumed that the three girls were Patrick's she didn't choose to correct them either. As far as she was concerned, he was more of a father to them than Lawrence had ever been. In the years after her first husband returned to America, he made no attempt to contact them or offer any kind of support.

Margaret and Patrick tried for children of their own, but without success. 'I'm so grateful to you,' he told her eventually. 'You've brought me a family I might otherwise never have had.'

But despite her happiness with Patrick, life wasn't always easy for Margaret. After several years in Switzerland, where she and her husband made the most of the skiing and beautiful mountain walks, she developed multiple sclerosis. It began with a trembling in her hands, but soon she was completely bedbound. She recovered well enough to walk with a pair of sticks, but then the disease came back. After three years of intermittent attacks it burned itself out, but Margaret was left in a wheelchair for the rest of her life.

Never one to let misfortune get the better of her, Margaret was determined to make the most of her life. She began teaching English report-writing skills to officials at the ILO and the United Nations, and wrote the organisations' official booklet on the subject. She also took a course in freelance journalism and was soon writing articles for *The Times* and the *Guardian*.

Although she tore all the photographs of Lawrence out of her family albums, Margaret stayed in touch with her former in-laws in America, in particular Lawrence's sister Ellen. From her, Margaret learned the sorry details of her ex-husband's later life – a repetitive cycle of achievement followed by catastrophe. He had worked in public relations for a Florida-based theme park, advised on a notoriously successful political smear campaign and even set up two successful magazines, *Outboard* and *Underwater*. But despite his various successes, his life would always unravel when he went back to the bottle. He had remarried in Panama City, and fathered a son and a daughter, but that marriage, too, had ended in divorce. In a drunken stupor he had wandered in front of a moving car, shattering the bones in his legs and leading to a long, miserable spell in a nursing home.

One day in 1974, Ellen wrote to tell Margaret that her brother had died. He had fallen from a moored-up boat on a Florida quayside and been dragged under by the mud. As Ellen put it, 'His soul went up and his body went down.' Whether he was drunk or sober at the time of the incident was a matter of dispute in the family.

In 1981 Patrick retired from his job at the ILO and he and Margaret returned to England, settling in Little Marlow, Buckinghamshire, in a beautiful single-storey house designed by his sister Elaine. At the age of seventy-five, Margaret fulfilled one of her life's great ambitions, taking a degree in Humanities with the Open University and achieving first-class honours.

Patrick died suddenly of a stroke in 2001, leaving Margaret to spend her final years alone. Throughout her life with him, she had rarely spoken about her first marriage, and many outside the family didn't even know that she had been a GI bride. But as time went on she grew more willing to share stories about her experiences in America.

Margaret died in January 2012, at the age of eighty-nine. With her at the end were her daughter Veronica and grand-daughter Nuala – who promised Margaret that she would tell her story, along with those of the other brave women who crossed an ocean for the men they loved.

Acknowledgements

This book would not exist without our core interviewees – Margaret Denby, Sylvia O'Connor, Lyn Patrino and Rae Zurovcik – sharing their stories with us. We thank them, and their families, for their generosity and patience. Although we have tried to remain faithful to what they have told us, at a distance of seventy years many memories are incomplete, and where necessary we have used our own research, and our imaginations, to fill in the gaps.

Our research took us all over America, tracking down GI brides. In three months, we covered 12,984 miles in a rented Fiat 500, passing through thirty-eight states. Over sixty brides and their relatives were kind enough to speak to us: Joy Beebe, Jane Bekhor, Elsie Blanton, June Blumenfeld, Jean Borst, Joyce Brown, Olga Brown, Mary Burkett, Doreen Burwell, Veronica Calvi, Dorothy Care, Lilah Contini, Pat Cracraft, Dorothy Cullins, Pamela Delleman, Phyllis Duerling, Catherine Fogarty, Thelma Fouts, Margie Franz, Doris Gallantine, Peggy Hamrick, Nancy Harrington, Eileen Harris, Doreen Heath, Bridget Henderson, Ivy Hettenhausen, Joyce Hinze, Daisy Hom, Joan James, Doreen Kamis, Betty Kranz, Doris Lindevig, Vera Long, Irene Maio, Elsie Mangan, Jessie McConnell, Dorothy McDaniel, Beryl McDonald, Edna McSpedden, Avril Meehan,

Edna Mewton, Jean Mobley, Margaret Moody, Patricia Murphy, Ruth Murtaugh, Linda Myers, Alma Naff, Eileen O'Connor, Rodger O'Connor, Annie Olsen, Eileen Pample, Hilda Peters, Betty Phipps, Rena Popivchak, Michael T. Powers, Edith Reiss, Donna Richardson, Frances Ross, Joyce Russell, Vince Schoenstein, Agnes Sekel, Kathleen Smoker, Miriam Stage, Joy Stanley, Liberty Webb, Linda Webb, Barbara Werner, Grace Whitcomb, Alice White, Eileen Whitney and Avice Wilson. You can find their stories, as well as pictures and audio clips of Margaret, Rae, Lyn and Sylvia, at **www.gibrides.com**.

We are hugely grateful to the World War II War Brides Association, in particular Erin Craig, Diane Reddy and Michele Thomas, for all their help, and for the warm welcome we received at their 2012 reunion in Boston. Thanks also to Francine Thomas from the Daughters of the British Empire and Jean McKinney from the TBPA for putting us in touch with their members.

As we travelled around America we were aided by local historians Larry Evans, David Giffels, Walter Patton and Ralph F. Witt. Glenn Booker, Neil Bromley, Ivan Cutting, Valerie Jackson, Jamie Lewis and Jo Stanley offered valuable research advice. We are grateful to the staff at NARA College Park, the Montana Historical Society, the American Red Cross, the University of Georgia Library, the United Steelworkers Archive, the McKeesport Heritage Center, the Early County Historical Society, the Akron Public Library and the University of Akron Archive.

In America, we received support and kindness from friends old and new: Kelly Barrett, Michael Barrett, Barbara Beebe Jensen, Jane Bloemer, Lawrence Cowart, Jeanneen Anderson Cowart, Vivian Beebe Brown, Billy Cissel, Judith Cissel, Spike

Cissel, Betsy Cissel Cosgrove, Melanie Cowait Collier, Gilly Furse, Dick Glendon, Annie Jones, Maria McCarthy, Lawrence Rambo III, Ellen Ross, Bruce Russell, Maureen Russell, Brooke Stearns and Daniel Walkowitz.

We are grateful to Becky Barry for her precise transcriptions, and to Clara Jones for research assistance. Thanks also to our agent Jon Elek, our editor Anna Valentine and our project editor Holly Kyte. For suggestions on the manuscript, we are indebted to Michèle Barrett, Nick Gill, Chris Rice and Jon Tillotson, as well as many of those already mentioned.

ENJOYED

GI Brides?

THE STORY'S NOT OVER...

Download this exclusive bonus ebook
to read more.

ALSO BY

DUNCAN BARRETT & NUALA CALVI

THE *SUNDAY TIMES* BESTSELLER

The
Sugar Girls

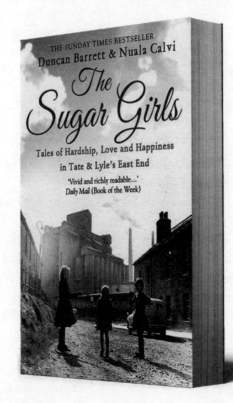

PRAISE FOR

The Sugar Girls

'This vivid and richly readable account of women's lives in and around the Tate & Lyle East London works in the Forties and Fifties is written as popular social history, played for entertainment. If it doesn't become a TV series to rival *Call the Midwife*, I'll take my tea with ten sugars.'

– BEL MOONEY, *The Daily Mail* (Book of the Week)

'Delightful, a terrific piece of nonfiction storytelling, and an authoritative and highly readable work of social history which brings vividly to life a fascinating part of East End life before it is lost forever.'

– MELANIE McGRATH, bestselling author of
Silvertown and *Hopping*

'Be sure to read *The Sugar Girls* – top social and female history, beautifully researched and written.'

– HEIDI THOMAS, *Call the Midwife* screenwriter

'An unlikely page-turner, synthesising a pacey narrative from what we assume must have been a bottomless well of memories and anecdotes from the surviving sugar girls. It reads like a novel. By the end, we half-wished we'd lived through those impoverished, crater-strewn days.'   – THE LONDONIST

'Do have the tissues close at hand when you get to the final chapter for the wrap-up of this remarkable, warm-hearted story ... [a] wonderful book.'   – LONDON HISTORIANS